LIS

D0440031

THE MINI ROUGH GUIDE

There are more than one hundred and fifty
Rough Guide travel, phrasebook, and music titles,
covering destinations from Amsterdam to Zimbabwe,
languages from Czech to Thai, and musics from
World to Opera and Jazz

Forthcoming titles include

Croatia • Cuba • Las Vegas
Rome • Switzerland

Rough Guides on the Internet

www.roughguides.com

Rough Guide Credits

Text editor: Gavin Thomas
Series editor: Mark Ellingham
Proof-reading: Carole Mansur
Typesetting: Link Hall
Cartography: Ed Wright

Publishing Information

This second edition published February 2000 by
Rough Guides Ltd, 62–70 Shorts Gardens, London WC2H 9AB

Distributed by the Penguin Group:

Penguin Books Ltd, 27 Wrights Lane, London W8 5TZ
Penguin Books USA Inc., 375 Hudson Street, New York 10014, USA
Penguin Books Australia Ltd, 487 Maroondah Highway,
PO Box 257, Ringwood, Victoria 3134, Australia
Penguin Books Canada Ltd, 10 Alcorn Avenue,
Toronto, Ontario, Canada M4V 1E4
Penguin Books (NZ) Ltd, 182–190 Wairau Road,
Auckland 10, New Zealand

Typeset in Bembo and Helvetica to an original design by Henry Iles.
Printed in Spain by Graphy Cems.

304pp, includes index
A catalogue record for this book is available from the British Library.
ISBN 1-85828-514-3

LISBON

THE MINI ROUGH GUIDE

by Matthew Hancock

with additional research by Amanda Tomlin,
Nicky Bailey and Bob Taylor

We set out to do something different when the first Rough Guide was published in 1982. Mark Ellingham, just out of university, was travelling in Greece. He brought along the popular guides of the day, but found they were all lacking in some way. They were either strong on ruins and museums but went on for pages without mentioning a beach or taverna. Or they were so conscious of the need to save money that they lost sight of Greece's cultural and historical significance. Also, none of the books told him anything about Greece's contemporary life – its politics, its culture, its people, and how they lived.

So with no job in prospect, Mark decided to write his own guidebook, one which aimed to provide practical information that was second to none, detailing the best beaches and the hottest clubs and restaurants, while also giving hard-hitting accounts of every sight, both famous and obscure, and providing up-to-the-minute information on contemporary culture. It was a guide that encouraged independent travellers to find the best of Greece, and was a great success, getting shortlisted for the Thomas Cook travel guide award, and encouraging Mark, along with three friends, to expand the series.

The Rough Guide list grew rapidly and the letters flooded in, indicating a much broader readership than had been anticipated, but one which uniformly appreciated the Rough Guide mix of practical detail and humour, irreverence and enthusiasm. Things haven't changed. The same four friends who began the series are still the care-takers of the Rough Guide mission today: to provide the most reliable, up-to-date and entertaining information to independent-minded travellers of all ages, on all budgets.

We now publish more than 150 titles and have offices in London and New York. The travel guides are written and researched by a dedicated team of more than 100 authors, based in Britain, Europe, the USA and Australia. We have also created a unique series of phrasebooks to accompany the travel series, along with an acclaimed series of music guides, and a best-selling pocket guide to the Internet and World Wide Web. We also publish comprehensive travel information on our Web site: **www.roughguides.com**

The Author

Matthew Hancock fell in love with Portugal and its people when he lived and worked in Lisbon in the early 1990s. He later returned to the country to complete a 775-mile walk along the Portuguese–Spanish border. Matthew has also lived in Athens and has travelled widely through Asia and the Middle East. He is now a freelance travel writer and editor based in London.

Acknowledgements

Many thanks to all the people who helped with this guide, especially Mandy for her support and ideas, Alex for checking out kids' facilities with gusto, and Olivia, who was –2 months old at the time. Also to Luke, Paula and Marianna for their Anglo-Portuguese hospitality and to Agostinho for use of his fantastic flat. I'm grateful for the after-hours work done by Bob Taylor and Nicky Bailey, and to Sapphire Flash for his insights into Lisbon's gay scene. Thanks too for the information supplied by Vitor Carriço, José Aragão, Mário Carneiro, Wilden Fonseca and Lucila Travassos; to Dr Manuel Duarte Fernandes; not to mention all the people who wrote in with their comments and suggestions. Also to everyone at Rough Guides, including Paul and Maxine, Link Hall for typesetting, Carole Mansur for proofreading, Ed Wright for patience and precision in the face of many maps, and particularly to Gavin for his excellent suggestions and dedicated editing.

Help Us Update

We've gone to a lot of effort to ensure that this second edition of *The Rough Guide to Lisbon* is as up to date and accurate as possible. However, if you feel there are places we've underrated or over-praised, or find we've missed something good or covered something which has now gone, then please write: suggestions, comments or corrections are much appreciated.

We'll credit all contributions, and send a copy of the next edition (or any other Rough Guide if you prefer) for the best letters. Please mark letters: "Rough Guide Lisbon Update" and send to:

Rough Guides, 62–70 Shorts Gardens, London WC2H 9AB, or
Rough Guides, 375 Hudson St, New York NY 10014.

Or send email to: **mail@roughguides.co.uk**
Online updates about this book can be found on
Rough Guides' Web site (see p.iv)

Readers' lettters

Thanks to Toby Ayer, Pauline Chester, Pauline K. Clendening, Kate Falloon, Nicola Farr, Mark Godber, Richard Heaton, Ian K. J. Jones, Ellen Kaptijn, Maya Kar, D.W. Money, F. Morris, Jonathan Ostler, Ventura Pobre, Roderick S. Pryde, Yizhar Regev, David Rowley, M. Schofield, Ted Stroll, C. Sutcliffe, Helen Thomas, Jeremy Thomas, Rene van der Vleuten, Maria Vourou, J. R. Watkins, Rachel Whiffen, Craig Wright

CONTENTS

Introduction

After many years as a sleepy backwater, **Lisbon** (Lisboa),
Europe's most westerly capital, has become in recent years
one of the continent's most happening cities, with hundreds
of lively bars, a vibrant nightlife and a growing number of
designer shops. Lisbon is also immediately likeable, gentler
than any capital should be; a big city that remains human in
pace and scale.

The unusual and startling cityscape is a big draw in itself.
At its heart is the eighteenth-century grid of the lower
town, the **Baixa**, enclosed by a switchback of hills above
the broad **Tejo** (in English, Tagus) estuary, and linked to
surrounding districts by a network of cobbled streets and a
system of trams and funiculars that crank their way up outrageous gradients. Down at the river, your gaze is lured
across to a vast, Rio-like statue of Christ, arms out-
stretched, whose embrace encompasses one of the grandest
of all suspension bridges, the Ponte 25 de Abril, and a fleet
of cross-river ferries. It's hard not to see the city as an urban
funfair, a sense heightened by the castle poised above the
Alfama district's medieval, whitewashed streets; by the fantasy Manueline architecture of Belém; and by the mosaics
of the central Rossio square and the city's Art Nouveau
shops and cafés.

Lisbon was once one of Europe's wealthiest cities, but many of its grandest buildings were destroyed in the Great Earthquake of 1755. The Romanesque **Sé** (cathedral), the Moorish walls of the **Castelo de São Jorge** and the extraordinary **Mosteiro dos Jerónimos** at Belém, are fine historic survivors of the earthquake, as is Lisbon's most atmospheric and traditional district, **Alfama**, a warren of narrow steps and alleys. Many of the city's more modern sites also demand attention: the **Fundação Calouste Gulbenkian**, a museum and cultural complex with superb collections of ancient and modern art; the **Museu Nacional de Arte Antiga**, effectively Portugal's national art gallery; and the futuristic **Oceanarium** at the Parque das Nações, the largest of its kind in Europe.

Beyond these, it's the central streets, avenues and squares, with their attendant comings and goings, that keep the interest high, along with a buoyant **nightlife** which ranges from the traditional fado clubs of the Bairro Alto and Alfama down to the glitzy clubs of Lisbon's redeveloped docklands. There's a superb array of Brazilian and African clubs and bands too, brought to the city by immigrants from Portugal's former colonies, and a panoply of international restaurants and bars.

All of which makes for a city that demands at least a few days out of anyone's itinerary. It is also the perfect base for day-trips and excursions into the surrounding area. The sea is close by, with the beach suburbs of **Estoril** and **Cascais** just half an hour's journey away by train; and slightly further, across the Tejo, are the miles of dunes along the **Costa da Caparica**. Northwest of the city, again easily reached by train, lie the lush wooded heights and royal palaces of **Sintra**, Byron's "glorious Eden". And if you're interested in Portuguese architecture, there are the rococo delights of the **Palácio de Queluz** and its gardens en route to Sintra, or the extraordinary monastery of **Mafra** to the north.

Lisbon's climate

| | °F | | °C | | Rainfall | |
| | Average daily | | Average daily | | Average monthly | |
	MAX	MIN	MAX	MIN	IN	MM
Jan	57	46	14	8	4.3	111
Feb	59	47	15	8	3.0	76
March	63	50	17	10	4.2	109
April	67	53	20	12	2.1	54
May	71	55	21	13	1.7	44
June	77	60	25	15	0.6	16
July	81	63	27	17	0.1	3
Aug	82	63	28	17	0.2	4
Sept	79	62	26	17	1.3	33
Oct	72	58	22	14	2.4	62
Nov	63	52	17	11	3.7	93
Dec	58	47	15	9	4.1	103

When to visit

Lisbon is comfortably warm from April to October: with its cooling Atlantic breezes it is less hot than Mediterranean cities on the same latitude, especially after sundown, though in terms of hours of sunshine it is one of Europe's brightest capitals. Most Lisbon residents take their holidays in July and August, which means that some shops, bars and restaurants close for the period, while the local beaches are heaving. September and October are good times to go, as is June, when the city enjoys its main saints' festivals. Lisbon's westerly position means that it gets its fair share of rainfall, most of which falls in the winter months, when the whole city seems to become saturated. However, when the sun does appear, it can be gloriously warm even in mid-winter. It is also worth noting that weather can be extremely localized – it can be pouring in Sintra but clear in Lisbon, or cloudy in Lisbon and sunny south of the Tejo.

THE GUIDE

Introducing
the city

I
t could hardly be easier to get your bearings in central Lisbon. At the southern end of the **Baixa** (Chapter 2), opening onto the River Tejo, is the broad, arcaded **Praça do Comércio**, with its ferry stations, trams for Belém, and grand triumphal arch. At the other end – linked by almost any Baixa street you care to take – stands Praça Dom Pedro IV, popularly known as **Rossio**, which connects to the east with **Praça da Figueira** and to the north with **Praça dos Restauradores**. These squares, filled with cafés, buskers, businesspeople and streetwise dealers, form the hub of central Lisbon's daily activity. Just west of the Baixa is **Chiado**, Lisbon's most elegant shopping area, largely rebuilt after the calamitous fire of 1988. East of the Baixa, the brooding landmark of the **Castelo de São Jorge** surmounts a leafy hill, with the **Alfama** district (Chapter 3) – the oldest, most interesting part of the city – sprawling below.

At night the focus shifts to the **Bairro Alto** (Chapter 4), high above and to the west of Chiado, and best reached by one of the city's *elevadores* (see p.14 and p.41).

Beyond the Bairro Alto lie the wealthy districts of **Estrela** and **Lapa** (Chapter 5), one of the city's main museums, the **Museu de Arte Antiga**, and the recently converted **Alcântara docks**, Lisbon's latest café and nightlife venue. Heading further out along the Tejo brings you to the historical suburb of **Belém** (Chapter 6), 6km west of the centre.

Heading north from Restauradores, the broad, tree-lined **Avenida da Liberdade** runs to the city's central park, **Parque Eduardo VII**, beyond which spreads the rest of the modern city, including the outstanding **Gulbenkian** museum (Chapter 7) and a string of lesser attractions. Five kilometres east of the capital lies the futuristic **Parque das Nações**, the former Expo 98 site at Olivais (Chapter 9), with its stunning **Oceanarium**, amongst many other attractions.

If you want to escape from Lisbon, the beautiful hilltop town of **Sintra** (Chapter 21), northwest of the city, is a popular excursion. West of Belém, a string of coastal resorts such as **Estoril** and **Cascais** make for wonderful day-trips

The euro and the escudo

Portugal is one of the eleven European Union countries which have opted to join together in economic and monetary union (EMU) and to adopt the single European currency, the **euro**. For the time being it is only possible to make paper transactions in the new currency (if you have, for example, a euro bank or credit-card account); euro notes and coins are scheduled to be issued at the beginning of 2002, and to replace the local currency entirely by July of that year.

At present, the Portuguese currency is the **escudo**; 1000 escudos is called a *conto*. Prices are written with the $ in the middle: thus 250$00 is 250 escudos; 1000$00 is a thousand escudos, or one *conto*.

(Chapter 22), while across the Tejo to the south are miles of dunes around **Caparica** (Chapter 23).

Arrival

When you arrive in Lisbon the first place to head for is **Rossio**, which is easily accessible by foot, bus or taxi.

By air

The well-equipped **airport** (Map 2, G2) is approximately 4km north of the centre. From here the easiest way into the city centre is by **taxi**, which should cost 1500–2000$00 to Rossio. Note that you'll be charged 300$00 extra for baggage, and that fares go up slightly at night from 10pm to 6am, at weekends and on public holidays.

Alternatively, catch the **Aerobus** (every 20min, 7am–9pm), which departs from outside the terminal, running to Praça Marquês de Pombal, Praça dos Restauradores, Rossio, Praça do Comércio and Cais do Sodré train station. The ticket, bought from the driver, also gives you one day's (450$00; free from the Welcome Desk for TAP passengers) or three days' (1100$00) travel on the city's buses and trams (see p.10 for more information). Cheaper **local buses** – #44 or #45 – leave from the main road outside the terminal to Praça dos Restauradores and Cais do Sodré (every 15min, 4am–1.40am; 160$00), although these are less convenient if you have a lot of luggage.

By train

Long-distance trains from Coimbra, Porto and the north

(and also from Madrid and Paris) use **Santa Apolónia station** (Map 4, K6; ℭ218 884 142), on the Gaivota metro line, about fifteen minutes' walk east of Praça do Comércio or a short ride on bus #9, #39, #46 or #90 from Praça dos Restauradores or Rossio. There's a helpful **information office** (Mon–Sat 9am–7pm) at the station, and an exchange bureau.

Trains from the Algarve and the south of Portugal involve a slightly more complicated approach. The rail lines terminate at **Barreiro station** (Map 1, G7; ℭ212 073 028), on the south bank of the Tejo, from where you catch a ferry (included in the price of the train ticket) to **Fluvial** terminal (Map 3, L3), next to Praça do Comércio. Buses #9, #39, #80 and #90 run up from Fluvial to Rossio, through the Baixa.

Local trains from Sintra or Queluz emerge right in the heart of the city at **Rossio station** (Map 3, C8; ℭ213 465 022), complete with shops, currency-exchange counters and left-luggage lockers. Trains to Belém, Estoril and Cascais leave from the fairly central **Cais do Sodré station** (Map 5, B8; ℭ213 470 181), to the west of the Baixa. This can be reached on the Gaivota metro line, or any one of buses #1, #2, #7, #32, #35, #43, #44 or #45 from Praça do Comércio.

By bus

Various bus companies have terminals scattered about the city, but the main one is at the old tram station on **Avenida João Crisostomo** (Map 9, G5; ℭ213 545 775), a short walk from metro Saldanha on the Girassol line, 2km to the north of the centre; there's an information office that can help with timetable enquiries. This terminal is also where most international bus services arrive; see p.217 for a list of other bus terminals in the city, or check with any tourist office for the latest details. Leaving Lisbon, you can usually buy tickets if you turn up half an hour or so in advance, though for summer express services to the Algarve it's best to book a seat (through any travel agent) a day in advance.

By car

Don't even think of **driving** in Lisbon: it takes years off your life, and at the beginning or end of public holiday weekends is to be avoided at all costs. Heading to or from the south on these occasions, it can take over an hour just to cross the Ponte 25 de Abril, a notorious traffic bottleneck which the recently opened Vasco da Gama bridge to the northeast of the city has done little to alleviate.

Parking is very difficult in central Lisbon. Pay-and-display spots get snapped up quickly, and some of the local unemployed get by on tips for guiding drivers into empty spots; reports suggest that scratches suddenly appear on cars whose drivers do not leave tips. So you'd be wise to head for an official car park: central locations include the underground one at Restauradores; Parque Mayer on Travessa do Salitre, off Avenida da Liberdade; Parque Eduardo VII; the underground car parks around the Gulbenkian such as Parking Berna on Rua Marquês de Sá da Bandeira; or the Amoreiras complex on Avenida Eng. Duarte Pacheco. Wherever you park, do not leave valuables inside: the break-in rate is extremely high.

If you're **renting a car**, it's best to wait until the day you leave the city to pick it up; see p.218 for car rental companies. If depositing a rented car at the airport at the end of your stay, follow the signs to the special rental car park and allow plenty of time for paperwork and bus transfers to the terminal.

Information

There's a helpful, English-speaking **tourist office** (*turismo*) at Rua Jardim do Regedor 50, off the eastern side of Praça dos Restauradores (Map 8, H7; ℂ213 433 672; daily 9am–1pm & 2–6pm), which can supply accommodation lists, bus timetables and maps. The main Portugal *turismo* is in Praça dos Restauradores (ℂ213 463 314; daily 9am–8pm), in the Palácio Foz, although this is better for information on the rest of the

Lisbon on the Internet

www.ccb.pt What's on at the Belém Cultural Centre (see p.57), with reviews in English.

www.nexus-pt.com.news Portugal's national on-line English-language newspaper.

www.parquedasnacoes.pt Up-to-date information on sites and events at the Parque das Naçoes.

www.portugal.org Government-run site with information on tourist attractions, sport and culture, and links to accommodation agencies.

www.portugal-turismo.com The best information on Portugal – with its own Lisbon section – though in Portuguese only, with information on everything from the weather to details on adventure sports, golf and what's showing at the cinema.

www.portugalvirtual.com One of the only Portugal-related sites in English, with lots of information in lists.

www.slbenfica.pt Official Web site of the Benfica soccer team, including match reports, fixtures and ticket details.

www.wiso/gwdg.de/ifbg/currency.html Escudos daily exchange rate.

www.yahoo.com/Regional_Information/Countries/Portugal/ Links to all things Portuguese.

country rather than for Lisbon itself. There's also a *turismo* at the airport, facing you as you leave customs (daily 6am–1am), which can help you find accommodation, and a few smaller tourist information kiosks dotted around town, such as the one in Martim Moniz (Wed–Sun 10am–2pm & 3–6pm), which have more limited information. A free telephone information line dispenses basic information in English (℘800 296 296; Mon–Sat 9am–midnight, Sun 9am–8pm).

For **listings** of events in the city, look in the free monthly magazines *What's On* and *Lisboa em* (in English), or in the *Agenda Cultural* (in Portuguese), published monthly by the city council. All are available from the tourist offices and larger hotels. For exhibitions and concerts, pick up a schedule of events from the reception desks at the Gulbenkian or the Cultural Centre in Belém. For other listings and reviews of forthcoming events, concerts, bars, clubs and restaurants, get hold of the Friday editions of the *Diário de Notícias* or *O Independente* newspapers – both have pull-out listings magazines. The expat newspaper, *The Anglo-Portuguese News*, is also useful for local news and reviews.

Free Lisbon

The following sites and museums are **free on Sunday** from 10am to 2pm, unless otherwise stated: Centro de Arte Moderna (all day); Igreja de Santa Engrácia; Mosteiro dos Jerónimos; Museu Antóniano (all day); Museu de Arqueologia; Museu do Chiado (all day); Museu da Cidade (all day); Museu dos Coches; Museu Gulbenkian (all day); Museu Militar (all day Wed); Museu Nacional de Arte Antiga; Museu Nacional do Azulejo; Museu Rafael Bordalo Pinheiro; Museus da Teatro e Traje; Palácio da Ajuda; Palácio de Mafra; Palácio Nacional, Sintra; Palácio da Pena, Sintra; Palácio de Queluz (until 1pm); Torre de Belém.

City transport

Central Lisbon is compact enough to explore on foot, though its hills tempt most people onto the **elevadores** that serve the steepest streets around the Bairro Alto and Avenida da Liberdade. Lisbon's **trams** ply the narrow streets around Alfama, the Baixa and out to Estrela. They're hardly the fastest form of transport (the modern tram to Belém being the exception) but, along with the *elevadores*, are undoubtedly the most fun. The city has a comprehensive network of **buses**: these can be useful for destinations not served by other forms of transport, although they often get snarled up in Lisbon's growing traffic congestion. Tram, bus and *elevador* stops are indicated by a sign marked *paragem*, which carries route details.

The most efficient way to get around, however, is on the **metro**, with stations close to most of the main sites and frequent trains. Finally, suburban **trains** run from Rossio out to Sintra and Queluz and from Cais do Sodré to Belém, Estoril and Cascais, while **ferries** link Lisbon to Cacilhas, with bus connections to the beach resort of Caparica, south of the Tejo.

Most forms of public transport operate from around 6.30am to midnight (1am for the metro); outside these hours there are usually plenty of inexpensive **taxis**, that can be hailed or phoned for in advance.

Tickets and passes

Probably the best-value **tickets** for buses, trams and *elevadores* are those which can be bought in advance from kiosks around the main bus terminals such as in Praça do Comércio and Praça da Figueira. The same tickets are valid on buses, trams and *elevadores* (though not on the metro or ferries); they can be bought either individually or in blocks of ten, cost 160$00 each, and are valid for two journeys within a single travel zone or one journey across two travel zones (such as from the city centre to Belém). Tickets are validated by putting them into the machine next to the driver when you board. Individual tickets for buses, trams and *elevadores* can also be bought on board. These too cost 160$00, but are valid for one journey only within a single travel zone – double the price of those bought in advance. Another option is to buy a one-day (450$00) or three-day (1100$00) **pass**, which you validate by punching in the machine next to the driver the first time you ride; it's then valid for 24 or 72 hours. All the above can be bought from kiosks around the main bus terminals, such as in Praça do Comércio and Praça da Figueira.

If you're planning some intensive sightseeing, it may be worth getting a **Lisbon Card** (Cartão Lisboa) (1900$00 for one day, 3100$00 for two, or 4000$00 for three). The card entitles you to unlimited rides on buses, trams, metro and *elevadores* and entry to 25 museums, including the Gulbenkian and Museu de Arte Antiga, plus discounts of around 25–50 percent to other main sites. It's available from the tourist office at Rua Jardim do Regedor 50 (Map 8, H7), the Mosteiro dos Jerónimos in Belém, and the Museu Nacional de Arte Antiga in Lapa. The **tourist pass** (Passe Turístico) (1700$00 for four days, 2400$00 for seven) allows unlimited travel on trams, buses, *elevadores* and the metro, and is available, on production of a passport, at kiosks by the Elevador Santa Justa, in Praça da Figueira and in Restauradores metro station, among other places. However, unless you plan to spend a lot of time on public transport, it's probably better to buy individual tickets for each mode of transport in advance.

The metro

Lisbon's **metro** – the *Metropolitano* – was drastically overhauled and extended in time for Expo 98 and is now the most efficient way of reaching the outlying districts. Its four colour-coded lines cover several useful routes (see box below and map 2); hours of operation are from 6.30am to

Useful metro stops

Lina da Caravela (green line)

Cais do Sodré, for the riverfront, ferries to Cacilhas and trains to Belém, Estoril and Cascais.

Baixa-Chiado, for the main shopping streets and the Elevador Santa Justa.

Rossio, for Praça da Figueira and the Baixa.

Martim Moniz, for tram connections to the Castelo de São Jorge and Alfama.

Alameda, for interchange to Linha do Oriente (red line) to Parque das Nações.

Roma, for the shops along Avenida de Roma.

Campo Grande, for Sporting Lisbon football club, Museu da Cidade and Museu Rafael Bordalo Pinheiro.

Linha da Gaivota (blue line)

Restauradores, for the tourist offices, the Elevador da Glória and trains to Sintra.

Marquês de Pombal or **Parque**, for Parque Eduardo VII.

S. Sebastião or **Praça de Espanha**, for the Gulbenkian (and Praça de Espanha for buses to Caparica).

Jardim Zoológico, for the zoo.

Colégio Militar-Luz, for Benfica football club and Colombo Shopping Centre.

Linha do Girassol (yellow line)

Saldanha, for the main bus station.

Campo Pequeno, for the bullring.

Campo Grande, for Sporting Lisbon football club, Museu da Cidade and Museu Rafael Bordalo Pinheiro.

1am. **Tickets** cost 100$00 per journey, or 800$00 for a ten-ticket *caderneta* – sold at all stations. If you think you're going to use the metro a lot, buy a **one-day pass** (260$00, valid on the metro). For those on longer stays, one-month passes are available, which also cover train journeys on the Cascais line (6720$00 for passes valid to Cascais, 5530$00 to Oeiras or 4490$00 to Belém).

Buses

Buses (*autocarros*) run just about everywhere in the Lisbon area, and can prove useful for getting to and from outlying attractions (see "Useful bus routes", below). A couple of **tourist bus tours** run during the summer months, departing from Praça do Comércio; details are given on p.15.

Useful bus routes

#1 Cais do Sodré to Charneca via Lumiar, Baixa, Avda da Liberdade, Picoas (for the youth hostel), Saldanha, Campo Pequeno and Campo Grande.

#8 Outside the airport to Largo Martim Moniz via Avda Almirante Reis and the Baixa.

#27 Marquês de Pombal to Belém via Rato, Estrela, Lapa and Alcântara.

#37 Praça da Figueira to Castelo de São Jorge via the Sé and Alfama.

#44/45 Outside the airport to Cais do Sodré via Entrecampos, Saldanha, Marquês de Pombal, Avda da Liberdade and the Baixa.

#46 Santa Apolónia station to near Palácio dos Marquêses de Fronteira via Praça do Comércio, the Baixa, Avda da Liberdade, Praça Marquês de Pombal and the Fundação Gulbenkian.

Trams and elevadores

Many of Lisbon's **trams** (*eléctricos*) have been taken out of service, and there are now just five tram routes, serving the area around the Castelo de São Jorge and west to Belém. Ascending some of the steepest urban gradients in the world, most are worth taking for the ride alone. The cross-city **tram #28** (see p.36) is among the best public transport rides in the city, although the central section of the route gets very busy and standing room only is the norm, while delays are common when cars park on the tracks. Another picturesque route is **#12**, which circles the castle area east of the city centre, via Alfama, Praça da Figueira and Largo Martim Moniz. Other useful routes are the modern air-conditioned "supertram" **#15** from Praça da Figueira to Belém (signed Algés), and **#18**, which runs from Rua da Alfândega (next to Praça do Comércio) via Praça do Comércio and Cais do Sodré to the Palácio da Ajuda. The remaining route, **#25**, runs from Rua da Alfândega to Campo Ourique via Praça do Comércio, Cais do Sodré, Lapa and Estrela.

From March to October you can take a **Tourist Tram Tour** in a revamped turn-of-the-century tram. The "Circuito Colinas" (Hills Tour) (March–June & Oct, two daily; July, four daily; Aug, five daily; Sept, three daily; 2900$00) takes passengers on a ninety-minute ride from Praça do Comércio round Alfama, Chiado and São Bento (information on ©213 632 021). You can, however, do virtually the same route for less money and in the company of locals by taking tram #28 from Largo Martim Moniz to Estrela and then hopping onto tram #25 back to Praça do Comércio.

Two funicular railways and one street lift, each known as an **elevador** or **ascensor**, offer exciting and quick access up to the Bairro Alto – for details, see p.41. There's a fourth *elevador* to the east of Avenida da Liberdade – see p.67.

Ferries

Ferries cross the Tejo from three main departure points. From **Praça do Comércio** (Estação Fluvial), passenger ferries cross to Cacilhas (every 10min, 6am–10.30pm; 110$00 one way), Barreiro (every 20–30min, same hours; 200$00) and Montijo (every 20–30min, same hours; 300$00). The journey to Cacilhas, in particular, is worth doing for the ride alone. Foot passengers can also take the

Sightseeing tours

Guided walks The *turismo* in Palácio Foz, Praça dos Restauradores (see p.8), is the starting point for a three-hour guided walk through the "medieval" suburbs of Chiado and Bairro Alto. Additional walks through "Old Lisbon" take in Alfama and the castle area, beginning from Casa dos Bicos on Praça da Ribeira. Minimum four people; two–three days' notice must be given. Information on © & fax 213 906 149, *jcabdo@ip.pt*.

River cruises Two-hour cruises up the Tejo depart from Estação Fluvial (daily April–Oct 11am & 3pm; 3500$00) to Belém. The price includes a drink and commentary, though the views are little different to those you get from the local ferry crossings.

Tourist open-top bus tour The "Circuito Tejo" (May–Sept hourly 11am–4pm; 2500$00) takes passengers round Lisbon's principal sites; a day ticket allows you to get on and off whenever you want. Tickets can be bought on board. Information on ©213 632 021.

For details of **tram tours**, see p.14.

CITY TRANSPORT

ferry from **Cais do Sodré** to Cacilhas (24hr service, every 20–30min during the day, 40–50min at night; 110$00 per person). From **Belém** there are services to Trafaria (every 30min–1hr: Mon–Sat 6.30am–11.30pm, Sun 7.30am–11.30pm; 150$00), from where you can catch buses to Caparica.

Taxis

Lisbon's cream – or the older black and green – **taxis** are inexpensive for journeys within the city limits; there's a minimum charge of 250$00 and an average ride will run to around 700$00 (or around 1200$00 from 10pm to 6am, at weekends and on public holidays). All taxis have meters, and tips are not expected; a green light means the cab is occupied. Outside the rush hour they can be found quite easily in the street, or alternatively head for one of the ranks in various central spots including outside the stations, Rossio, Praça da Figueira, at the southern end of Avenida da Liberdade and Estação Fluvial. At night it's usually best to get a restaurant or bar to phone one for you, or phone yourself (which entails 150$00 extra charge): try Rádio Taxis (✆218 155 061), Autocoope (✆217 932 756) or Teletaxi (✆218 152 076).

The Baixa, Chiado and Cais do Sodré

arly eighteenth-century prints show a Lisbon of tremendous opulence and mystique, its skyline characterized by towers, palaces and convents. Then, in November 1755, the greater part of the city was devastated by what came to be known as the Great Earthquake. Given orders following the disaster to "Bury the dead, feed the living and close the ports", the king's minister, the Marquês de Pombal, first restored order, then embarked on a complete rebuilding of the heart of the city on the plan of a Neoclassical grid, an austerely impressive example of eighteenth-century town-planning.

This central area, the **Baixa**, adheres to Pombal's ideals of simplicity and economy. Individual streets were assigned to particular crafts and trades, and the whole enterprise shaped around public buildings and squares. Only **Rossio**, the city's main square since medieval times, remains in its original place, slightly off-centre in a symmetrical design that runs between it and the adjacent **Praça da Figueira** at its northern end, and the arcaded **Praça do Comércio** at its southern.

West of here is the affluent **Chiado** district, housing some of Lisbon's most famous cafés and designer boutiques. By contrast, the streets around **Cais do Sodré** station, south of Chiado, retain their earthy origins in a bustling commercial district epitomized by the **Mercado da Ribeira**, one of Lisbon's most colourful markets.

....

**The area covered by this chapter is shown in detail
on colour maps 3 and 5.**

....

The Great Earthquake

The **Great Earthquake** – which was felt as far away as Scotland and Jamaica – struck Lisbon at 9.30am on November 1, 1755, All Saints' Day, when most of the city's population was at Mass. Within the space of ten minutes there had been three major tremors. Fires – spread by the candles of a hundred church altars – raged throughout the capital, and a vast tidal wave swept the seafront, where refugees had sought shelter. In all, 40,000 of a population of 270,000 died. The destruction of the city shocked Europe, with Voltaire, who included an account of it in his novel *Candide*, leading an intense debate with Rousseau on the operation of providence. For Portugal, and for the capital, it was a disaster that in retrospect seemed to seal an age and marked the end of Lisbon's role as arguably the most active port in Europe. Many people feel that it is only a matter of time before a quake of similar magnitude strikes Lisbon again – a soothsayer's recent prediction that an earthquake was imminent virtually emptied the city for a weekend.

THE BAIXA

The **Baixa** (pronounced *bye-sha*) houses many of the country's government departments, banks and business offices, as well as some of its most interesting shops. Europe's first great example of Neoclassical urban planning, it remains an imposing quarter of rod-straight streets, some streaming with traffic, although an increasing number – concentrated around the broad Rua Augusta – have been cobbled underfoot and turned over to pedestrians, street performers and pavement artists.

For listings of the Baixa's best restaurants and hotels, see p.92 and p.111.

Praça do Comércio

Map 3, J5–K6.

At the southern end of the Baixa, on the waterfront, the **Praça do Comércio** represents the climax of Pombal's design, surrounded by classical buildings – once a royal palace, now government offices – and centred on an exuberant bronze equestrian statue of Dom José, monarch during the earthquake and the capital's rebuilding. The square – popularly known as **Terreiro do Paço** after the royal palace which stood here before the earthquake, and whose steps still lead up from the Tejo – has played an important part in the country's history. In 1908, King Carlos I and his eldest son were shot dead here, opening the way to the declaration of the Republic two years later.

The square is earmarked for a redevelopment which will ultimately see the whole area pedestrianized, freeing it for cultural and political functions – as was its original purpose – although in the meantime the riverfront side remains a constant stream of cars, while the northern end forms a bus and tram interchange. New museums, galleries and cafés are also planned for the arcades around the square, though for now the only refreshment spot is the old-world café *Martinho da Arcada* (see p.145), one of the haunts of Portugal's greatest twentieth-century poet, Fernando Pessoa. Rebuilding work permitting, the square's riverfront provides a natural focus for the area, especially an hour or two before sunset, when people gather in the golden light to watch the orange ferries ply between the Estação Fluvial and Cacilhas on the opposite side of the Tejo.

For more on Fernando Pessoa, see p.49.

Just to the northeast of here, the attractive **Praça do Município** (Map 3, J7) is the site of the Neoclassical nineteenth-century Câmara Municipal, or **City Hall**, where the Portuguese Republic was declared in 1910. Flatteringly described by Pessoa as "one of the finest buildings in the city", it houses Pombal's plans for rebuilding Lisbon after the earthquake. From here, it's a short walk west to Cais do Sodré (see p.26) down **Rua do Arsenal**, which is packed with smelly shops selling dried cod and grocers selling cheap wines, port and brandies.

North from the Praça do Comércio

Back on Praça do Comércio, a huge arch depicting statues of historical figures – Pombal is one – marks the beginning of the pedestrianized route north along Rua Augusta across the Baixa grid. The lower town has always been the core of Lisbon: building work on the BCP bank in Rua dos Correeiros revealed the remains of a Roman fish-preserving industry, a fifth-century Christian burial place and Moorish ceramics. These varied exhibits can be viewed in the tiny

Núcleo Arqueológico at Rua dos Correeiros 9 (Map 3, H5; Thurs 3–5pm, Sat 10am–noon & 3–5pm; free), a fascinating insight into the lives of Lisbon's early inhabitants.

In the upper reaches of the Baixa, from the western end of Rua de Santa Justa, the iron-lattice Elevador de Santa Justa (Map 3, E7; see p.42) street lift has superb views from its upper terrace.

One of the major appeals of today's Baixa is the survival of more recent traditions. Many of the streets in the grid, such as Rua da Prata (Silversmiths' Street), Rua dos Sapateiros (Cobblers' Street), Rua do Ouro (Goldsmiths' Street, now better known as Rua Aurea) and Rua do Comércio (Commercial Street) maintain their crafts and businesses as Pombal devised. These, along with the mosaic-embellished squares, are a visual delight, with tiled Art Deco shopfronts and elaborately decorated *pastelarias* (pastry shops) still surviving here and there. The best streets to explore are the pedestrianized ones running south to north – Rua Augusta, Rua dos Correeiros and Rua dos Douradores – and the smaller Rua de Santa Justa, Rua da Assunção, Rua da Vitória and Rua de São Nicolau, which run east to west. Look out, too, for the northern end of Rua dos Sapateiros, which is linked to Rossio by a low arch.

Rossio

Map 3, C7–D6.

Until the beginning of the century, Praça Dom Pedro IV, popularly known as **Rossio**, sat at the edge of the city limits; beyond were the vineyards of Palhavã and the wine estates of Campo Pequeno and Campo Grande. During the nineteenth century Rossio's plethora of cafés attracted Lisbon's painters and writers, and though many of the artists'

THE BAIXA

haunts were converted to banks in the 1970s, the huge square still provides a focus for the city's social life, sporting atmospheric and popular cafés most of which have outdoor seating, though the traffic and bustle can be offputting.

For reviews of the best Baixa cafés, see p.144.

The square's single concession to grandeur is the **Teatro Nacional de Dona Maria II**, built along its north side in the 1840s. Prior to the earthquake this was the site of the Inquisitional Palace, in front of which bullfights, public hangings and *autos-da-fé* (ritual burnings of heretics) took place. The nineteenth-century statue atop the central column of Rossio is officially of Dom Pedro IV – after whom the square is named – though in fact it was cast originally as Emperor Maximilian of Mexico. The statue just happened to be in Lisbon en route from France to Mexico when news came through of Maximilian's assassination in 1867, and it was decided that since Maximilian would have no further use for it, it would do just as well for Dom Pedro. The statue is now the focus of a weekly **flower market** (Sat 7am–2pm). Above the square is the stylish, horseshoe-shaped entrance to Rossio station, a mock-Manueline complex with the train platforms an improbable escalator-ride above the street-level entrances. It's now part of a new train-and-metro interchange which links Rossio with the neighbouring square of Restauradores. Look out for the modern decorative azulejo panels by Lima de Freitas in the underground hall.

The **Igreja de São Domingos** (Map 3, C6; daily 8am–7pm), immediately to the east of Rossio, stands on the site of the Convento de São Domingos, where the Inquisition read out its sentences – one terrible pronouncement in 1506 instigated the massacre of much of the city's Jewish population. Formerly the venue for royal marriages and christenings, the church was gutted by a fire in the 1950s. It's recently undergone restoration, though the cavernous interior and scarred pillars remain powerfully atmospheric.

The road and square outside the church, at the bottom of Rua das Portas de Santo Antão (see p.66), is a popular meeting place: the local African population hangs out on the street corner; commuters get their shoes cleaned at the rank of small metal booths; while everyone from businessmen to Lisbon's lowlife frequent the various *ginginha* bars (see p.155).

Praça da Figueira

Heading south, Largo de São Domingos runs into **Praça da Figueira** (where Rossio metro also has exits), much quieter than Rossio, despite being one of the city's main bus and tram stops. Its western side is lined with shops and cafés, including the famous *Café Suiça* (see p.145), whose outdoor seats are particularly appealing, with views of the green slopes of the Castelo de São Jorge above. From the northeastern corner of Praça da Figueira, Rua da Palma leads through to **Largo Martim Moniz**, a concrete expanse not much improved by its water features and odd modernist craft kiosks.

From the Largo Martim Moniz, it's possible to reach the Mouraria district and the eastern entrance to the Castelo de São Jorge using tram #12.

CHIADO

On the west side of the Baixa, stretching up the hillside towards the Bairro Alto, lies the area known as **Chiado** – it's said that the district was named after the sixteenth-century poet António Ribeiro, who was known as "O Chiado" (literally "squeaking" or "hissing"). The area was greatly damaged by a fire in August 1988, which destroyed all but the facade of the Grandella department store and many old shops in Rua do Crucifixo, as well as the Museum of Contemporary Art, (subsequently reborn as the Museu do Chiado – see below). After years of dallying, the authorities have restored most of the area's gutted buildings under the direction of eminent Portuguese architect Alvaro Siza Vieira, in keeping with Chiado's traditions; soaring marble facades consciously mimic those destroyed in the fire.

At the top end of Rua Garrett, you can take tram #28 to São Bento and Estrela (see p.47) or head up Rua Nova da Trindade to the Bairro Alto (see p.41).

Despite the fire damage, Chiado remains one of the city's most affluent quarters. From Rossio, the easiest approach is along Rua do Carmo, virtually rebuilt from scratch after the 1988 fire and home to some of the area's best shops (as well as offering an alternative route to the Elevador de Santa Justa; see p.41). At the end of Rua do Carmo are the fashionable shops and old café-tearooms of **Rua Garrett**. Of these, *A Brasileira*, at no. 120, is the most famous, having been frequented by generations of Lisbon's literary and intellectual leaders – Fernando Pessoa and novelist Eça de Queiroz among them. While on Rua Garrett, take a stroll past **Igreja dos Mártires** (Map 5, E6), built on the site of a burial ground created for English Crusaders killed during the siege of Lisbon.

Museu do Chiado

Map 5, F7. Tues 2–6pm, Wed–Sun 10am–6pm; 400$00. Metro Baixa–Chiado or bus #58 or #100 from Cais do Sodré.

CHIADO

Development and destruction

In recent years Lisbon has experienced some of the most radical **redevelopment** since the Marquês de Pombal rebuilt the shattered capital after the 1755 earthquake. This building boom began in the wake of Portugal's joining the European Community in 1986, when grants and foreign investment poured into the capital, and continued during the lead-up to Expo 98, which saw further chunks of old Lisbon disappearing under new roads and train lines, while tramlines were removed to provide space for faster roads.

Complicated **rent laws** have also been bad news for the city's older buildings. Until recently, landlords whose tenants were installed before the 1974 Revolution received insufficient income to maintain properties, making the option of selling up to developers a tempting one. As a result, many of the city's beautiful old mansions and tenement buildings are either in a state of decay or have been demolished to make way for office buildings. Ironically, it is beyond Pombal's statue at Praça Marquês de Pombal that most of the redevelopment work is being done, with some fairly grim housing developments out in the newer suburbs. Most of these are a result of a longstanding chronic housing problem that – combined with the rent laws – has made new property in Lisbon among the most expensive in Europe.

But not all of old Lisbon is lost, and older buildings' facades are now protected by law – though developers often tack modern developments onto them, such as the extraordinary Heron Castillo building at Rua Braacamp 40 near Rato. Meanwhile, EU funding continues to help restore and upgrade many historic buildings, particularly in Lisbon's oldest quarters, **Alfama** – many of whose houses previously had no bathrooms – and the **Bairro Alto**, while much of the Tejo riverfront has been transformed from industrial wasteland to a thriving area of cafés and clubs. The most obvious sign of renovation is in the streets of **Chiado**, burned out in the 1988 fire but now beautifully restored to their original design.

CHIADO

25

Just beyond the Igreja dos Mártires, Rua Serpa Pinto veers steeply downhill past Lisbon's main opera house, the Teatro Nacional de São Carlos, to the contemporary art museum, the **Museu do Chiado**. Opened in 1994, this stylish building, with a pleasant courtyard café (see p.146) and rooftop terrace, incorporates the former Museum of Contemporary Art. Constructed around a nineteenth-century biscuit factory, the new museum displays works by some of Portugal's most influential artists since the nineteenth century and is recommended even for those with little knowledge of Portuguese art. Highlights include the beautiful sculpture *A Viúva* (The Widow) by António Teixeira Lopes, António Costa Pinheiro's painting of Fernando Pessoa, and some evocative Lisbon scenes by Carlos Botelho and José Malhoa. Look out too for the wonderful decorative panels by José de Almada Negreiros, recovered from the São Carlos cinema. There is also a small collection of French sculpture, including Rodin's *The Bronze Age*.

CAIS DO SODRÉ

Ten minutes' walk west of the Baixa along the riverfront, or a steep walk down Rua do Alecrim from Chiado, is **Cais do Sodré** metro and station (Map 5, B8), from where trains run out to Estoril and Cascais, and car ferries cross to Cacilhas. It's not the most elegant of areas, though its waterfront warehouses are slowly being converted into upmarket cafés and restaurants (see p.117) and by day, in particular, a stroll along its atmospheric riverfront is very enjoyable. Look out for the characterful vendors outside the station, in particular the *varinas* – fishwives from Alfama – who usually appear from dawn to around midday from Monday to Saturday, and the colourfully dressed women from Cape Verde, who bargain for and then cart off great baskets of wares on their heads.

> An enjoyable, if somewhat industrial, walk of
> around an hour is to head west from Cais do Sodré
> along the waterfront; apart from a few detours, it's
> possible to stroll all the way along the docks to the
> Ponte 25 de Abril suspension bridge, ending up at
> the cafés and bars of Doca de Santo Amaro
> (see p.150 and p.168).

Just north of Cais do Sodré, take a look inside the domed **Mercado da Ribeira** (Map 5, A7–B7; Mon–Sat 6am–noon; metro Cais do Sodré or tram #15 from Praça da Figueira). Even if you're not tempted by the array of food – least of all perhaps by the gruesome slabs of flesh and innards – the fruit, flower, spice and vegetable displays on the upper storey are impressive. Just above the market, with its entrance tucked into an arch on Rua de São Paulo, is the bottom end of the precipitous **Elevador da Bica** (Map 5, A6–C4; Mon–Sat 7am–10.45pm, Sun 9am–10.45pm; 160$00), a funicular leading up to the Bairro Alto district via a steep residential street with drying washing usually draped from every window – it's worth taking the *elevador* for the ride alone. Take a left at the top and then the second left down Rua M. Saldanha and you'll reach the **Miradouro de Santa Catarina**, with spectacular views over the city and, in summer, a handy drinks kiosk with outdoor tables.

CAIS DO SODRÉ

Alfama
and around

ounded by the Moors on a hill to the east of the Baixa and remodelled by the Christians after their reconquest of the city in 1147, the **Castelo de São Jorge** became during the Middle Ages the hub of a walled city that circled the castle and spread downhill as far as the river. Today it is these districts – **Alfama**, **Mouraria** and **Santa Cruz** – which are the oldest and perhaps most interesting areas of Lisbon, retaining a quiet, village-like quality, particularly in the maze-like streets of Alfama, which remain devoid of traffic and largely free of tourist boutiques.

To the south of the castle is the city's cathedral, the **Sé**, while to the east, around the **Campo de Santa Clara**, are the churches of Santa Engrácia and São Vicente de Fora, best visited on a Tuesday or Saturday to coincide with the chaotic Feira da Ladra flea market. East from here are three mildly interesting **museums**: the Museu da Militar (Military Museum), the tiny Museu da Água (Water Museum), and the more interesting Museu do Azulejo, a beautiful tile museum.

....

The area covered by this chapter is shown in detail on colour map 4.

....

THE SÉ AND AROUND

Map 4, B8. Cathedral: daily 8.30am–6pm; free. Cloisters: Mon–Sat 10am–5pm; 100$00. Sacristy: same hours as cloisters; 400$00. Tram #28 from Rua da Conceição in the Baixa.

Lisbon's cathedral – the **Sé** – stands stolidly on a hill overlooking the Baixa. Founded in 1150 to commemorate the city's reconquest from the Moors (and occupying the site of the principal mosque of Moorish Lishbuna), it's a Romanesque structure with a suitably fortress-like appearance, extraordinarily restrained in both size and decoration. The great rose window and twin towers form a simple and effective facade, although there's nothing very exciting inside: the building was once splendidly embellished on the orders of Dom João V, but his rococo whims were swept away by the earthquake and subsequent restorers. All that remains is a group of Gothic tombs behind the high altar and the decaying thirteenth-century cloister.

The Baroque **sacristy** holds a small museum of treasures including the relics of Saint Vincent, brought to Lisbon in 1173 by Afonso Henriques in a boat which, according to legend, was piloted by ravens. Ravens were kept here for centuries until the last one died in 1978. To this day, they remain one of the city's symbols.

Opposite the Sé, have a look at the church of **Santo António**, said to have been built on the spot where the city's most popular saint was born. If you want to find out more about Saint Anthony of Padua, as he is more commonly known, the neighbouring **museum** (Tues–Sun 10am–1pm & 2–6pm; 175$00, free on Sun)

THE SÉ AND AROUND

chronicles the saint's life, including his enviable skill at fixing marriages.

Just south of the Sé, on Rua dos Bacalhoeiros, stands the curious **Casa dos Bicos** (Map 4, B9), whose walls, set with diamond-shaped stones, offer an image of the richness of pre-earthquake Lisbon. Built in the 1520s for the son of the Viceroy of India, the building is not regularly open to the public, though it sees fairly frequent use as a venue for cultural exhibitions.

Further west, a couple of blocks from Praça do Comércio, along Rua da Alfândega, is the church of **Conceição Velha**, severely damaged by the earthquake of 1755, but retaining its flamboyant Manueline doorway. It once formed part of a *misericórdia* (almshouse) – you'll find one of these impressive structures in almost every town or city in Portugal.

ALFAMA

The oldest part of Lisbon, tumbling from the walls of the castle down to the Tejo, **Alfama** was buttressed against significant damage in the 1755 earthquake by the steep, rocky mass on which it's built. Although none of its houses dates from before the Christian Reconquest, many are of Moorish design, and the *kasbah*-like layout is still much as the English priest Osbern of Bawdsley described it in the 12th century, with "steep defiles instead of ordinary streets . . . and buildings so closely packed together that, except in the merchants' quarter, hardly a street could be found more than eight foot wide".

In Moorish times, this was the grandest part of the city, but as the city expanded the new Christian nobility moved out, leaving it to the local fishing community. Today, it is undergoing some commercialization, the latest scheme being to reintroduce fado houses into the area which helped give birth to the music. But although antique shops and restaurants are moving in, they are far from taking over – indeed the tourist board still cautions against wandering around the area alone at night. Certainly the quarter retains a largely traditional life, with cheap local cafés, the twice-weekly flea market at Campo de Santa Clara and, during June, the "Popular Saints" festivals, above all the *festa* of Saint Anthony on June 12, when makeshift tavernas appear on every corner.

For more on fado, see p.175.

From the Sé, Rua Cruz de Sé leads onto **Rua de São João da Praça** – the only road hereabouts wide enough for cars – which leads down into the heart of Alfama. The steep defiles, alleys and passageways are known as *becos* and *travessas* rather than *ruas*, and it would be futile to try to follow any set route. At some point in your wanderings around the quarter, though, head for **Rua de São Miguel** – off which run some of the most interesting *becos* – and for the lower, parallel **Rua de São Pedro**, where *varinas* sell the fish catch of the day from tiny stalls, right down to the **Largo do Chafariz de Dentro**, a lively square at the bottom of the hill and site of the area's main springs. Along these streets and alleys, life continues much as it has done for years: kids playing ball in tiny squares; people buying groceries and fish from hole-in-the-wall stores; householders stringing washing across narrow defiles and stoking small outdoor charcoal grills; and elderly men idling away the hours on decrepit wooden benches.

TOWARDS THE CASTELO DE SÃO JORGE

Returning from Alfama to the Sé, it's an uphill walk towards the Castelo de São Jorge along Rua Augusto Rosa. En route, you'll pass the sparse ruins of a **Roman theatre** (57 AD), set behind a grille just to the left at the junction of Rua de São Mamede and Rua da Saudade (Map 4, B7). Further uphill, the church of Santa Luzia marks the entry to the **Miradouro de Santa Luzia** (Map 4, D7), a spectacular viewpoint where elderly Lisboans play cards and tourists gather their breath for the short, steep final ascent to the castle.

Just beyond here, at Largo das Portas do Sol 2, is the Espírito Santo Silva Foundation, home of the **Museu Escola de Artes Decorativas** (Map 4, D6; Tues–Sun 10am–5pm; 900$00), a seventeenth-century mansion stuffed with what was once the private collection of banker Ricardo do Espírito Santo Silva, who gave it to the nation in 1953. On display are unique pieces of furniture, major collections of silver and porcelain, paintings, textiles and azulejo panels – in short, some of the best examples of seventeenth- and eighteenth-century applied art in the country. To get an idea of the best of contemporary crafts-manship, look out for the beautiful Arraiolos carpets from Arraiolos in the Alentejo district of Portugal. You can usually see craftsmen plying their trades in the attached workshops, which form part of the museum school.

Over the road, the **views** from the terrace-café in Largo das Portas do Sol are tremendous: a solitary palm rising from the stepped streets below, the twin-towered facade of Graça convent, the dome of Santa Engrácia, and the Tejo beyond.

CASTELO DE SÃO JORGE

Map 4, C4. Daily: May–Oct 9am–9pm; Nov–April 9am–6pm; free.
Tram #28 to Miradouro de Santa Luzia then follow the signs uphill, or bus #37 from Praça do Comércio.

Reached by a confusing – but well-signed – series of twisting roads, the **Castelo de São Jorge** is perhaps the most spectacular building in Lisbon, though as much because of its position as anything else. Beyond the small statue of Afonso Henriques, triumphant after the siege of Lisbon (see box on p.34), the entrance leads to the gardens, walkways and viewpoints within the old Moorish walls. The first Portuguese kings took up residence in the Alcáçova, the old Muslim palace within the castle, although by the time of Manuel I they had moved to the new royal palace on Praça do Comércio. After this, the castle was for a time used as a prison, and then as an army barracks until as recently as the 1920s, although the walls were partly renovated by Salazar in the 1930s, and further restored for Expo 98. It's an enjoyable place to wander about in for a couple of hours, looking down on the city from its ramparts and towers. One of these, the Tower of Ulysses, now holds a **Câmara Escura** (daily every 30min, weather permitting, 10am–4.30pm; 300$00), a kind of periscope which projects sights from around the city onto a white plate with commentary in English, though unless you like being holed up in darkened chambers with up to fifteen other people, you may prefer to see the view in the open air.

Olisipónia

Map 3, 2E. Daily 10am–6pm; 600$00.

Of the old Moorish Alcáçova, only a much-restored shell remains. This now houses **Olisipónia**, a multimedia history show in three underground chambers, including the one in which Vasco da Gama was once received by Dom Manuel. Portable headsets give a 35-minute commentary on aspects of Lisbon's development presented through film, sounds and images. The presentations overlap somewhat and gloss over a few of the city's less savoury chapters, such as slavery and the Inquisition, but are a useful introduction to the city. The final, 36-monitor "Quadroscope" show is the best part, offering insights into Salazar's regime and interesting archive footage.

CASTELO DE SÃO JORGE

The siege of Lisbon

The siege of the Moorish castle and walled city of Lisbon remains an uneasy episode in the city's history. Although an important victory, which led to the Muslim surrender at Sintra and throughout the surrounding district, it was not the most Christian or glorious of Portuguese exploits. A full account survives, written by one Osbern of Bawdsley, an English priest and Crusader, and its details, despite the author's judgemental tone, direct one's sympathies to the enemy.

The attack, in the summer of 1147, came through the opportunism and skilful management of Afonso Henriques, already established as "king" at Porto, who persuaded a large force of French and British Crusaders to delay their progress to Jerusalem for more immediate goals. The Crusaders – scarcely more than pirates – came to terms and in June the siege began. Osbern records the Archbishop of Braga's demand for the Moors to return to "the land whence you came" and, more revealingly, the weary and contemptuous response of the Muslim spokesman: "How many times have you come hither with pilgrims and barbarians to drive us hence? It is not want of possessions but only ambition of the mind that drives you on." For seventeen weeks the castle and walled inner city stood firm, but in October its walls were breached and the citizens – including a Christian community coexisting with the Muslims – were forced to surrender.

The pilgrims and barbarians, flaunting the diplomacy and guarantees of Afonso Henriques, stormed into the city, cut the throat of the local bishop and sacked, pillaged and murdered Christian and Muslim alike. In 1190 a later band of English Crusaders stopped at Lisbon and, no doubt confused by the continuing presence of Moors, sacked the castle and city a second time.

Santa Cruz and Mouraria

Crammed within the castle's outer walls is the tiny medieval quarter of **Santa Cruz**, very much a village in itself, with kids playing in the streets and women chatting on doorsteps – though it is currently undergoing substantial redevelopment, with a new hotel due for completion shortly. Leaving Santa Cruz, a tiny arch at the end of Rua do Chão da Feira leads through to Rua dos Cegos and down to Largo Rodrigues de Freitas. At 19a is the **Museu da Marioneta** (Map 4, D4; daily 10am–1pm & 2–7pm; 500$00; tram #12 from Largo Martim Moniz), a small museum displaying satirical puppets dating back to the time of the Inquisition. The museum hosts occasional weekend puppet shows, too, but is unlikely to enthral unless you have a keen interest in puppetry.

From the Museu da Marioneta, you can re-enter the castle through its eastern entrance to the left of the museum as you face it. Alternatively, catch tram #12 down the steep Calçada de Santo André to central Lisbon.

Largo Rodrigues de Freitas marks the eastern edge of **Mouraria**, the district to which the Moors were relegated after the seige of Lisbon – hence the name. Today Mouraria is an atmospheric residential area with some of the city's best African restaurants (see p.120), especially around **Largo de São Cristóvão** (Map 3, E4), a ten-minute walk west from the Museu da Marioneta along Costa do Castelo and then Rua das Farinhas. From Largo de São Cristóvão it's a short stroll back to Praça da Figueira and the Baixa down Rua das Farinhas towards the river, then first right into busy Rua da Madalena.

Tram #28

The picture-book **tram #28** is one of Lisbon's greatest rides. With a tourist pass (see p.11), you can hop on and off at the various spots along its route at no extra cost. The central section of its route runs from Rua da Conceição in the Baixa, past the Sé and up Rua Augusto Rosa, before rattling through some of Lisbon's steepest and narrowest streets – at times you are so close to the shops you could almost take a can of sardines off the shelves. The route is of less interest after you reach Rua de Voz do Operário, from where it's a short walk down to the church of São Vicente and the Feira da Ladra market (see p.37), or get off at the next stop in Largo da Graça where you can admire the superb views over Lisbon and the castle from the Miradouro da Graça.

CAMPO DE SANTA CLARA AND BEYOND

Map 4, I3.

An alternative route from the Museu da Marioneta is to head east down Rua de Santa Marinha and Rua de São Vicente towards Campo de Santa Clara. On the way you'll pass the church of **São Vicente de Fora** (daily 9am–12.30pm & 3–6.30pm; free), whose name – "Saint Vincent of the Outside" – is a reminder of the extent of the sixteenth-century city. An older church, where Saint Anthony of Padua took his religious vows in 1210, was built here in 1185 on the site of a crusader burial ground, while Afonso Henriques pitched camp on this spot during his siege and conquest of Lisbon.

The current church was built during the years of Spanish rule by Philip II's Italian architect, Felipe Terzi (1582-1629); its severe geometric facade was an important Renaissance innovation. Through the cloisters, decorated with azulejos, you can visit the old monastic refectory, which since 1855 has formed the **pantheon of the Bragança dynasty** (Tues–Sun 10am–6.30pm; 400$00). Here, in more or less complete (though unexciting) sequence, are the bodies of all Portuguese kings from João IV, who restored the monarchy in 1640, to Manuel II, who lost it and died in exile in England in 1932. Among them is Catherine of Bragança, the widow of England's Charles II. The monastery has a café with a cosy indoor room, a pretty outdoor courtyard and a small roof terrace with spectacular views over Alfama and the river beyond.

Just east of São Vicente, **Campo de Santa Clara** is home to the twice-weekly **Feira da Ladra** ("Thieves' Market"), Lisbon's rambling and ragged flea market (Tues & Sat 7am–6pm; tram #28 from Rua da Conceição in the Baixa to Rua da Voz do Operário, or bus #12 from Santa Apolónia station or Praça Marquês de Pombal). It's not the world's greatest market, but it does turn up some interesting things, like oddities from the former African colonies and old Portuguese prints. Out-and-out junk – broken alarm clocks and old postcards – is spread on the ground above Santa Engrácia, and half-genuine antiques at the top end of the *feira* around the covered market building, whose upstairs restaurant (see p.124) is particularly lively on market days.

While at the flea market, take a look inside **Santa Engrácia** (May–Oct 10am–6pm; Nov–April 10am–5pm; closed Mon; 250$00), whose dome makes it one of the most recognizable buildings on the city skyline. The loftiest and most tortuously built church in the city, it has become synonymous with unfinished work – begun in 1682, it was finally completed only in 1966. Ask nicely and you may be allowed to take the elevator to the dome, from where you can look down on the empty church and out over the flea market, port and city.

Museu Militar and Museu da Água

A couple of blocks south of Santa Engrácia stands the

Portuguese azulejos

Fans of azulejos – brightly coloured, decorative ceramic tiles – have plenty to enjoy in Lisbon, where you can see a variety of styles spanning five hundred years inside and outside houses, shops, monuments and even metro stations. Though influenced by Moorish and Spanish glazed tiles – the early sixteenth-century tiles in the Palácio Nacional in Sintra typify Moorish geometric patterns – **Portuguese azulejos** developed their own style around the mid-sixteenth century, when a new Italian method allowed images to be painted onto the clay (rather than using coloured clay) – those in the Igreja de São Roque (p.43) reflect the religious imagery favoured at this time. Later, by the seventeenth century, decadent and colourful images were all the rage, and the wealthy commissioned large azulejo panels displaying battles and hunting scenes.

Soon, new Dutch techniques produced a higher standard of azulejo, although their colour was limited to just blue and white; those on the Palácio dos Marquêses de Fronteira (see p.77) and São Vicente de Fora (see p.36) are typical of this new style. Competition with the Dutch meant that local tile makers had to raise their standards in order to survive, and the early eighteenth century saw trained artist "masters" producing highly decorated ceramic mosaics, culminating in Rococo themes as seen in Madre de Deus, now the tile museum (see p.39).

Following the Great Earthquake, more prosaic tiled facades, often with Neoclassical designs, were considered good insulation devices, as well as protecting buildings from rain and fire. By the mid-nineteenth century, mass-produced azulejos were being used to decorate shops and factories – the tiles on the front of the Fábrica Viúva Lamego (p.197), for example, are of this type, while the end of the century saw the reappearance of figures on tiles, typified by the work in the *Cervejaria da Trindade*

(p.127). The nineteenth century also saw the arrival of individual-
ists such as Rafael Bordalo Pinheiro (p.76), who used azulejos
for comical and satirical purposes. Art Deco took hold in the
1920s, while more modern, works can be admired in Lisbon's
underground stations – Campo Pequeno, Colégio Militar and
Cidade Universitária, among others.

imposing Corinthian facade of the city's military museum,
the **Museu Militar** (Map 4, J6; Tues–Sun 10am–5pm;
300$00, free Wed; bus #9 from Praça do Comércio or #39
from Restauradores), though this is very traditional in layout – old weapons in old cases – and lacks appeal unless
you've an unusual interest in historical military campaigns
and weaponry.

Some ten minutes' walk beyond the Museu Militar at
Rua do Alviela 12, a side street off Calçada dos
Barbadinhos, stands the **Museu da Água** (Map 2, H8;
Mon–Sat 10am–6pm; 350$00; bus #105 from Praça da
Figueira), a limited but surprisingly engaging museum
devoted to the evolution of the city's water supply. It is
housed in an attractive old pumping station, built in 1880
to pump water up Lisbon's steep hills. If you get a kick
out of watching demonstrations of nineteenth-century
beam engines, this is the place for you. While here, you
can arrange a visit to the Aqueduto das Águas Livres (see
p.78).

Museu Nacional do Azulejo

Map 2, H8. Tues 2–6pm, Wed–Sun 10am–6pm; 400$00, free on
Sun; bus #104 from Praça do Comércio, bus #105 from Praça da
Figueira.

A little over 1.5km to the east of the Museu da Agua (and
linked to it by buses #104 and #105) stands one of Lisbon's

CAMPO DE SANTA CLARA AND BEYOND

most interesting small museums, the **Museu Nacional do Azulejo**, which traces the development of the distinctive Portuguese azulejo tiles from Moorish styles to the present day. It is installed in the church and cloisters of Madre de Deus, whose eighteenth-century tiled scenes of the life of Saint Anthony are among the best in the city. Upstairs there are temporary exhibitions. The highlight, however, is Portugal's longest azulejo – a wonderfully detailed 40-metre panorama of Lisbon, completed in around 1738. Look out, too, for the meat-and-game imagery on the tiled walls of the museum café-restaurant, a great spot for lunch, with its own leafy garden.

The Bairro Alto

igh above and to the west of the city centre is the **Bairro Alto**, the upper town. By day, the quarter's narrow seventeenth-century streets feel essentially residential, with children playing in the cobbled streets and old people sitting in doorways. After dark, the area takes on a very different character, thrumming with drinkers, clubbers and diners visiting its wonderful fado houses, bars and restaurants. Reached by **elevadores** that are a treat in themselves, the area is also home to two of the city's most interesting churches, the **Convento do Carmo** and **São Roque**. Heading north towards the district of Rato, the leafy **Praça do Príncipe Real** is a foretaste of the exotic **Jardim Botânico** botanical gardens, which roll down the hill below the **museums of science and natural history**.

For listings of the Bairro Alto's best bars and clubs,
see p.159 and p.165.

THE ELEVADORES

Unless you want to take the prosaic bus #58 from Cais do Sodré, it's best to approach the Bairro Alto via one of the area's three **elevadores**. Two of these are funicular-like electric trams – the **Elevador da Bica** (Map 5, A6–C4; see p.27) and the **Elevador da Glória** (Map 5, G2; see p.44). It's the **Elevador de Santa Justa** (Map 3, E7; daily 7am–11.45pm), however, which offers the most startling ascent. Built in 1902 by Raul Mésnier, this is one of the city's most eccentric and captivating structures: a giant lift which whisks you up the innards of a latticework metal tower before depositing you on a platform high above the Baixa with a rooftop café. The exit at the top of the *elevador* – which leads out beside the Convento do Carmo – has been temporarily closed during the construction of a new metro line, but is due to reopen shortly. To reach the Convento from the Baixa on foot, head up the steep Calçada do Carmo, off the southwest side of Rossio, or the gentler route along Rua do Carmo behind the Elevador de Santa Justa, into Rua Garrett, then first right up Calçada do Sacramento. Both walks take about five minutes.

Tickets for all the *elevadores* cost 160$00 each way.

CONVENTO DO CARMO

Map 3, E8. Mon–Sat: April–Sept 10am–6pm; Oct–March 10am–1pm & 2–5pm; 500$00.

Leaving by the top exit of the Elevador Santa Justa brings you to the pretty, enclosed Largo do Carmo, where you'll find the ruined Gothic arches of the **Convento do Carmo**. Once the largest church in the city, this was half-destroyed by the Great Earthquake, but is perhaps even more beautiful as a result.

In the nineteenth century its shell was used as a chemical factory. Today it houses the splendidly miscellaneous **Museu Arqueológico do Carmo** (currently closed while metro tunnelling is completed underneath, but due to reopen soon). Inside, the entire nave is open to the elements, with roses growing up the aisle columns and tombs and statuary scattered in all corners. On either side of what was the main altar are the most notable exhibits, centred on a series of tombs of great significance. Largest is the beautifully carved stone tomb, two metres high, containing the bones of Ferdinand I; nearby, that of Gonçalo de Sousa, chancellor to Henry the Navigator, is topped by a recumbent statue of Gonçalo, his clasped arms holding a book, signifying his learning. Other pieces include a jasper sculpture from Brazil of the Virgin Mary, with cherubs clinging to the stand for dear life and, more alarmingly, two pre-Columbian mummies, which lie curled up in glass cases alongside the preserved heads of a couple of Peruvian Indians. Elsewhere there are flints, arrowheads, prehistoric ceramics, thirteenth-century coins and Roman inscriptions all well labelled in English and endearingly positioned cheek-by-jowl with little thought of thematic progression.

SÃO ROQUE

Map 5, G3. Church: daily 8.30am–6pm; free. Museu de São Roque: May–Oct Tues–Sun 10am–5pm; Nov–Apr daily 10am–noon & 1–5pm; 150$00, free Sundays. Bus #58 from Cais do Sodré.

Heading north from the Convento do Carmo it's around five minutes' walk to the Bairro Alto's other main site – go left along Rua da Trindade, then right up Rua Nova da Trindade, which brings you to Largo T. Coelho, with a diminutive statue of a postman loping across the square. To the left sits the **Igreja de São Roque**. From the outside, this looks like the plainest church in the city, its bleak Renaissance facade (by Filipo Terzi, architect of São Vicente) having been further simplified by the earthquake. But inside lie an astonishing succession of side chapels, lavishly crafted with azulejos, multi-coloured marble and Baroque painted ceilings.

The highlight is the **Capela de São João Baptista**. This chapel, one of the most extravagant commissions of its age, is estimated for its size to be the most expensive ever constructed. It was ordered from Rome in 1742 by Dom João V to honour his patron saint and, more dubiously, to gratify the pope, whom he had persuaded to confer a patriarchate upon Lisbon. Designed by the papal architect, Vanvitelli, and using the most costly materials available, including ivory, agate, porphyry and lapis lazuli, it was erected at the Vatican for the pope to celebrate Mass in, before being dismantled and shipped to Lisbon at the then vast cost of some £250,000. If you take a close look at the four "oil paintings" of John the Baptist's life, you'll find that they are in fact intricately worked mosaics. Today, the lapis lazuli and more valuable parts of the altar front are kept in the adjacent **museum**, which also displays sixteenth- to eighteenth-century paintings and the usual motley collection of vestments, chalices and bibles which have been bequeathed to the church over the centuries.

AROUND PRAÇA DO PRÍNCIPE REAL

Map 8, D7.

Just behind São Roque on Rua de São Pedro de Alcântara lies the top end of the **Elevador da Glória** (Map 5, G2; daily 7am–12.55am). Built in 1885, this funicular-style *elevador* links the Bairro Alto directly with the Baixa, taking off from just behind the tourist office in Praça dos Restauradores. From the gardens by the top end there's a superb view across the city to the castle, whilst immediately over the road is the *Instituto do Vinho do Porto* (see p.160), one of the city's most famous bars.

Continuing north along Rua Dom Pedro V brings you to **Praça do Príncipe Real**, one of the city's loveliest squares. The central fountain is built over a covered reservoir that – improbably – hosts occasional art exhibitions. At weekends the square is full of elderly locals playing cards around a superb cedar tree, whose extensive branches are propped up to form a natural shelter. By night, the square takes on a somewhat different air as the focal point of Lisbon's best gay nightclubs (see p.171).

The square also has a handy play area for children, near the outdoor tables of the *Esplanada do Prínçipe Real* – a lovely drinks stop, though the food is overpriced.

Continuing along the busy Rua Escola Politécnica towards the district of Rato, you'll come to the classical-fronted former technical college, now housing the museums of Natural History and Science. The former, the **Museu da Historia Natural** (Mon–Fri 10am–noon & 1–5pm, closed Aug; free; bus #15 or #58 from Cais do Sodré), houses a rather sorry collection of stuffed animals, eggs and shells representing plant and animal life in the Iberian peninsula, though temporary exhibitions held in the adjacent rooms can be more diverting. The **Museu da Ciência** opposite (Mon–Fri 10am–1pm & 2–5pm, Sat 3–6pm, closed Aug; free) has more absorbing geological exhibits and a low-tech interactive section where you can balance balls on jets of air and swing pendulums among throngs of school kids.

Jardim Botânico

Map 8, D5. May–Oct Mon–Fri 9am–8pm, Sat–Sun 10am–8pm; Nov–April same hours until 6pm; 250$00.

Just beyond the museums lies the entrance to the city's nineteenth-century **Jardim Botânico** (botanical gardens). Almost entirely invisible from the surrounding streets –

there's another entance tucked into Rua da Alegria – the gardens are an oasis of green, packed with twenty thousand neatly labelled exotic plants from around the world. Steep, shady paths lead downhill under overbearing palms and luxuriant shrubs, a tranquil escape from the city bustle. To get back into town from here, leave through the garden's bottom exit into Rua da Alegria and walk downhill to Avenida da Liberdade; alternatively, it's five minutes' walk north along Rua da Escola Politécnica at the top of the gardens to Rato metro.

Estrela, Lapa and Alcântara

W est of the Bairro Alto extend some of Lisbon's most affluent areas. Beyond **São Bento** – home to the impressive Palácio da Assembléia, Portugal's parliamentary building – lies the attractive district of **Estrela**, best known for its **gardens** and enormous **basilica**, one of Lisbon's most attractive churches, whose white dome can be seen from much of the city. To the north are the **Cemitério dos Ingleses** – the English Cemetery – and the former home of one Lisbon's greatest writers, Fernando Pessoa, now a cultural centre.

To the south of Estrela lies the opulent suburb of **Lapa**, whose tranquil streets are the favoured homes of diplomats and Lisbon's rich. The one key sight here is the wonderful collection of paintings and artefacts in the **Museu Nacional de Arte Antiga**. West of Lapa, a tangle of busy roads leads towards Ponte 25 de Abril and the **Alcântara docks**, now home to some of Lisbon's liveliest bars and restaurants.

The area covered by this chapter is shown in detail on colour map 6.

ESTRELA AND SÃO BENTO

São Bento

Map 6, H3. Tram #28 from Rua da Conceição in the Baixa. Bus #6 from Praça Marquês de Pombal.

En route to Estrela, the district of **São Bento** is worth a brief stopover to peer at the **Palácio da Assembléia**, home to Portugal's parliament. The classical facade was originally the Mosteiro de São Bento, a Benedictine monastery which the government took over in 1834 after the abolition of religious orders. The building has been tarted up in recent years, making it stick out like even more of a sore thumb in an otherwise nitty-gritty residential area which houses some good ethnic restaurants (see p.131).

Estrela

Estrela is one of Lisbon's more attractive and traditional districts. Tramlines from Campo de Ourique, Lapa and Chiado converge at the spacious Praça da Estrela, over-looked by the impressive **Basílica da Estrela** (Mon–Sat 8am–7pm, Sun 9am–7pm; tram #28 or bus #13 from Praça do Comércio), a vast monument to late-eighteenth century Neoclassicism, constructed by order of Queen Maria I (whose tomb lies within) and completed in 1790. Opposite is the **Jardim da Estrela** public garden. Lisbon takes its gardens seriously and this is among its most enjoyable: a quiet refuge with a pondside café, a well-equipped children's playground and even a library kiosk for those who fancy a spot of Portuguese literature under the palms.

North of the park on Rua de São Jorge you'll find the gate to the **Cemitério dos Ingleses** (English Cemetery) (Map 6, G2 – ring loudly for entry) where, among the cypresses, lie the remains of Henry Fielding, author of *Tom Jones*, whose imminent demise may have influenced his verdict on Lisbon as "the nastiest city in the world".

A little further uphill from here at Rua Coelho da Rocha 16 stands the **Casa Museu Fernando Pessoa** (Map 6, G1; Mon–Wed & Fri 10am–6pm, Thurs 1–8pm; free), where Fernando Pessoa lived for the last fifteen years of his life. As well as housing Almada Negreiros's famous painting of the writer, it contains a few of Pessoa's personal belongings

Fernando Pessoa

In common with many other great artists, **Fernando Pessoa** was largely unrecognized until after his death, but is now Portugal's most celebrated modern poet. Born in Lisbon in 1888, Pessoa spent most of his childhood in South Africa with his mother, and he subsequently wrote many of his poems in English. Returning alone to Lisbon aged seventeen, he lived mostly in spartan rented rooms, contributing poetry to literary magazines. He soon became known as a modernist, influenced by the European avant-garde, Cubists, Futurists and others. With his distinctive gold-rimmed glasses, bow tie and hat, the quirky poet was a conspicuous figure in the Baixa cafés where he wrote. Unfortunately, his need to smoke and drink while he worked contributed to a short life, and he died in 1935, a year after the appearance of *Mensagem*, the only one of his books published during his lifetime. Since his death, researchers have unearthed several intriguing but previously unpublished works, many written under pseudonyms including Alberto Caeiro, Alvaro de Campos, Ricardo Reis and, for his prose, Bernardo Soares. Each pseudonym represented a different persona, a different literary style; but each one was equally learned and inspired, embodiments of the different personalities the enigmatic Pessoa believed we all possess.

such as his glasses and diaries. There are also exhibits by artists influenced by Pessoa.

LAPA

From Estrela, tram #25 passes through the well-heeled suburb of **Lapa** en route to Praça do Comércio, stopping at the end of Rua das Janelas Verdes, which houses the Museu Nacional de Arte Antiga. If you want to explore Lapa's opulent streets more closely, you could walk all the way from the Praça da Estrela along the tramlines to the top of Rua de São Domingos à Lapa. A detour to the left along Rua da Lapa reveals steep side streets offering lovely views over the Tejo below. You can continue downhill along Rua de São Domingos à Lapa all the way to the museum (take a right along Rua do Prior and left along Rua do Conde). Alternatively, for a real taste of Lapa opulence, head right along Rua do Sacramento à Lapa, past grand embassy buildings and stunning mansions. Turn left into Rua do Pau da Bandeira where you'll find the luxurious *Hotel da Lapa* (see p.100) at no. 4. It's worth saving some escudos for a drink here in one of Lisbon's plushest and most tasteful hotels. From here, it's a ten-minute walk (from Rua do Pau da Bandeira, go left into Rua do Prior and then first right into Rua do Conde), downhill all the way, to the Museu Nacional de Arte Antiga.

Museu Nacional de Arte Antiga

Map 6, F6. Tues 2–6pm, Wed–Sun 10am–6pm; 500$00, free on Sun 10am–2pm. Bus #40 or #60 from Praça do Comércio, or bus #27 or #49 from Belém. Tram #25 from Alcântara.

The **Museu Nacional de Arte Antiga**, in effect Portugal's national gallery, is the one Lisbon museum that stands comparison with the Gulbenkian. The museum fea-

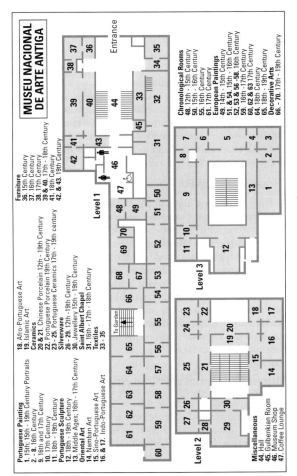

MUSEU NACIONAL DE ARTE ANTIGA

Entrance

Level 1
Level 2
Level 3

To Garden

Saint Albert Chapel

Portuguese Painting
1. 15th; 15th - 19th Century Portraits
2. - 8. 16th Century
9. 16th and 17th Century
10. 17th Century
11. 18th - 19th Century

Portuguese Sculpture
12. 18th - 19th Century
13. Middle Ages; 16th - 17th Century

Oriental Art
14. Namban Art
15. Sino-Portuguese Art
16. & 17. Indo-Portuguese Art

18. Afro-Portuguese Art
19. Islamic Art

Ceramics
20 & 21. Chinese Porcelain 12th - 19th Century
22. Portuguese Porcelain 19th Century
23 - 25. Portuguese Ceramics 17th - 19th century

Silverware
26 - 29. 12th - 19th Century
30. Jewellery 15th - 19th Century

Saint Albert Chapel
31. 16th - 17th - 18th Century

Textiles
33 - 35

Furniture
36. 15th Century
37. 16th Century
38. 17th Century
39 & 40. 17th - 18th Century
41. 18th Century
42. & 43. 19th Century

Chronological Rooms
48. 12th - 15th Century
50. 15th - 16th Century
55. 16th Century
61. 17th Century

European Paintings
49. 14th - 15th Century
51. & 54. 15th - 16th Century
52, 53 & 56 & 58. 16th Century
59. 16th - 17th Century
60, 62 & 63 17th Century
64. 18th Century
65. 18th - 19th Century

Decorative Arts
66. - 70. 17th - 19th Century

Miscellaneous
44. Hall
45. Gulbenkian Room
46. Museum Shop
47. Coffee Lounge

LAPA

51

tures the largest collection of Portuguese fifteenth- and six-teenth-century paintings in the country, European paintings from the fourteenth century to the present day, and a rich display of applied art showing the influence of Portugal's colonial explorations. All of this is well displayed in a beautifully converted seventeenth-century palace once owned by the Marquês de Pombal, with a café complete with outdoor tables in attractive formal gardens overlooking the Tejo. The palace was built over the remains of the Saint Albert monastery, most of which was razed during the 1755, although its chapel can still be seen today.

Gonçalves and the Portuguese School

Starting on the top floor (level 3), **Nuno Gonçalves** and other painters of the so-called **Portuguese School** span that indeterminate and exciting period in the second half of the fifteenth century when Gothic art was giving way to the Renaissance. Their works, exclusively religious in concept, are particularly interesting in their emphasis on portraiture, transforming any theme into a vivid observation of local contemporary life (notably Gregório Lopes's *Martyrdom of São Sebastião*, and Frei Carlos's *Annunciation*). Stylistically, the most significant influences upon them were those of the Flemish Northern Renaissance painters: Jan van Eyck, who came to Portugal in 1428, Memling and Mabuse (both well represented here), and Roger van der Weyden. As two of the main maritime powers of the time, there were close trade links between Portugal and Flanders, and many Flemish painters visited or settled in Lisbon.

The acknowledged masterpiece is Gonçalves's altarpiece for Saint Vincent (1467–70) in room 1, a brilliantly marshalled composition depicting Lisbon's patron saint receiving homage from all ranks of its citizens. On the two left-hand panels are Cistercian monks, fishermen and pilots;

on the opposite side the Duke of Bragança and his family, a helmeted Moorish knight, a Jew (with book), a beggar, and a priest holding Saint Vincent's own relics (a piece of his skull, still kept by the cathedral). In the epic central panels the moustachioed Henry the Navigator, his nephew Afonso V (in black and green), and the youthful (future) Dom João II, pay tribute to the saint. Among the frieze of portraits behind them, that on the far left is reputed to be Gonçalves himself; the other central panel shows the Archbishop of Lisbon. **Later Portuguese painters** – from the sixteenth to the eighteenth century – are displayed too, most notably António de Sequeira and Josefa de Óbidos. The latter, though born in Seville (in 1634), is considered one of Portugal's greatest women painters, spending most of her life as an etcher, miniaturist and religious painter in the convent of Óbidos, around 70km north of Lisbon.

The rest of the collection

After Gonçalves and his contemporaries, the most interesting exhibits are on the bottom floor (level 1), where there are works by **Flemish and German** painters – Cranach, Bosch and Dürer. The highlight for most people is Hieronymus Bosch's stunningly gruesome *Temptation of St Anthony* in room 57. Elsewhere on this level there are miscellaneous gems: an altar panel depicting the Resurrection by Raphael, Zurbarán (*The Twelve Apostles*) and a small statue of a nymph by Rodin. Look out, too, for the Baroque Saint Albert Chapel by room 31, beautifully decorated with azulejos.

Level 2 contains extensive applied art sections. Here, you'll find Portuguese **furniture** and **textiles** to rival the European selection in the Gulbenkian, and an excellent collection of **silverware** and **ceramics**. The **Oriental art collection** shows the influence of Indian, African and Oriental

LAPA

designs derived from the trading links of the sixteenth century. Other colonially influenced exhibits include inlaid furniture from Goa and a supremely satisfying series of late sixteenth-century **Japanese namban screens** (room 14), showing the Portuguese landing at Nagasaki. The Japanese saw the Portuguese traders as southern barbarians (*namban*) with large noses – hence their Pinocchio-like features.

ALCÂNTARA

Steps beside the Museu Nacional de Arte Antiga lead down to Avenida 24 de Julho, where you can brave crossing the railway lines to reach the **Alcântara docks**, one of the city's most vibrant areas. Formerly in a state of decline until, during the mid-1990s, it was realized that these docks would make the perfect, traffic-free alternative to the clubs of the Bairro Alto and the Avenida 24 de Julho. The scale of their success has set in motion a development boom that is turning many of Lisbon's riverfront warehouses all the way from Belém to Santa Apolónia into smart bars and restaurants.

To reach Alcântara and the docks from the city centre, catch a train from Cais do Sodré to Alcântara Mar (Map 6, C6). Alternatively, tram #15 from Praça da Figueira goes along Avenida 24 de Julho, just north of the docks.

At present the **Doca de Alcântara** (Map 6, C6–E7) is liveliest at night, when its boat-bars and restaurant–clubs like *Kings and Queens* and *Indochina* (see p.169) come into their own. A better bet by day is to head west to the more intimate **Doca de Santo Amaro** (Map 6, B7), nestling right under the Ponte 25 de Abril. This small, almost completely enclosed dock is filled with bobbing sailing boats and lined with tastefully converted warehouses. There's the odd restaurant around here, but many more cafés, with prices considerably higher that usual in Lisbon. For more on these, see p.150.

Back inland, over the busy Avenida da Índia, the suburb of **Alcântara** itself is a traditional district of shops and houses wedged between railway lines and the major traffic arteries that pass along and over the river – a suitably grungy zone for some of Lisbon's coolest clubs and restaurants (see p.167).

Just north east of here lie the steep, green expanses of the **Jardim da Tapada das Necessidades** (Map 6, D4–E3; Mon–Sat 10am–6pm). The gardens belong to the Palácio Real das Necessidades, a former royal residence now used by the government (not open to the public). The gardens have somewhat hard-to-find entrances on Rua do Borja and Largo das Necessidades; inside, the wooded slopes – eerily deserted and unkempt – offer some impressive semi-tropical plants and fine views over the Ponte 25 de Abril.

Palácio da Ajuda

Daily except Wed 10am–5pm; 400$00, free Sun morning 10am–2pm; tram #18 from Praça do Comércio and Alcântara, bus #60 from Praça da Figueira or #14 from Belém.

From Alcântara it's a short ride on tram #18 from Avenida 24 de Julho to the **Palácio da Ajuda.** The palace was built by those crashingly tasteless nineteenth-century royals, Dona Maria II and Dom Ferdinand, and like their Pena Palace folly at Sintra is all over-the-top aristocratic clutter. The banqueting hall, however, is quite a sight, as is the lift, decked out with mahogany and mirrors. Next to the palace is the attractive **Jardim Botânico** (Mon–Fri 8am–5pm), dating back to the time of Pombal – a fine example of formal Portuguese gardening boasting some great views over Belém.

ALCÂNTARA

Belém

Two kilometres west of the towering Ponte 25 de Abril lies one of Lisbon's most historic areas: **Belém**. It was from here in 1497 that Vasco da Gama set sail for India, and here too that he was welcomed home by Dom Manuel "the Fortunate" (O Venturoso), bringing with him a small cargo of pepper which was enough to pay for his voyage sixty times over. The monastery subsequently built here – the **Mosteiro dos Jerónimos** – stands as a testament to his triumphant discovery of a sea route to the Orient, which initiated the beginning of a Portuguese golden age.

The River Tejo at Belém has receded with the centuries. When the monastery was built it stood almost on the beach, within sight of the caravels moored ready for expeditions, and of the **Torre de Belém**, which guarded the entrance to the port. This, too, survived the earthquake, and is along with the monastery Lisbon's other showpiece of the Manueline style, a maritime-influenced architectural manner with its characteristic nautical motifs. Both monastery and tower lie in what is now – despite being bisected by the road and railway – a pleasant waterfront suburb, 6km west of the city centre, close to a small group of museums set up by Salazar during the wartime Expo. There are also some fine cafés and restaurants, most within sight of a more recent celebration of Portuguese explorers, the large concrete **Monumento dos Descobrimentos.**

Belém is easily reached by tram – the fast supertram #15 (signed Algés) runs from Praça da Figueira via Praça do Comércio, taking about twenty minutes – the route goes through Alcântara via Rua Fradesso da Silveira and Rua 1° de Maio, not along the riverfront; from the Palácio da Ajuda it's a short hop on bus #14.

The area covered by this chapter is shown in detail on map 7.

AROUND PRAÇA DO IMPÉRIO

Several of Belém's major sights are clustered around **Praça do Império** (Map 7, E5), a square with an impressive fountain laid out by Salazar during World War II. The controversial pink marble **Centro Cultural de Belém** (Map 7, D5; daily 11am–8pm; ©213 612 400) on its western side was hurriedly built to host Lisbon's 1992 presidency of the EU. It's now an arts complex containing a design museum (see p.58) and hosting regular photography and art exhibitions, as well as concerts and live entertainment at weekends – jugglers, mime artists and the like; at other times, its concrete expanse takes on a rather desolate air. For the best views of the surroundings, drop into *Café Quadrante* on the first floor, whose roof-garden overlooks the river and the Monumento dos Descobrimentos.

Note that many of Belém's sites are closed on Mondays.

Just east of the square down Rua de Belém are the seemingly never-ending rooms of the *Antiga Confeitaria de Belém* (see p.151), which bills itself as the only producer of *pastéis de Belém* – delicious flaky tartlets filled with custard-like cream. If you want something more to eat, head for the attractive traditional buildings along nearby Rua V. Portuense, where there's a row of restaurants with outdoor seating (see p.134). North of here, garden lovers will enjoy the **Jardim do Ultramar** (Map 7, H3; daily 10am–5pm), a green oasis with hothouses, ponds and towering palms – the entrance is on Calçada do Galvão.

Museu do Design

Map 7, D5. Daily 11am–8pm (last entry 7.15pm); 500$00.

Opened in the Centro Cultural's Exhibition Centre in 1999, the **Museu do Design** (Design Museum) is the first in the city dedicated to contemporary household design. The collection was amassed by former stockbroker and media mogul Francisco Capelo (who also helped found the Museu de Arte Moderna in Sintra) and contains over 160 design classics embracing furniture, glass and jewellery from 1937 to the present. Exhibits are displayed chronologically in three sections entitled "Luxo" (Luxury), "Pop" and "Cool". "Luxo" contains one-off luxury and later, industrially produced designs from the 1930s to the 1950s, including classic fibreglass chairs from Charles and Ray Eames, and Marshmallow and Coconut chairs by the American George Nelson. "Pop" features fun designs from the 1960s and 1970s, including bean bags, kitsch moulded plastic furniture and wonderful Joe Colombo trolleys. "Cool" contains designs from the 1980s and 1990s, including the Memphis Group's Tawaraya bed, Phillipe Starck's chair and the works of established Portuguese designers such as Tomás Tavira and Alvara Siza Vieria.

The Mosteiro dos Jerónimos

Map 7, F4. June–Sept 10am–6pm; Oct–May 10am–5pm; closed Mon. Entry to the monastery is free; entry to the cloister costs 500$00 but is free Sun 10am–2pm.

Even before the Great Earthquake, the **Mosteiro dos Jerónimos**, flanking the northern side of Praça do Império, was Lisbon's finest monument: since then, it has stood quite without comparison. Begun in 1502, the monastery is the most ambitious and successful achievement of Manueline architecture. It was built on the site of the Ermida do Restelo, a hermitage founded by Henry the Navigator at which Vasco da Gama and his companions spent their last night ashore in prayer before leaving for India. Dom Manuel made a vow to the Virgin that he would build a monastery should da Gama return successfully. And successful he was: the monastery's funding came from a five percent tax on all spices imported from the East other than pepper, cinnamon and cloves, whose import had become the sole preserve of the Crown.

The daring and confidence of the monastery's design is largely the achievement of two outstanding figures: **Diogo de Boitaca**, perhaps the originator of the Manueline style with his Igreja de Jesus at Setúbal, and **João de Castilho**, a Spaniard who took charge of construction from around 1517. It was Castilho who designed the **main entrance** to the church, a complex hierarchy of figures clustered around Henry the Navigator (on a pedestal above the arch). In its intricate and almost flat ornamentation it shows the influence of the then current Spanish style, Plateresque (literally, the art of the silversmith). Yet it also has distinctive Manueline features – the use of rounded forms, the naturalistic motifs in the bands around the windows – and these seem to create both its harmony and individuality. They are also unmistakably outward-looking, evoking the new forms discovered in the East, a characteristic that makes each Manueline building so new and interesting, and so much a product of its particular and expansionist age.

This is immediately true of the church itself, whose breathtaking sense of space alone places it among the great triumphs of European Gothic. Here, though, Manueline developments add two extraordinary fresh dimensions. There are tensions, deliberately created and carefully restrained, between the grand spatial design and the areas of intensely detailed ornamentation. And, still more striking, there's a naturalism in the forms of this ornamentation that seems to extend into the actual structure of the church. Once you've made the analogy, it's difficult to see the six central columns as anything other than palm trunks, growing both into and from the branches of the delicate rib-vaulting.

Manueline architecture

This elaborate architectural style known as **Manueline** was a development of the Gothic and evolved during the reign of Manuel 1 (1495–1521), after whom it is named. This was the age of Portugal's maritime explorations, and it was these that supplied the inspiration for the distinctive Manueline motifs, drawn from ropes, anchors, ships' wheels and the exotic plant and animal life encountered abroad, and which typically adorn Manueline buildings' windows, doors and columns. It would be hard to imagine an art more directly reflecting the achievements and preoccupations of an age. Another peculiarity of Manueline buildings is the way in which they can adapt, enliven, or encompass any number of different styles. João de Castilho's columns in the Mosteiro dos Jerónimos, for example, show the influence of the Renaissance, while the Torre de Belém has Moorish touches.

Here, the basic structure is thoroughly Gothic, though Castilho's ornamentation on the columns is much more Renaissance in spirit. So too is the semicircular apse (around the altar), added in 1572, beyond which is the entrance to the remarkable double cloister.

Vaulted throughout and fantastically embellished, the **cloister** is one of the most original and beautiful pieces of architecture in the country, holding Gothic forms and Renaissance ornamentation in an exuberant balance. The rounded corner canopies and delicate twisting divisions within each of the arches lend a wave-like, rhythmic motion to the whole structure, a conceit extended by the typically Manueline motifs drawn from ropes, anchors and the sea.

The only time that entry to the church is restricted is during Mass and on Saturday mornings, when there seems to be an endless procession of flamboyant weddings, whose photo calls spill out onto Praça do Império.

The monastery museums

In the wings of the monastery are two museums. The enormous **Museu da Marinha** (Marine Museum) (June–Sept 10am–6pm; Oct–May 10am–5pm; closed Mon; 300$00, free Sun 10am–2pm), in the west wing, is more interesting than many of its kind, packed not only with models of ships, naval uniforms and a surprising display of artefacts from Portugal's oriental trade and colonies, but also with real vessels – among them fishing boats and sumptuous state barges – a couple of seaplanes and even some fire engines. There's also a **Museu das Crianças** (Children's Museum) within the museum – see p.209 for details.

The **Museu de Arqueologia** on Praça do Império (Tues 2–6pm, Wed–Sun 10am–6pm; 400$00, free Sun 10am–2pm), a Neo-Manueline extension to the monastery added in 1850, has a small section on Egyptian antiquities, but concentrates on Portuguese archaeological finds – rather a sparse collection and, apart from a few fine Roman mosaics unearthed in the Algarve, thoroughly unexceptional.

The Monumento dos Descobrimentos

Map 7, E6. Tues–Sun 9.30am–6.30pm; 330$00.

South of Praça do Império, and reached via an underpass beneath the busy Avenida da Índia and railway line, the **Monumento dos Descobrimentos** (Discoveries Monument) is an angular slab of concrete erected in 1960 to commemorate the five-hundredth anniversary of the death of Henry the Navigator. An impressive statue of Henry appears on the prow along with Camões and other Portuguese heroes. Within the monument is a small exhibition space, with interesting temporary exhibits on the city's history – the entrance fee also includes a ride in the lift to the top for some fine views of the Tejo and the Torre de Belém. Just in front of the monument, the pavement is decorated with a map of the world charting the routes taken by Portuguese explorers, while the adjacent **Doca de Belém** shelters some upmarket restaurants (see p.134).

Heading west along the riverfront, you'll pass the **Museu de Arte Popular** (Map 7, D6; Mon–Sat 10am–12.30pm & 2–5pm; 300$00), a province-by-province display of Portugal's diverse folk arts housed in a shed-like building on the waterfront. As well as farm implements there are regional costumes, pieces of furniture, bagpipes from northern Portugal and some interesting ceramics. From here, you can continue west past another dockland development, the **Doca de Bom Sucesso**, to the Torre de Belém.

AROUND PRAÇA DO IMPÉRIO

Torre de Belém

Map 7, A7. June–Sept 10am–6pm; Oct–May 10am–5pm; closed Mon; 400$00, free on Sun 10am–2pm.

The **Torre de Belém**, still washed by the sea, is 500m west of the monastery, fronted by a little park with a café. Whimsical, multi-turreted and with a real hat-in-the-air exuberance, it was built over the last five years of Dom Manuel's reign (1515–20) to defend the mouth of the Tejo – before an earthquake shifted its course in 1777, it stood near the middle of the great river. As such, it is the one completely Manueline building in Portugal, the rest having been adaptations of earlier structures or completed in later years.

Its architect, Francisco de Arruda, had previously worked on Portuguese fortifications in Morocco, and a Moorish influence is very strong in the delicately arched windows and balconies. Prominent also in the decoration are two great symbols of the age: Manuel's personal badge of an armillary sphere (representing the globe) and the cross of the military Order of Christ, once the Templars, who took a major role in all Portuguese conquests. The tower's interior is unremarkable except for the views from it and a "whispering gallery"; it was used into the nineteenth century as a prison, notoriously by Dom Miguel (1828–34), who kept political enemies in the waterlogged dungeons.

EAST TOWARDS ALCÂNTARA

Returning to Praça do Império and heading east down Rua de Belém brings you to the second of the area's two main squares, **Praça Afonso de Albuquerque**. On the northern side of the square is the **Museu dos Coches** (Map 7, H4; June–Sept Tues–Sun 10am–5.30pm; 450$00, free Sun 10am–2pm). The museum, housed in the attractive former riding school of the President's palace, was opened in 1905 on the initiative of Queen Dona Amélia and contains one of the largest collections of carriages and saddlery in the world, although the interminable line of royal coaches – Baroque, heavily gilded and sometimes beautifully painted – hardly warrants the museum's claim to be one of the most visited tourist attractions in Lisbon.

Regular ferries depart from Belém's Estação Fluvial (every 30min Mon–Fri 6.30am–11.30pm, Sun 7.30–11.30pm), on the riverfront south of Praça Afonso de Albuquerque, to Trafaria, which is a short bus ride from the beaches of Caparica. Alternatively, get off at the first stop, Porto Brandão, where there are some good fish restaurants and views back to Belém.

Now that work on the new railway line beneath the Ponte 25 de Abril suspension bridge has been completed, it is possible to walk the 2km along the relatively traffic-free riverfront all the way from Belém to Alcântara's Doca de Santo Amaro (see p.54). Another option is to **cycle**; the kiosk by the Belém ferry terminal hires out bikes for around 800$00 an hour. En route is the extraordinary **Museu da Electricidade** (Tues–Sun 10am–12.30pm & 2-5.30pm; 300$00; Belém station from Cais do Sodré), an early twentieth-century electricity generating station whose museum highlights include "steam turbines, high pressure generators and low pressure generators"; looking like something from the science-fiction film *Brazil*, it is actually more interesting than it sounds.

Avenida da Liberdade to the Gulbenkian

F or a gradually rising view over the Baixa, head up the central strip of the grand, palm-lined **Avenida da Liberdade**, still much as Fernando Pessoa described it: "the finest artery in Lisbon . . . full of trees from beginning to end . . . small gardens, ponds, fountains, cascades and statues". This leads up to the city's principal park: **Parque Eduardo VII**. Just north of here, the Fundação Calouste Gulbenkian combines one of Europe's richest art collections, the **Museu Gulbenkian**, with Portuguese comtemporary art in the **Centro de Arte Moderna**.

The area covered by this chapter is shown in detail
on colour maps 7 and 8.

AVENIDA DA LIBERDADE

Map 8, D2–G6.

The middle section of **Avenida da Liberdade**, from the new metro interchange at Restauradores to metro Avenida, has some of the city's nicest outdoor cafés, under the shade of trees that help cushion the roar of the passing traffic. The upper end of the avenue is home to many of the city's grander hotels (see p.100), banks, airline offices and designer shops, although after dark the leafy central strip is a favourite hangout for prostitutes.

For listings of the best restaurants on and around the Avenida da Liberdade, see p.137.

One block parallel to the east is the atmospheric **Rua das Portas de Santo Antão**, well known for its seafood restaurants (see p.135 for reviews). If you manage to coincide with a tour, take a look inside the **Geographical Society** at no. 100 (tours on Mon, Wed & Fri 11am & 3pm; free), which preserves snake spears, African instruments and other exotic ethnographic relics from Portugal's former colonies in Africa and the East. Next door is the domed **Coliseu**: opened in 1890 as a circus, it's now one of Lisbon's main concert venues.

PARQUE EDUARDO VII

Map 8, A6–C8. Metro Marquês de Pombal or Parque, or any bus to Rotunda (officially called Praça Marquês de Pombal), or about twenty minutes' walk from Praça dos Restauradores, at the bottom end of Avenida da Liberdade in the Baixa.

At the top of Avenida da Liberdade is the steep, formally laid-out **Parque Eduardo VII**, named after Britain's Edward VII, who visited the city in 1903. The big attractions

A backstreet stroll

The following walk doesn't pass any particular sights, but does lead you down some of Lisbon's most characterful streets. It should take about an hour.

Starting at Praça Marquês de Pombal (Map 8, D2), head down the left-hand side of Avenida da Liberdade and take the first left into Rua Alexander Herculano (Map 8, C2). The second turning on the right is the narrow **Rua de Santa Marta**, which passes the Hospital de Santa Marta before heading downhill. Here you'll find an amazing collection of tiny shops selling port and antiques, as well as some of the city's cheapest lunchtime restaurants (see p.137). The road becomes Rua de São José as it descends past the grand military cooperative and government buildings on the left, whose gardens spill down the slopes.

At Largo de Anunciada (Map 8, G6), just before the road becomes Rua das Portas de Santo Antão, have a rest in the beautifully decorated *Pastelaria Anunciada* (see p.152). Directly opposite here is the **Elevador do Lavra** funicular (Mon–Sat 7am–10.45pm, Sun 9am–10.45pm; 160$00 one way), opened in 1882 and still Lisbon's least touristed *elevador*. Take a ride to the top of the precipitous Calçada do Lavra, where a brief detour to the left, on Travessa do Torel, takes you to Jardim do Torel, a tiny park offering exhilarating views over Lisbon.

Going right at the top of the *elevador* along Rua Câmara Pestana, then turning right again, brings you on to the long **Calçada de Santa Ana** (Map 8, H6). This road's top end is surrounded by the Hospital de São José, but heading downhill, it becomes residential; some of the city's most reasonable restaurants are at the foot of the road, as it bears to the left. Continuing from here, the road dips downhill, becoming Calçada de Garcia (Map 8, I7) and ending at Largo São Domingos, next to Rossio.

PARQUE EDUARDO VII

here are the two *estufas* (Map 8, A7; daily 9am–4.30pm; 100$00), huge buildings with an appealingly ad hoc and tatty look, filled with tropical plants, pools and endless varieties of palms and cacti. Of the two, the **Estufa Quente**, the hothouse, has the more exotic plants; the **Estufa Fria**, the coldhouse, hosts occasional rock and classical concerts and an antiques fair.

Just south of the entrance, below the duck pond, is the **Parque Infantil** (summer 9am–7pm, winter 9am–5.30pm), a play area for children built round a mock galleon and overlooked by a handy café. There's an eye-catching gym complex next door, though you'll have to pay through the nose to use the facilities. Opposite the *estufas* on the eastern side of the park sits an ornately tiled sports pavilion which doubles as a venue for occasional concerts and cultural events. A good spot to aim for just north of here is the tranquil pond-side park café. Above the café, two concrete poles mark a **viewing platform** with commanding views over Lisbon; on clear days, the view stretches to the hills south of the Tejo. Beyond here, the top end of the park consists of an appealing grassy hillock complete with its own olive grove. This newly planted area means that it is now possible to walk through greenery virtually all the way from Praca Marquês de Pombal to the Gulbenkian Museum.

THE FUNDAÇÃO CALOUSTE GULBENKIAN

Map 7, B4–C4. Tues–Sun 10am–5pm; Museu Gulbenkian: 500$00, free on Sun; Centro de Arte Moderna: 500$00, free on Sun. Bus #31 or #46 from Rossio, bus #51 from Belém, or metro to Praça de Espanha or São Sebastião.

The **Fundação Calouste Gulbenkian** is the great cultural centre of Portugal – the wonder is that it's not better known internationally. Housed in a superb complex just

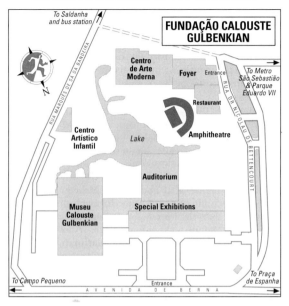

north of Parque Eduardo VII, the foundation is set in its own park and features a museum whose collections seem to take in virtually every great phase of Eastern and Western art – from Ancient Egyptian scarabs to Art Nouveau jewellery. In a separate building across the park, a modern Portuguese art museum touches on most twentieth-century styles.

Astonishingly, all the main museum exhibits were acquired by just one man, the Armenian oil magnate **Calouste Gulbenkian** (1869–1955), whose legendary art-market coups included the acquisition of works from the Hermitage in St Petersburg following the Russian

Revolution. In a scarcely less astute deal made during World War II, Gulbenkian auctioned himself and his collections to the European nations: Portugal bid security, an aristocratic palace home (a *marquês* was asked to move out) and tax exemption, acquiring in return one of the most important cultural patrons of the century.

The Gulbenkian maintains a "Centro Artístico Infantil" in its gardens (entrance just off Rua Marquês de Sá de Bandeira), well stocked with toys and offering free childcare for four to twelve-year-olds Mon–Fri 9.30am–5.30pm.

Today the Gulbenkian Foundation has a multi-million dollar budget sufficient to run an orchestra, three concert halls and two galleries for temporary exhibitions in the capital alone. It also finances work in all spheres of Portuguese cultural life – there are Gulbenkian museums and libraries in even the smallest towns – and makes charitable grants to a vast range of projects.

Museu Gulbenkian

The **Museu Gulbenkian** is divided into two parts: the first devoted to Classical and Oriental art; the second to European. The collections aren't immense or particularly imaginative in layout, but each contains pieces of such outstanding individual interest that, ideally, you'll probably want to take them in on separate visits. Refreshments are well provided for by the basement café-bar and gardens.

Classical and Oriental art

It seems arbitrary to pick out particular highlights from the **Classical and Oriental Art** section, but they must

THE FUNDAÇÃO CALOUSTE GULBENKIAN

include the entire contents of the small **Egyptian room**, which covers almost every period of importance from the Old Kingdom (2700 BC) to the Roman period. Particularly striking are a carved ivory spoon from the time of Amenophis III and an extraordinarily lifelike Head of a Priest from the Ptolemaic period. Other exhibits from the ancient Near East include two cylinder seals from **Mesopotamia**, one dating from before 2500 BC, and **Assyrian** alabaster bas reliefs.

Fine statues, silver and glass from the **Romans** and intricate gold jewellery from ancient **Greece** follow, along with a particularly extensive collection of Greek coins. Next are some remarkable illuminated manuscripts and ceramics from **Armenia**, and works from **China**, including an impressive pair of Qing (in Portuguese, "Ts'ing") Dynasty porcelain jars and some ornate eighteenth-century jade and crystal pieces. The beautiful **Japanese** prints and lacquerwork are set off by the backdrop of the museum's Japanese-style stepped gardens. **Islamic arts** are magnificently represented by ornamented texts, opulently woven carpets, glassware and precious bindings from India. Look out in particular for the colourful Persian carpets and tapestries, the stunning fourteenth-century Syrian painted glass, and the surprisingly contemporary-looking Turkish azulejos and sixteenth-century ceramic work.

European art

The **European Art** section contains work from many of the major schools, starting with a group of French medieval ivory diptychs (particularly interesting are six scenes depicting the Life of the Virgin) and a thirteenth-century manuscript of St John's prophetic *Apocalypse*, produced in Kent and touched up in Italy. From **fifteenth-century Flanders** there's a pair of panels by van der Weyden, while from the same period in Italy comes Ghirlandaio's *Portrait of a Young Woman*. The **seventeenth century** yields two exceptional portraits: Rubens' of his second wife, Helena Fourment, and Rembrandt's *Figure of an Old Man*, plus works by van Dyck, Frans Hals and Ruïsdael. **Eighteenth-century** works include a good Fragonard, *The Gardens of Tivoli*, and works by Gainsborough, Turner and Sir Thomas Lawrence. Don't miss the **Venetian section**, with no fewer than nineteen paintings of the Italian city by Francesco Guardi. Finally, there's a good showing from **nineteenth- and twentieth-century France**, with works by Monet, Degas and Renoir, a selection of snowy countryside scenes by Corot, and the particularly fine wintery landscape of Manet's *O'Degelo*.

Sculpture is poorly represented on the whole, though a French sixteenth-century statue of Mary Magdalene, a fifteenth-century medallion of Faith by Luca della Robbia, a 1780 marble Diana by Jean-Antoine Houdon, and a couple of Rodins all stand out, as does the beautiful marble statue of a child by Jean-Baptiste Pigalle, dating from the eighteenth century. Elsewhere, you'll find **ceramics** from Spain and Italy; **furniture** from the reigns of Louis XV and Louis XVI; fifteenth-century Italian bronze **medals** (by Pisanello, in particular); and assorted Italian **tapestries and textiles**. Among the eighteenth-century works from French **gold- and silversmiths**, don't miss the two silver epergnes (ornamental centrepieces for a table), one draped with cherubs drinking and eating grapes, the other intertwined with a selection of fish. Last, but definitely not least, is the stunning **Art Nouveau collection** of 169 pieces of fantasy jewellery and crystal works by René Lalique, a close friend of Gulbenkian. The crystal vases are impressive but are outshone by the hairpieces, brooches and necklaces inlaid with precious and semi-precious stones. Look out for the beautiful orchid hairpiece, and the fantastical *mulher-libélula*

Paula Rego

Paula Rego shot to prominence internationally in 1990 when she was appointed the first associate artist of the National Gallery in London. Though now living in England, her formative years were spent in Salazar's Lisbon. Her sheltered childhood was passed in the confines of a wealthy family home, and she still feels bitter about the way her mother became a "casualty" of a society which encouraged wealthy women to be idle, leaving work to their servants. Her women are portrayed as typical of the servants of her childhood: stocky and solid. She avoids graceful forms, preferring hairy, bony yet powerful female figures. Power and dominance are major themes of her work; she revives the military outfits of post-war Portugal for her men and dresses many of her women like dolls in national costume. Several of her pictures convey sexual opposition, the result perhaps of a background dominated by the regimes of the Roman Catholic church and a military dictatorship. Her images are rarely beautiful, but are undoubtedly amusing, disturbing and powerful. Her work is often displayed at galleries and temporary exhibitions around Lisbon.

brooch, half woman, half dragonfly, decorated with enamel work, gold, diamonds and moonstones.

Centro de Arte Moderna

The high-ceilinged, airy **Centro de Arte Moderna** (Museum of Modern Art) lies across the gardens with their specially commissioned sculptures (including a Henry Moore). Confusingly, to get into the museum, you need to exit the garden and enter from the main entrance on Rua Dr Nicolau de Bettencourt. The museum displays big names on the twentieth-century Portuguese scene, includ-

THE FUNDAÇÃO CALOUSTE GULBENKIAN

ing Almada Negreiros, the founder of *modernismo* (look out for his self-portrait, set in the café *A Brasileira*), Amadeu de Sousa Cardoso and Guilherme Santa-Rita (both of Futurist inclinations), and Paula Rego (one of Portugal's leading contemporary artists; see box on p.73). Some international figures are also represented, including the American abstract-expressionist Arshile Gorky and French artists Maria Vieira da Silva and Arpad Szenes. The museum also stages high-profile temporary exhibitions. The adjacent shop is a good source of art books and posters, while the museum's self-service restaurant is a good lunch stop (see p.139).

THE FUNDAÇÃO CALOUSTE GULBENKIAN

Outer Lisbon

Few visitors explore the bustling modern areas north and west of the Gulbenkian. Out around **Campo Grande**, though, are some mildly diverting **museums**, while over to the northwest of the Gulbenkian, in the suburb of **Sete Rios**, further peripheral attractions are provided by the **Jardim Zoológico** (the city's zoo) and the nearby **Palácio dos Marquêses de Fronteira**. Heading back into town from here, it's difficult to miss the **Amoreiras** centre, Lisbon's brashest modern landmark, which towers over the more historic **Aqueduto das Águas Livres**, Lisbon's traditional source of water.

CAMPO GRANDE AND BEYOND

Map 2, E3.

Campo Grande (literally, "the big field") is one of Lisbon's main traffic arteries. This was once an extensive park, and though urban sprawl has severely diminished its extent, the central grassy strip between the carriageways, filled with trees, cafés, tennis courts and a lake, makes a surprisingly pleasant escape. Just south of the bottom end of Campo Grande sits the **Feira Popular** (Map 2, E5; Mon–Fri 7pm–midnight, Sat & Sun 3pm–1am; 300$00, rides extra; metro Entrecampos), a fairground which makes a fun afternoon out for kids; its restaurants are also pretty good.

To the west of Campo Grande spread the campuses of the city's **university**; at the top end are two museums. The **Museu da Cidade** (Tues–Sun 10am–1pm & 2–6pm; 350$00, free on Sun; bus #1 from Cais do Sodré via Rossio, or metro Campo Grande) details the development of the city from the restoration of Independence in 1640 to the advent of the Republic in 1910. Installed in the eighteenth-century Palácio Pimenta, its principal interest lies in an imaginative collection of prints, paintings and an impressive model of pre-1755 Lisbon. Enjoyable, too, are various azulejo panels showing scenes of the city throughout history.

A death-defying crossing of the road leads you to another lovely mansion housing the **Museu Rafael Bordalo Pinheiro** (Tues–Sun 10am–1pm & 2–6pm; 270$00). Pinheiro (1846–1905) was an architect, ceramicist and political caricaturist. Upstairs, exhibits include his amazing collection of ornate dishes crawling with ceramic crabs and lobsters, frogs and snakes. The paintings, cartoons and sketches downstairs are of less interest.

Some 2km further north of the Museu da Cidade in the suburb of Lumiar, the **Museu do Traje** (Costume Museum) (Map 2, E1; Tues–Sun 10am–6pm; joint ticket with Museu do Teatro 400$00; free on Sun) occupies another eighteenth-century palace, the Palácio do Monteiro-Mor. The museum's extensive collections are drawn upon for temporary thematic exhibitions – excellent if costume is your subject, less gripping if you're not an aficionado of faded fabrics. To get there, take bus #1 from Rossio, #3 from Campo Grande, #7 from Cais do Sodré or Praça da Figueira. The small **Museu do Teatro** (Theatre Museum) (Map 2, D1; Tues 2–6pm, Wed–Sun 10am–6pm; tickets as for Museu do Traje) nearby is of truly specialist interest, displaying photos of famous actors, theatrical props and costumes. For more casual visitors, the surrounding park (daily until 5pm) is at least as big an attraction – one of the lushest areas of the city, and with a good restaurant and café.

SETE RIOS

Map 2, C4.

West of Campo Grande, the district of Sete Rios's main attraction, at Estrada da Benfica 158–160, is the **Jardim Zoológico** (April–Sept 10am–8pm; Oct–March 10am–6pm; 1800$00). This has been spruced up but remains one of the least inspiring of European zoos, exhibiting unhappy captives in utterly miserable conditions. On the other hand it's really as much a rambling garden as anything else and in this, and in its peculiarly Portuguese eruptions of kitsch (an extraordinary dogs' cemetery, for instance), makes for an enjoyable afternoon's ramble, with a small *teleferique* or cable car (daily from 11am until closing time), a reptile house (10am–noon & 1–6pm) and performing dolphins as further diversions. To get there, take bus #31 from Rossio, #41 from Praça de Espanha, or the metro to Jardim Zoológico station.

Palace enthusiasts might like to visit the **Palácio dos Marquêses de Fronteira** (Map 2, B5), a private former hunting lodge built in the late seventeenth century and famed for its azulejos. It's around twenty minutes' walk west from the zoo, or take bus #46. After passing the bland housing development on Rua de São Domingos de Benfica, the fantastic gardens of this small, pink country house feel like an oasis, complete with topiary, statues and fountains. Inside, there is period furniture along with more stunning azulejos. The allegorical panels on the lower level, taken from Camões's tale of the *Doze da Inglaterra* ("The Twelve Englishmen"), mark a historic moment in the history of azulejos when, in the mid-seventeenth century, the Portuguese dropped the formal Moorish methods of design (as in the upper level) and turned to painting straight onto tiles. From the palace, bus #46 goes back to Rossio, #58 to Cais do Sodré via the Bairro Alto and Amoreiras (see below).

Because the Palácio dos Marquêses de Fronteira is still inhabited, visiting hours are limited. Currently, from June to September, Monday to Saturday there are four tours daily at 10.30am, 11am, 11.30am and at noon; the rest of the year, there are only two, at 11am and at noon. Entrance costs 500$00 (gardens only) or 1500$00 (palace and gardens). Call ✆217 782 023 to check the latest details.

AMOREIRAS

Map 2, C7.

From the Palácio dos Marquêses de Fronteira, bus #58 heads to Cais do Sodré via **Amoreiras**, Lisbon's eye-catching postmodern shopping centre, visible on the city skyline from almost any approach despite the growing number of blocks around it. The complex, designed by Tomás Taveira, is Portugal's most adventurous – and most entertaining – modern building: a wild fantasy of pink and blue, sheltering ten cinemas, sixty cafés and restaurants, 370 shops and a hotel. Most of the shops here stay open until midnight, seven days a week; Sunday sees the heaviest human traffic, with entire families descending for an afternoon out. To get here directly from the city centre, take bus #11 from Rossio or Restauradores.

AQUEDUTO DAS ÁGUAS LIVRES

Map 2, C6.

Heading north, bus #11 connects Amoreiras with the imposing arches of the **Aqueduto das Águas Livres** –

(buses from Praça de Espanha to Caparica also pass underneath it). The aqueduct was opened in 1748, bringing reliable drinking water to the city for the first time. It stood firm during the 1755 earthquake and later gained a more notorious reputation thanks to one Diogo Alves, a nineteenth-century serial killer who threw his victims off the top – a 70m drop. Pessoa called the aqueduct "a real national monument, and perhaps the most remarkable of its kind in Europe", even if the recent road that has been ploughed through its central arches detracts from its grandeur. For an unusual walk and some amazing views, you can stroll over the top of the aqueduct to scruffy Monsanto Park – for details of tours, enquire at the Museu da Água (©218 135 522; see p.39), which is owned by the water company that still services the aqueduct. The entire structure stretches some 60km, mostly underground; sections of it are visible either side of the tracks on the train line to Sintra. While in the vicinity of the Amoreiras side of the aqueduct, don't miss the former **Mãe d'Água** water cistern, which holds water from the aqueduct at Rua das Amoreiras, close to metro Rato on Largo do Rato. Completed in 1843, the chunky, castellated structure nowadays hosts occasional exhibitions.

Parque das Nações

Now rechristened the **Parque das Nações** – the Park of Nations – the former Expo 98 site, 5km to the east of the city, remains a huge attraction for Lisboans, especially at weekends (Map 1, G5; Mon–Thurs & Sun 9.30am–1am, Fri & Sat 9.30am–3am; free). Its appeal is clear: the series of flat, wide, traffic-free walkways lined with fountains, palms, cafés and futuristic buildings make a complete contrast to the narrow, precipitous streets of old Lisbon. The main highlight is the world's second-largest **Oceanarium**, one of Lisbon's most impressive landmarks. The **Virtual Reality Pavilion** is another key draw, while the educational exhibits in the **Centre of Live Science** are also rewarding. Other attractions include water gardens, a cable car, a viewing tower, two of Lisbon's largest concert venues and a diverse array of bars, shops and restaurants, many with outdoor seating overlooking Olivais docks and the astonishing 17km-long Vasco da Gama bridge over the Tejo.

> **The easiest way to reach the Parque is by taking the metro to Oriente (red line from Alameda).**

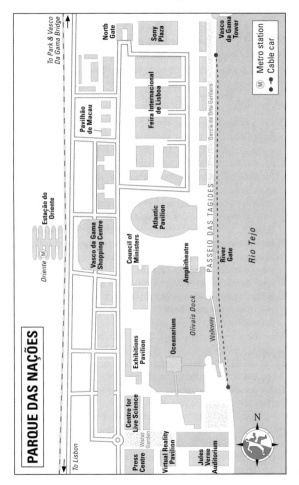

PARQUE DAS NAÇÕES

To Lisbon

To Park & Vasco Da Gama Bridge

Oriente Ⓜ Estação do Oriente

North Gate

Sony Plaza

Vasco da Gama Tower

Pavilhão de Macau

Feira Internacional de Lisboa

Vasco da Gama Shopping Centre

Council of Ministers

Atlantic Pavilion

Garcia de Orta Gardens

Exhibitions Pavilion

Oceanarium

Olivais Dock

Amphitheatre

PASSEIO DAS TAGIDES

River Gate

Rio Tejo

Centre for Live Science

Water Garden

Virtual Reality Pavilion

Press Centre

Jules Verne Auditorium

Walkway

N

Ⓜ Metro station
●—● Cable car

Expo 98 and after

The **Expo 98 site** was built as a giant maritime-influenced theme park in 1998 to coincide with the 500th anniversary of Vasco da Gama's arrival in India and the UN's "Year of the Oceans". The event was a huge success that placed Lisbon firmly in the international spotlight – for a year at least. But the funds raised for and generated by the event have also had a lasting impact on Lisbon as a whole, providing the impetus for a city-wide facelift. Virtually every city monument was touched up, and substantial improvements were carried out to the city's transport infrastructure, including a drastic expansion of the metro, a new rail line under the Ponte 25 de Abril, and a brand new bridge over the Tejo, the Ponte Vasco da Gama.

While the Parque das Nações is evolving into a thriving entertainment zone, it forms only part of one of the most ambitious urban regeneration projects ever undertaken. An area of three square kilometres around the Parque is in the process of being transformed into a large-scale business and residential zone, complete with a mammoth riverside park, with the aim of redirecting Lisbon's sprawling suburbs in a more planned fashion towards the east of the city; completion is due in the next ten years.

Arrival

Stepping off the metro, you arrive in the bowels of the **Estação do Oriente**, a stunning glass-and-concrete bus-and-train interchange designed by Spanish architect Santiago Calatrava; from here, there are also overground trains to Santa Apolónia station, and buses to towns north and south of the Tejo. Leaving the station, it's easy to be drawn into the substantial Vasco da Gama shopping centre opposite, a medley of international and local stores; otherwise, take a right and the Parque entrance is a short walk away on the left.

The Parque has a distinct lack of shade; if visiting in high summer, wear a hat, while in winter an umbrella is a good precaution.

Here you can either turn right into the **southern** half of the Parque – where you'll find the Oceanarium, Virtual Reality Pavilion, and Centre of Live Science – or left into the **northern** half, to the Vasco da Gama tower and water-front gardens. Alternatively, jump on the free **toy train** which trundles clockwise round the whole site every twenty minutes or so to get an idea of what's on offer.

PARQUE SOUTH

Heading south alongside the calm waters of Olivais docks you'll pass the **Exhibitions Pavilion** (Pavilhão das Exposições), with temporary exhibitions on themes as diverse as individual artists to the tea trade, and arrive at the **Centre of Live Science** (Centro da Ciência Viva) (Tues–Sun 10am–6pm; 800$00). Run by Portugal's Ministry of Science and Technology (which shares the premises), the centre hosts temporary exhibitions on subjects such as cutting-edge technology and multimedia – absorbing, if twiddling knobs and clicking a mouse is your thing. Behind lies the **Water Garden** (Jardim da Água), crisscrossed by riverlets and ponds linked by stepping stones, with various fountains gushing cooling spray and enough water gadgets and pumps to keep kids occupied for hours.

At the foot of the gardens stands the **Virtual Reality Pavilion** (Pavilhão da Realidade Virtual) (Tues–Sun 1pm–7pm; "Voyage to Oceania" 1000$00; "Voyage to Virtual Oceanarium" 300$00; combined tickets 1200$00).

Tickets go on sale at midday and it's worth getting here then as this has become one of the Parque's most popular attractions, and the virtual reality technology is certainly impressive. There are two shows: the forty-minute "Voyage to Oceania" is the better, taking visitors into the sea through an imaginative recreation of the lost world of "Oceania", while the Virtual Oceanarium is exactly what its name suggests, so you're probably better off heading for the real thing next door.

On the riverfront side of the Virtual Reality Pavilion is the **Jules Verne Auditorium**, the Parque's main venue for classical music and opera. Beyond here, more cafés sprawl along the waterfront to the south, while to the north, a narrow walkway leads across Olivais docks below the ski-lift-style **cable car** (Mon–Fri noon–7pm, Sat & Sun 10am–8pm; 500$00), which shuttles you to the northern side of the Parque, giving commanding views over the site on the way.

Lisbon Oceanarium

Daily 10am–7pm; 1500$00.

Designed by Peter Chermaeff and looking like something off the set of a James Bond film, the **Lisbon Oceanarium** (Oceanário de Lisboa), Europe's largest, contains some 25,000 fish and marine animals. Its main feature is the enormous central tank, the size of four Olympic-sized swimming pools, which you can look into from different levels for close-up views of the various creatures that live on the surface, including sharks, which circle the main body of the water, down to the rays burying themselves into the sand on the sea bed. Almost more impressive, though, are the recreations of various ocean ecosystems, such as the Antarctic tank, containing frolicking penguins, and the Pacific tank, where otters bob about and play in the rock pools. These areas are separated from the main tank by invisible acrylic sheets, giving the impression that all the marine creatures are swimming together in the same space. On the darkened lower level, smaller tanks contain shoals of brightly coloured tropical fish and other warm-water creatures. Find a window free of school parties and the whole experience becomes the closest you'll get to deep-sea diving without getting wet.

> **The Oceanarium attracts hefty queues, particularly at weekends; get there early or expect to wait up to an hour to get in.**

PARQUE NORTH

The cable car from the Oceanarium takes you to **Garcia de Orta Garden** (Jardim Garcia de Orta), a leafy waterside strip displaying plant species collected from Portugal's former colonies. But the main draw on this side of the Parque is a lift ride to the top of the **Vasco da Gama Tower** (Torre Vasco da Gama) (daily 10am–8pm; 500$00), formerly part of an oil refinery, whose viewing platform gives a 360° panorama over Lisbon, the Tejo and into the Alentejo to the south. The summit also holds a pricey restaurant (see p.141). Opposite the tower is the **Sony Plaza**, Lisbon's largest purpose-built outdoor arena, which hosts concerts and sports events; there's also a giant screen showing live soccer or pop videos most evenings. Opposite here, Lisbon's trade fair hall, the **Feira Internacional de Lisboa** (FIL), has moved into the space formerly occupied by Expo 98's international pavilions, and hosts various events including a handicrafts fair displaying ceramics and crafts from round the country (usually in July). At the back of FIL, the mock-colonial **Pavilion of Macau** (Pavilhão de Macau)

(Tues–Sun 10am–6pm; 250$00) is the only international pavilion remaining from Expo 98, displaying traditional and modern aspects of the former Portuguese colony – which was handed back to China in 1999 – including a Chinese garden.

Heading back towards Olivais docks you'll pass the bulk of the impressive **Atlantic Pavilion** (Pavilhão Atlântico), officially Portugal's largest indoor arena and the venue for major visiting bands and sporting events. From here it's a short walk back to Oriente station or to the waterfront cafés and restaurants of Olivais docks (see p.140 for reviews).

LISTINGS

Accommodation

Nearly every part of Lisbon offers some sort of accommodation, though if you're after affordable modern comforts you may need to move slightly away from the central Baixa grid. There are three basic types of accommodation: **pensions** (*pensões*; singular *pensão*), **guesthouses** (*residenciais*; singular *residencial*), and **hotels** – the only difference between the first two is that some *pensões* serve meals, while *residenciais* do not. Pensions and guest houses are officially graded from one to three stars. One-star hotels are much the same as three-star *pensões,* but hotels with two stars and above are markedly better in terms of facilities and accordingly more expensive.

There are scores of small, inexpensive pensions and guesthouses, often in tall tenement buildings in the central parts of the city. The most obvious and accessible – but also noisiest – accommodation area is at the **northern end of the Baixa** around Rossio, Praça dos Restauradores and Praça da Figueira. North of here, the streets parallel to **Avenida da Liberdade** (particularly Rua Portas de Santo Antão and Rua da Glória) are where you're most likely to find a cheap bed at busy times of year. The **central Baixa** has a fair selection of places, too, and there are a couple of more upmarket choices in **Chiado**. **Bairro Alto** is one of the more interesting parts of the city to stay in – though rooms in its few pensions can be hard to come by and noisy nightlife goes on late. For atmosphere, there are a few attractive places on the periphery of **Alfama**, and up towards the castle. A number of more expensive places are located away from the city centre, either in the prosperous suburb of **Lapa**, around **Parque Eduardo VII** or in the business area of **Saldanha**, near the Gulbenkian. Further north, around **Avenida Almirante Reis** – the streets between Anjos and Arroios metros in particular – there are some handy places for an early flight, though nowhere in central Lisbon is much more than half an hour's taxi ride from the airport.

....

Our listings are divided into the following areas: Baixa (p.92); Chiado (p.96); Alfama and Castelo (p.97); Bairro Alto and around (p.98); Lapa (p.99); Belém (p.100); Around Avenida da Liberdade (p.100); Parque Eduardo VII and Saldanha (p.104); Around Avenida Almirante Reis (p.106).

....

There are three **youth hostels** (*pousadas de juventude*) in and around Lisbon: one in the city a short walk from metro Picoas, one out at Oeiras, overlooking the sea, and another

Disabled access

Lisbon accommodation with **disabled access** includes: Hotel Fenix (p.104); Hotel da Lapa (p.100); Hotel Lisboa Plaza (p.102); Meridien Portugal (p.105); Hotel Mundial (p.95); Parque Municipal de Campismo (p.107); Pousada de Dona Maria; Hotel Real Parque (p.105); Ritz Four Seasons (p.106); Tivoli Lisboa (p.103); and the pousada da juventude (youth hostel) at Picoas (p.96).

in Sintra – see p.96 and p.238. For those wanting to **camp**, the main, well-equipped city campsite is in the giant hilltop Parque Florestal de Monsanto 6km out of the city, and there are also some decent, reasonably priced campsites within commuting distance of Lisbon on the Atlantic coast at Caparica, Guincho and Praia Grande; see p.107 for a complete listing.

The main **turismo** offices (see p.8 for details) can provide accommodation lists, but won't reserve rooms for you. In the summer months in particular, fax or telephone a reservation at least a week in advance; most owners speak English. It is also advisable to reconfirm any booking a day or two in advance, and ideally to get written confirmation, as some places have been known to deny all knowlege of verbal reservations during busy times. At Easter, and even more so in midsummer, **room availability** is often stretched to the limit, with prices artificially inflated. At this time you should be prepared to take anything vacant and look around the next day, if need be, for somewhere better or cheaper. Fortunately, during most of the year you should have little difficulty in finding a room, and you can always try to knock the price down at quieter times, especially if you can summon a few good-natured phrases in Portuguese.

To phone Lisbon from abroad, dial the international access code followed by 351, followed by the subscriber's number.

When doing the rounds, be warned that pensions tend to occupy upper storeys of tall buildings – leaving one person downstairs with all the bags is a good idea if you're in company. **Addresses** are written in the form "Rua do Crucifixo 50–4°", meaning the fourth storey of no. 50, Rua do Crucifixo. Don't be unduly put off by some fairly insalubrious staircases, but do be aware that rooms facing onto the street can often be unbearably noisy.

THE BAIXA

Hotel Duas Nações

Map 3, G6. Rua da Vitória 41 ⓒ213 460 710, fax 213 470 206. Classy, pleasantly faded nineteenth-century hotel with a secure entrance and helpful, English-speaking reception. Surprisingly quiet for so central a location. Rooms without bath ②, en suite ③.

Pensão Galicia

Map 3, H7. Rua do Crucifixo 50–4°ⓒ213 428 430.
Entered past a shoe-repair stall, this top-storey pension has some sweet rooms with sunny balconies and wooden floors, although the atmosphere is somewhat spoilt by too many house rules and smelly drains. ②

Accommodation price codes

Apart from information on youth hostels (when actual prices are given), all the accommodation prices in this book have been coded using the symbols below. The symbols represent the price of the **cheapest double room in high season**.

① under 4000$00
② 4000$00–7000$00
③ 7000$00–11,000$00
④ 11,000$00–15,000$00
⑤ 15,000$00–20,000$00
⑥ 20,000$00–25,000$00
⑦ 25,000$00–30,000$00
⑧ 30,000$00–40,000$00
⑨ over 40,000$00

Residencial Insulana

Map 3, F6. Rua da Assunção 52 ℗ & fax 213 427 625.
Reached via a series of underwear shops, this is one of the more upmarket Baixa options, with carpeted entrance hall, smart en-suite rooms, English-speaking staff and its own bar overlooking a quiet pedestrianized street. Good breakfasts too. ③

Pensão Moderna

Map 3, E6. Rua dos Correeiros 205–4° ℗213 460 818.
Situated at the top of an off-putting stairwell, but once inside you'll find big, clean rooms crammed with elderly furniture. It could do with a lick of paint, but is fine for the bargain-basement price. Some rooms have (rickety) balconies overlooking the pedestrianized street. Shared bathrooms. ①

Pensão Prata

Map 3, H5. Rua da Prata 71–3° ℗213 468 908.
You'll need mountaineering experience to climb the stairs to this pension, which has small rooms in a welcoming, family-run apartment – you pass to and fro via their TV lounge. Some rooms have showers, others share a clean bathroom. Book in advance as it's popular. ②

ROSSIO AND AROUND

Pensão Arco da Bandeira

Map 3, E6. Rua dos Sapateiros 226–4° ℗213 423 478.
Highly recommended and friendly *pensão* with half a dozen comfortable rooms, some overlooking Rossio. The shared bathrooms are spotless. The entrance is just through the arch at the southern end of the square. Don't be put off by the dingy stairway, or by the fact it's opposite a porn cinema (actually Lisbon's oldest film house). ③

Hotel Avenida Palace

Map 3, C7. Rua 1° de Dezembro ℗213 460 151, fax 213 422 884.
Lisbon's grandest downtown hotel, wedged between Rossio and

Praça dos Restauradores, has recently undergone renovation but maintains an elegant nineteenth-century style, with very comfortable rooms sporting high ceilings, traditional furnishings and marble bathrooms. ⑧

Pensão Beira Minho

Map 3, C5. Praça da Figueira 6–2° ℂ213 461 846.
Rooms (with and without bath) are small but clean, and some have fine views, especially on the upper floors, though the cheaper ones don't even have a window. ②

Pensão Coimbra e Madrid

Map 3, D6. Praça da Figueira 3–3° ℂ213 421 760, fax 213 423 264.
Large, decently run if faintly shabby *pensão*, above the *Pastelaria Suíça* (see p.145), with superb views of Rossio, Praça da Figueira and the castle beyond from (street-honkingly noisy) front-facing rooms, which come with shower or bath; there's a TV room, too, and breakfast is included in the price. Best choice on the square. ③

Pensão Estação Central

Map 3, D8. Calçada do Carmo 17–2° ℂ213 423 308.
After climbing interminable flights of stairs you're greeted by small and musty rooms, some with diminutive bathrooms. It is, however, one of the cheapest places in town; it's also handy for the Bairro Alto. ①

Pensão Ibérica

Map 3, D5. Praça da Figueira 10–2° ℂ218 867 026.
Central location and lots of rooms, most with TVs, but it's a bit ramshackle and the decor is gloomy and uninspiring. The rooms overlooking the square have the best views and most air, but are very noisy. Reception's open 24hr – useful for those planning a late night out. ③

Pensão Imperial

Map 3, A7. Praça dos Restauradores 78–4° ℂ213 420 166.
In a sunny position at the bottom of Restauradores (by Rua Jardim

Regedor), with a fine blue-tiled facade. Enter through an optician's and climb to the top floor for small rooms, some with showers, and with a view up Avenida da Liberdade. ②

Hotel International

Map 3, D6. Rua da Betesga 3 ℂ213 466 401, fax 213 478 635.
This is a smart central choice, and if you get one of the rooms with a balcony overlooking the city, you'll not be disappointed. Rooms come with air conditioning, TVs and a safe. There's also a bar and a friendly reception. ④

Hotel Metrópole

Map 3, D7. Rossio 30 ℂ213 469 164, fax 213 469 166.
Turn-of-the-century hotel, very centrally located and with an airy lounge bar – and most rooms – offering superb views over Rossio and the castle beyond. Comfortable en-suite rooms, but you pay for the location, and the square can be pretty noisy at night. ⑤

Hotel Mundial

Map 3, C5. Rua Dom Duarte 4 ℂ218 863 101, fax 218 879 129.
Central four-star hotel popular with businesspeople, with around three hundred rooms. There's a rooftop pool, and great views from its eighth-floor restaurant and terrace. Neat rooms, all with plush bathrooms and mod cons. Buffet breakfast included. Disabled access. ⑤

Hotel Portugal

Map 3, C4. Rua João das Regras 4 ℂ218 877 581, fax 218 867 343.
Amazing old hotel which has suffered an appalling conversion, with its high decorative ceilings chopped up by new wall partitions. Nevertheless, the rooms are comfortable and air conditioned, the bathrooms are marble-lined, and there's a lovely ornate TV room with period furniture. ④

Residencial do Sul

Map 3, C7. Rossio 59 ℂ213 422 511, fax 218 132 697.

ROSSIO AND AROUND

Entered through a small shop, this is very close to Rossio station and the National Theatre. A good first choice if you want a view of Rossio from your room, but be prepared for the noise. It's very clean and there are quieter back rooms, though some of these don't have any windows. ②

CHIADO

Hotel Borges
Map 3, F9. Rua Garrett 108 ℭ213 461 951, fax 213 426 617.

Youth hostels

The central booking office for Portugal's youth hostels (*pousadas de juventude*) is Movijovem, near metro Saldanha at Avda Duque d'Avila 137 ℭ213 138 820, fax 213 528 621, *movijovem@mail.telepac.pt* For details of the youth hostel at Sintra, see p.238.

Pousada de Juventude de Catalazete (Map 1, D6), Estrada Marginal, Oeiras ℭ214 430 638. Small, attractive hostel overlooking the beach at Oeiras, between Belém and Cascais. It is best reached by bus #44 from the airport, or take a train from Cais do Sodré to Oeiras station, then a taxi for the last 2km. Reception is open 6am–11pm and there's a midnight curfew. although you can get a pass to stay out later. Dorm rooms from 1500$00.

Pousada de Juventude de Lisboa (Map 9, E7). Rua Andrade Corvo 46 ℭ213 532 696. This is the main city hostel, with good facilities, no curfew, and 24hr reception. There are doubles as well as dormitory beds and disabled access. The price includes breakfast, while lunch and dinner are served at bargain prices. Dorm beds from 2900$00, double rooms from 4700$00.

A traditional hotel in a handy position in Chiado's main street, though the rooms are very ordinary and the hotel often fills with tour groups. Breakfast included. ④

Residencial Nova Silva

Map 3, J9. Rua Vítor Cordon 11 ©213 424 371, fax 213 427 770. Clean, friendly and good-value option, though rooms are small – try to get one at the rear of the building, ideally on the top floor, for stunning views of the Tejo. ②

ALFAMA AND CASTELO

Albergaria Senhora do Monte

Map 2, G8. Calçada do Monte 39 ©218 866 002, fax 218 877 783. Comfortable, modern hotel in a beautiful location with views of the castle and Graça convent from the south-facing rooms, some of which have terraces. Breakfast is included, and private parking is available. To get there, head north from Largo do Graça, taking the first right into Rua Damasceno Monteiro – Calçada do Monte is the first left. ⑥

Pensão Ninho das Águias

Map 4, B3. Costa do Castelo 74 ©218 867 008. Beautifully sited in its own view-laden terrace-garden on the street looping around and below the castle. Climb up the staircase and past the birdcages. Rooms are bright and white; some have en-suite facilities. Book in advance. ③

Pensão São João da Praça

Map 4, C9. Rua São João da Praça 97–2° ©218 862 591, fax 218 881 378. Attractively painted town house with street-facing wrought-iron balconies. It's a clean, quiet and friendly choice immediately below the cathedral. Rooms with and without en suite, and meals can be provided. ④

Sé Guest House

Map 4, C9. Rua São João da Praça 97–1° ©218 864 400, fax 263 271 612.

Beautifully done-up town house with wood floors and bright, airy rooms in same building as the *Pensão São João da Praça*. Communal bathroom. ③

BAIRRO ALTO AND AROUND

Residencial Camões

Map 5, E4. Trav. do Poço da Cidade 38–1° ©213 467 510, fax 213 464 048.

Small, pretty rooms, some with balconies, right in the heart of the Bairro Alto. Breakfast is served in a pleasant dining room, and the English-speaking owners are very friendly. Without bathroom ②, en suite ③.

Casa de São Mamede

Map 8, C5. Rua da Escola Politécnica 159 ©213 963 166, fax 213 951 896.

Slightly away from the Bairro Alto on a busy street north of Praça do Príncipe Real, this is a superb seventeenth-century town house with period fittings, bright breakfast room and even a grand stained-glass window. Rooms are rather ordinary, but all come with private bathrooms and TV. ⑤

Pensão Duque

Map 5, G4. Calçada do Duque 53 ©213 463 444.

Near São Roque church, down the steps off Largo T. Coelho heading down to Rossio, so clear of the nightlife noise. It has basic but usually spotless rooms, with shared bathrooms. ②

Pensão Globo

Map 5, F2. Rua do Teixeira 37 ©213 462 279.

Attractive house in a relatively quiet street, bang in the middle of the Bairro Alto. Rooms are simple but clean and reasonably large, though those right at the top are a little cramped. Helpful management, too. ②

Pensão Londres

Map 8, E7. Rua Dom Pedro V 53 ℂ213 465 523, fax 213 465 682. Wonderful old building with high ceilings. The rooms are uninspiring, though pleasant enough, and spread across a couple of price ranges (mostly ③) and floors. Some come with tiny bathrooms, and breakfast is included. ②–③

Pensão Luar

Map 5, F4. Rua das Gáveas 101–1° ℂ213 460 949.
Polished interior whose decently furnished rooms (with and without shower) are comfortable but somewhat noisy. Some are much larger than others, so ask to see. ③

Hotel Prínçipe Real

Map 8, E6. Rua da Alegria 53 ℂ213 460 116, fax 213 422 104.
Reached via steps off Praça do Prínçipe Real, this four-star hotel is in a characterful street by the lower entrance to the botanical gardens. Its 24 small but comfortable rooms have balconies, though the only decent views are from the rooftop restaurant, which is open to non-residents. ⑥.

LAPA

As Janelas Verdes

Map 6, F5. Rua das Janelas Verdes 47 ℂ213 968 143, fax 213 968 144, *heritage.hotels@mail.telepac.pt.*
Highly recommended, this discreet, welcoming eighteenth-century town house, where Eça de Queirós wrote *Os Maios* (see p.276), is just metres from the Museu de Arte Antiga. Well-proportioned rooms come with marble bathrooms, period furnishings and pictures, and breakfast is served in the delightful walled garden.

Top-floor rooms command spectacular river views. Bookings recommended. ⑦

Hotel da Lapa
Map 6, E5. Rua do Pau da Bandeira 4 ℂ213 950 005, fax 213 950 665, *reservas@hotelapa.com*.
Justifiably considered Lisbon's top hotel, this stunning nineteenth-century mansion is set in its own lush gardens, with dramatic vistas over the Tejo. Rooms are luxurious, and those in the Palace Wing are each decorated in a different style, from Classical to Art Deco. In summer, grills are served by the outside pool. There's also an indoor health club and disabled access. ⑨

Residencial York House
Map 6, G5. Rua das Janelas Verdes 32 ℂ213 962 435, fax 213 972 793.
Located in a sixteenth-century convent, rooms come with rugs, tiles and four-poster beds. The best are grouped around a beautiful interior courtyard, where drinks and meals are served in summer. The highly rated restaurant (see p.132) is open to non-residents. ⑧

BELÉM

Hotel da Torre
Map 7, F2. Rua dos Jerónimos 8 ℂ213 636 262, fax 213 645 995.
Well-positioned, pleasant hotel right by the monastery in the heart of Belém. Rooms are en suite and breakfast is included. ⑤

AROUND AVENIDA DA LIBERDADE

Residencial 13 da Sorte
Map 2, E8. Rua do Salitre 13 ℂ & fax 213 531 851.
Popular option set in an attractive building in a good location. Rooms are well decorated and come with TVs and bathrooms. ③

Residencial Alegria

Map 8, F6. Praça Alegria 12 *Ⓒ*213 475 522, fax 213 478 070.
Great position, facing the leafy Praça Alegria, with spacious and
spotless rooms with TVs; those with bath are more expensive than
those with showers. ②–③

Hotel Britania

Map 8, E3. Rua Rodrigues Sampaio 17 *Ⓒ*213 155 016, fax 213 155
021, *heritage.hotels@mail.telepac.pt.*
Designed in the 1940s by influential architect Cassiano Branco, this
is a smart option with good-sized rooms and classic Art Deco
interior. A buffet breakfast is included, and children under 12 stay
free. ⑥

Hotel Flamingo

Map 8, C2. Rua Castilho 41 *Ⓒ*213 862 191, fax 213 861 216.
Small, rather unattractive-looking hotel, but with an appealing
atmosphere, off the top of the avenue. It's popular with tour groups
so can get booked up. ④

Residencial Florescente

Map 8, H7. Rua das Portas de Santo Antão 99 *Ⓒ*213 426 609, fax
213 427 733.
One of this pedestrianized street's best-value establishments; some
rooms come with TV and small bathroom. There's a large selection
across four floors, so if you don't like the look of the room you're
shown, ask about alternatives. Breakfast is not included. ③

Pensão Iris

Map 8, G7. Rua da Glória 2a–1° *Ⓒ*213 423 157.
Through the extremely off-putting entrance are English-speaking
proprietors and large, clean, if shabby rooms (triples available),
some with shower, and a couple overlooking the main avenue.
Those at the side are a bit too close to the clanking street funicular
for comfort. ②

Hotel Lisboa Plaza

Map 8, F5. Trav. Salitre 7 ©213 463 922, fax 213 471 630, *heritage.hotels@mail.telepac.pt.*
Just off Avenida da Liberdade in front of a theatre park, this bright, polished, four-star hotel is a real treat – dried flowers everywhere, marble bathrooms, bar, restaurant (good breakfast included), and views of the botanical garden from the rear rooms. Disabled access. ⑦

Pensão Monumental

Map 8, F6. Rua da Glória 21 ©213 469 807, fax 213 430 213.
A backpackers' favourite, with a mixed bag of rooms in a rambling old building; the hot water supply is a little erratic, but it's handy if you fancy a night out at the *Ritz Club* (see p.180) up the road. ③

Pensão Portuense

Map 8, G6. Rua das Portas de Santo Antão 153 ©213 464 197, fax 213 424 239.
Singles and doubles in a family-run place that takes good care of its guests. The spacious bathrooms are meticulously clean, the water stays hot, and breakfast is provided. ③

Hotel Suisso-Atlântico

Map 8, F6. Rua da Glória 3–19 ©213 461 713, fax 213 469 013.
Clean, modern hotel in a good location around the corner from the *elevador*, just off Avenida da Liberdade. Standard mid-range accommodation; rooms have showers, and some come with balconies looking down onto seedy Rua da Glória. The bar's the best bit, an intriguing mock-baronial number. ④

Hotel Tivoli Jardim

Map 8, E4. Rua Júlio César Machado ©213 539 971, fax 213 556 566, *htjardim@mail.telepac.pt.*
Related to the nearby *Tivoli Lisboa* (whose pool and gardens you're allowed to use), the *Tivoli Jardim* is a large modern block set back in a quiet street. Most rooms come with spacious balconies. ⑦

Tivoli Lisboa

Map 8, E4. Avda da Liberdade 185 ℂ213 198 900, fax 213 198 950, *htlisboa@mail.telepac.pt*.
Flash hotel with cavernous lobby-lounge, three hundred sound-proofed rooms, an outdoor pool, tennis courts and garden. Breakfast is included and there's a top-floor grill-restaurant with superb city views. Disabled access. ⑧.

Hotel Veneza

Map 8, E4. Avda da Liberdade 189 ℂ213 522 618, fax 213 526 678. Historic nineteenth-century former town house which combines a traditional feel and decor with plush, comfortable rooms, each with a minibar and en-suite bathroom. ⑥

Self catering

Hotel Impala (Map 9, D5), Rua Filipe Folque, Saldanha 49 ℂ213 148 914, fax 213 575 362. One of the few relatively inexpensive self-catering options. Small, simple apartments sleep up to four (though are better sized for two). Pension-standard bedrooms are attached to small kitchen-cum-living rooms with TVs. There are also laundry facilities. ④ per apartment.

Orion Eden (Map 3, A8), Praça dos Restauradores 18–24 ℂ213 216 600, fax 213 216 666, *eden.lisboa@mail.telepac.pt*. Four-star studios and apartments sleeping up to four people, mainly geared to business visitors, are available on the upper floors of the impressively converted Eden Theatre. Get a ninth-floor apartment with a balcony and you'll have the best views and be just below the surreal rooftop pool and break-fast bar. All studios come with dishwashers, microwaves and TVs. ⑥ for studios and double apartments; ⑦ for larger apartments.

SELF CATERING

PARQUE EDUARDO VII AND SALDANHA

Residencial Avenida Alameda

Map 9, D8. Avda Sidónio Pais 4 ℭ213 532 186, fax 213 526 703.
Very pleasant three-star *residencial* with air-conditioned rooms, all
with park views and bath; breakfast included. ④

Residencial Canadá

Map 9, G5. Avda Defensores de Chaves 35 1–4° ℭ213 521 455, fax
213 542 922.
Very near the main bus station, this is excellent value for money,
with satellite TV and private bathrooms in biggish and airy rooms
which are kept immaculate by a bevy of charming ladies. There's
also a sunny breakfast room and lounge area. Recommended. ④

Hotel Eduardo VII

Map 9, D8. Avda Fontes Pereira de Melo 5 ℭ213 530 141, fax 213
533 879.
Close to the park, this renovated 1930s hotel is in an unattractive
block on a noisy road, but has all mod cons, plus a rooftop bar and
restaurant. ⑤

Pensão Embaixatriz

Map 9, E6. Rua Pedro Nunes 45–2° ℭ213 531 029.
Welcoming management make this a perennially popular place. It's
hardly luxurious, but is clean and inexpensive – rooms with showers
are even cheaper than those with baths. The entrance is a little hard
to find, on the other side of the road to the maternity hospital. ②

Hotel Fenix

Map 8, D1. Praça Marquês de Pombal 8 ℭ213 862 121, fax 213 860
131, *h@fenixip.pt*.
Large four-star hotel on the giant square, with double-glazed windows to keep out the noise. The rooms, with armchairs and TVs,

overlook the square or the park, and English newspapers are available in the lobby. There's also a restaurant and bar, and disabled access. **⑥**

Meridien Portugal
Map 9, A8. Rua Castilho 149 ©213 830 900, fax 213 890 505, *reservas.lisboa@lemeridien.pt.*
Ghastly modern exterior shelters a superior luxury hotel, with an impressive atrium, bright café-lounge and top-quality rooms. There's also a health club, music bar and disabled access. **⑧**

Miraparque
Map 9, D8. Avda Sidónio Pais ©213 524 286, fax 213 578 920, *miraparque@isoterica.pt.*
Housed in an attractive building overlooking Parque Eduardo VII, *Miraparque* has a traditional feel, though the reception staff can be a bit brusque. All rooms come with TV, and there's a decent bar and restaurant. **⑤**

Residencial Pascoal de Melo
Map 2, F6. Rua Pascoal de Melo 127–131 ©213 577 639, fax 213 144 555.
A spotless and airy three-star *residencial* near Largo Dona Estefânia with friendly staff and a characterful, azulejos-lined entry hall. Rooms are neat and come with attached bathroom, television and balcony. **②**

Pensão Pátria
Map 9, F5. Avda Duque d'Ávila 42 5–6° ©213 150 620, fax 213 578 310.
Close to the main bus station, this cheerful establishment has plenty of nice little rooms with wooden floors and clean bathrooms – some also come with rooftop views, others with small glassed-in verandas – and there's also a sunny breakfast room. **②**

Hotel Real Parque
Map 9, D5. Avda Luís Bívar 67 ©213 570 101, fax 213 570 750, *realparque@mail.telepac.pt.*

PARQUE EDUARDO VII AND SALDANHA

Four-star modern block in a quiet part of town near Parque Eduardo VII, complete with its own restaurant, coffee shop and bar. Unimaginative but comfortable rooms with mod cons including pay TV channels, plus off-street parking and disabled access. ⑥

Hotel Rex

Map 9, A8. Rua Castilho 169 ℂ213 882 161, fax 213 887 581, *rex@rex.pt.*

Smart hotel, newly renovated, which is nicer from the inside as you can't see the modern exterior. The front rooms have large balconies overlooking Parque Eduardo VII. ⑥

Ritz Four Seasons

Map 9, A8. Rua Rodrigo da Fonseca 88 ℂ213 832 020, fax 213 831 783, *ritzfourseasons@mail.telepac.pt.*

On the west side of Parque Eduardo VII, this vast modern block is perhaps the grandest – and most expensive – hotel in the city, with huge airy rooms, terraces overlooking the park, and public areas replete with marble, antiques, old masters and overly attentive staff. Disabled access. ⑨

Residencial São Pedro

Map 2, F6. Rua Pascoal de Melo 130 ℂ213 578 765, fax 213 578 865. A heavy, dark-wood interior gives this a rather sombre mood, but the rooms are clean and comfortable enough and it's only a short walk from the cenral bus station. ③

AROUND AVENIDA ALMIRANTE REIS

Pensão Fernandinha

Map 2, G6. Rua António Pedro 52–1° ℂ213 536 379.

Just off Praça do Chile (head west down Rua A. P. Carrilho – Rua António Pedro is the first on the left), and a handy option for the airport. Don't be put off by the rather alarming faded Sixties furnishings. Bathroom is communal. ②

Campsites

The Portuguese camping organization Orbitur have 21 campsites throughout the country, including two in the Lisbon region. For membership and information contact them at Rua Diogo do Couto 1-8 ☏218 117 070, fax 218 148 045, *info@orbitur.pt*, or visit their Web site on *www.orbitur.pt*.

Camping Praia Grande (Map 1, A4), Praia Grande ☏219 290 581. Well-equipped campsite on the beach at Praia Grande, west of Sintra. Bus #441 runs from Sintra train station to here.

Orbitur Guincho (Map 1, A5), EN 247, Lugar da Areia, Guincho ☏214 871 014, fax 214 872 167, *info@orbitur.pt*. Attractive campsite set among pine trees close to Guincho beach, served by regular bus from Cascais. The well-equipped site also has bungalows and caravans for hire. Orbitur members get a ten percent discount.

Orbitur Costa de Caparica (Map 1, E7), Avda Afonso de Albuquerque, Quinta de St António, Monte de Caparica ☏212 901 366, fax 212 900 661, *info@orbitur.pt*. Well-positioned a short, tree-shaded walk from the beach, this is one of the few campsites in Caparica open to non-members, but tents, caravans and bungalows are crammed in cheek-by-jowl; facilities are good, but it's not for those looking for solitude.

Parque Municipal de Campismo (Map 2, A6), Parque Florestal de Monsanto ☏217 609 620, fax 217 609 633. The main city campsite – well-equipped, with disabled facilities, a swimming pool and shops – is 6km west of the city centre, in the expansive, hilltop Parque de Monsanto. The entrance is on Estrada da Circunvalação on the park's west side. Bus #43 runs to the campsite from Praça da Figueira via Belém. Though the campsite is relatively secure, take care in the park after dark.

Pensão Lar do Areeiro

Map 2, G5. Praça Dr Francisco de Sá Carneiro 4–1° ℭ218 493 150, fax 218 406 321.

Respectable and well-run *pensão*, if a little old-fashioned. It's right on the *praça*, opposite Areeiro metro, which means it's noisy; ask for a room at the back. All rooms have attached bath, and breakfast is included. ③

Residencial O Paradouro

Map 2, G6. Avda Almirante Reis 106–7° ℭ218 153 256, fax 218 155 445.

Smart English-speaking establishment in a residential neighbourhood, opposite the fine *Portugália* restaurant (see p.139). All rooms come with TV, and some have balconies; breakfast included. ③

Eating

Lisbon has some of the best-value **restaurants** of any European city, serving large portions of good Portuguese food at sensible prices. A set menu (*ementa turística*) at lunch or dinner will get you a three-course meal for 1800–2500$00 anywhere in the city, though you can eat for considerably less than this by sticking to the ample main dishes and choosing the daily specials.

At their finest, Portuguese dishes can be a revelation, with fresh ingredients bursting with flavour, despite the absence of elaborate sauces. Grilled meats and fish tend to be the best bets, usually accompanied by chips or rice and salad. But unless you go upmarket, don't expect sophisticated sauces or delicate touches: stews in particular are not for the faint-hearted, offal features highly on most menus and even the ever-present bacalhau (dried salted cod) can be pretty heavy going if you choose the wrong variety (and there are reputedly 365). If you want to try specialities from the Lisbon area itself, go for *lulas fritas* (fried squid), *iscas* (marinated liver, often cooked with ham and potatoes) or *santola recheada* (stuffed spider crab).

Unless you have a big appetite, you may find a *meia doce* (half portion) sufficient for a main course, or order one dish between two people. You will also usually be presented with starters of olives, cheeses, spreads and sometimes cold meats or seafood when you sit down. You'll be charged for anything you eat; if you don't take anything, make sure it's not put on your bill. If you do have room for desserts, don't expect a great variety: ice cream (*gelado*), fruit (*fruta*), crème caramel (*pudim flan*) and rice pudding (*arroz doce*) are fairly ubiquitous.

The city, naturally, features some of the country's best (and most expensive) restaurants, specializing for the most part in a hybrid French-Portuguese cuisine. It also has a rich vein of inexpensive foreign restaurants, particularly those featuring food from the former colonies (see box on p.119), as well as an increasing number from Japan, Argentina, Mexico and Italy. Seafood is widely available, if generally more expensive than other dishes – an entire central street, **Rua das Portas de Santo Antão** (see p.135), specializes in it, as does an enclave of restaurants across the River Tejo at **Cacilhas**. Several traditional restaurants also survive, most notably some beautifully tiled *cervejarias* (literally "beer halls"), where the emphasis is often as much on drinking as eating.

By day there are plenty of restaurants scattered around the **Baixa**, offering set lunches to office employees, and there are some good places in all the other areas in which you're likely to be sightseeing, especially in **Alfama** and **Belém**. By night the obvious place to be is the **Bairro Alto**, which

Restaurant prices

The listings below have been coded into three categories: **inexpensive** (less than 2500$00); **moderate** (2500–4000$00); and **expensive** (above 4000$00). These prices refer to the cost of a two-course meal including wine, but excluding tips. All the places listed accept major credit cards unless specifically stated.

hosts several of the city's trendiest restaurants, as well as some more basic venues which are great value for money. Note that many restaurants are closed on **Sunday evenings**, while on Saturday nights in midsummer you may need to book for the more popular places; phone numbers are given below where necessary.

For the best vegetarian options see p.116; for a list of restaurants with great views see p.117; for restaurants with outdoor seating see p.123; for restaurants serving cuisines from Portugal's former colonies see p.119.

BAIXA

Beira Gare
Map 3, B7. Rua 1° de Dezembro 5.
Daily 6.30am–1am. No credit cards. Inexpensive.
Well established snackbar-restaurant opposite Rossio station, serving stand-up Portuguese snacks, and cheap lunches and dinners. Constantly busy, which is recommendation enough.

If you'd prefer to make your own meals, see p.202 for details of the best places to buy food.

A Berlenga
Map 3, C5. Rua Barros Queiroz 29.

Daily 8am–midnight. Moderate to expensive.

A *cervejaria*-restaurant with a window stuffed full of crabs and seafood. Early-evening snackers munch prawns at the bar, giving way later on to local diners who eat meals chosen from the window displays, as well as some meat dishes. The *ementa turística* at 2500$00 offers the best value, otherwise expect to pay 3500$00 and up.

Celeiro
Map 3, D7. Rua 1° de Dezembro 65.

Mon–Fri 9am–7pm. No credit cards. Inexpensive.

Just off Rossio, this self-service restaurant in the basement of a health-food supermarket offers tasty vegetarian spring rolls, quiches and the like. Go for the food, not the decor.

João do Grão
Map 3, E6. Rua dos Correeiros 220–228 ℂ213 424 757.

Daily 1–10pm. Moderate.

Appealing outdoor tables on this pedestrianized street tempt you to sample the reasonably priced Portuguese favourites and interesting salads, though the marble- and azulejos-decorated interior is just as attractive.

Leão d'Ouro
Map 3, C7. Rua 1° de Dezembro 105 ℂ213 426 195.

Daily noon–midnight. Moderate to expensive.

Cool and attractive azulejos-covered restaurant specializing in seafood and grilled meats. Prices are quite high, but then so is the quality. It gets busy early, so book ahead if you can.

Martinho da Arcada
Map 3, J5. Praça do Comércio 3 ℂ218 879 259.

Mon–Sat 7–11pm. Moderate to expensive.

Beautiful traditional restaurant tucked into the arcade around the square, with starched white tablecloths and attentive waiters, little changed from the beginning of the century when it was frequented by writer Fernando Pessoa.

Sol Posto
Map 3, B6. Calçada de Sant'Ana 11.
Daily 9am–midnight. No credit cards. Inexpensive.
Popular spot for huge *arroz* (rice) dishes – *marisco* (seafood) and *pato* (duck) rice are two specialities – and fellow diners are more likely to be from the neighbourhood than a tour coach.

Yin-Yang
Map 3, H5. Rua dos Correeiros 14–1°.
Mon–Fri noon–1pm & 6–8pm. No credit cards. Inexpensive.
Macrobiotic vegetarian meals, including tofu dishes, fruit juices and crepes. It's great value and tasty – the hard part is to catch it while it's open.

Some essentials

Almoço	Lunch	*Jantar*	Dinner
Arroz	Rice	*Legumes*	Vegetables
Assado	Roasted	*Manteiga*	Butter
Batatas fritas	Chips	*Mexido*	Scrambled
Conta	Bill	*Ovos*	Eggs
Copo	Glass	*Queijo*	Cheese
Cozido	Boiled	*Pão*	Bread
Ementa	Menu	*Pequeno almoço*	Breakfast
Estrelado	Fried	*Pimenta*	Pepper
Frito	Fried	*Piri-piri*	Chilli sauce
Garrafa	Bottle	*Sal*	Salt
Grelhado	Grilled	*Salada*	Salad

SOME ESSENTIALS

Portuguese foods and dishes

Arroz de marisco	Seafood rice
Atum	Tuna
Bacalhau à brás	Salted cod with egg and potatoes
Bife à portuguesa	Thin beef steak with a fried egg on top
Borrego	Lamb
Caldeirada	Fish stew
Caldo verde	Cabbage soup
Camarões	Shrimp
Carapau	Mackerel
Cataplana	Fish, shellfish or meat stewed in a circular metal dish
Cozido à portuguesa	Boiled casserole of meats and beans, served with rice and vegetables
Espetada mista	Mixed meat kebab
Febras	Pork steaks
Frango no churrasco	Barbecued chicken
Gambas	Prawns
Lulas grelhadas	Grilled squid
Pato	Duck
Pescada	Whiting
Porco à alentana	Pork cooked with clams
Presunto	Smoked ham
Salmão	Salmon
Sardinhas na brasa	Charcoal-grilled sardines
Sopa de peixe	Fish soup
Truta	Trout
Vitela	Veal

CHIADO

1° de Maio
Map 5, D5. Rua da Atalaia 8 ℂ213 426 840.
Mon–Fri 9am–4pm & 7pm–midnight, Sat 9am–4pm.
Moderate.
Characterful, buzzing traditional *adega* (wine cellar) at the bottom end of Rua da Atalaia, with a low arched ceiling, excellent dishes of the day and an array of sizzling grilled meat and fish dishes. Fills up early so book ahead.

Associação Católica
Map 5, E8. Trav. Ferragial 1.
Mon–Fri noon–3pm. No credit cards. Inexpensive.
Go through the unmarked door on a small road just off Rua do Ferragial and head to the top floor for this self-service canteen offering different dishes each day. The chief attraction is the price and the fine rooftop terrace with views over the Tejo.

Belcanto
Map 5, F7. Largo de São Carlos 10 ℂ213 420 607.
Mon–Fri noon–3pm & 7–11pm, Sat 7–11pm. Expensive.
Favoured by government ministers and local business folk, this intimate wood-panelled restaurant exudes an air of sophistication and tradition. Good bacalhau dishes and home-made desserts.

O Canteiro
Map 5, E8. Rua Vitor Cordon 8–10.
Mon–Fri 7.30am–8.30pm. No credit cards. Inexpensive.
On a steep street served by tram #28, the wonderful, cool, azulejos-covered interior shelters a self-service counter feeding local workers with a fine range of dishes such as tuna and black-eyed bean salad, bacalhau rissoles and strawberries. Particularly busy at lunchtimes.

CHIADO

L'Entrecôte
Map 5, E6. Rua do Alecrim 121 ©213 428 343.
Mon–Sat 12.30–3pm & 8pm–midnight, Sun 12.30–3pm & 8–11pm.
Moderate to expensive.
A relaxing and informal, French-influenced restaurant, one of the new breed of tasteful places opening up round the city. Its spacious, wood-panelled interior with soaring ceilings is an excellent place to enjoy a steak washed down by fine wines.

Tágide
Map 5, F8. Largo Academia das Belas Artes 18–20 ©213 420 720.
Mon–Fri 12.30–2.30pm & 7.30–10.30pm. Expensive.
One of Lisbon's priciest restaurants, serving superb regional dishes in a dining room with sweeping city views that are hard to beat. Book ahead, especially for a window seat. At least 6000$00 per person.

Tavares Rico
Map 5, F5. Rua da Misericórdia 37 ©213 421 112.
Mon–Fri 9am–midnight, Sun 7pm–midnight. Expensive.

Vegetarian restaurants

All the following restaurants are reviewed in this chapter – not all of them are purely vegetarian, but all offer good meat-free options.

VEGETARIAN RESTAURANTS

Gloriously ornate restaurant, one of Lisbon's oldest, where you can dine like a king in exclusive, chandeliered splendour on lobster, duck and sole cooked to perfection.

CAIS DO SODRÉ

Cais da Ribeira
Map 5, B9. Armazém A, Porta 2. ©213 463 611/213 423 611.
Wed–Fri noon–midnight, Sat, Mon & Tues 6pm–midnight.
Expensive.
Part of the newly improved area around the back of Cais do Sodré station, this attractive, recently converted warehouse with river views serves superior fish, meat and seafood straight from the market.

Marisqueira do Cais do Sodré
Map 5, A9. Cais do Sodré ©213 422 105.
Daily noon–3.30pm & 7.30–11.30pm; closed last week in Oct.
Expensive.
Big seafood restaurant by the station, complete with bubbling fish tanks. Try the *caldeirada de tamboril* (monkfish stew), the *caril de gambas* (curried prawns) or the seafood medley, *parrilhada*.

Restaurants with views

Associação Católica	Chiado, p.115
Atira-te ao Rio	Cacilhas, p.258
O Barbas	Caparica, p.261
Casa do Leão	Castelo, p.121
Já Sei	Belém, p.134
O Muchaxo	Guincho, p.254
Tágide	Chiado, p.116
Via Graça	Graça, p.124

Porto de Abrigo
Map 5, B8. Rua dos Remolares 16–18 ☎213 460 873.
Tues–Sun noon–3pm & 7–10.30pm. No credit cards.
Inexpensive.
Old-style tavern-restaurant serving fish fresh from the market at reasonable prices. It's a basic place, but it sits in one of Lisbon's most atmospheric areas.

ALFAMA AND AROUND

AROUND THE SÉ

Adega Triunfo
Map 3, I3. Rua dos Bacalhoeiros 129.
Tues–Sun noon–midnight. No credit cards. Inexpensive.
One of several no-frills, paper-tablecloth café-restaurants along this street, which is downhill from the Sé towards the river. This has a changing menu of meat and fish, pricier seafood, and cheap house wine. The *feijoada* (bean stew) is a good bet.

Delhi Palace
Map 3, I3. Rua da Padaria 18–20 ☎218 884 203.
Daily 9am–midnight. Moderate.
Bizarre combination of decent curries and pretty passable pizza and pasta, all served in attractive tiled restaurant. Friendly, English-speaking Indian owners.

Estrela da Sé
Map 3, I3. Largo S. António da Sé 4.
Mon–Sat 7am–midnight. No credit cards. Moderate.
Beautiful azulejos-covered restaurant just uphill from the Sé serving inexpensive and tasty dishes like *alheira* (chicken sausage) and salmon. Not exactly undiscovered, but with a traditional feel nonetheless.

Portuguese colonial food

Portugal's former status as a great trading nation has had a great influence on world cuisine. Along with port, the Portuguese are credited with introducing foodstuffs such as marmalade (though Portuguese *marmelada* is made from quince), Japanese tempura and even Indian curries such as vindaloo – indeed, the use of chillies in the East began only when the Portuguese started to import them from Mexico. Despite this global culinary influence, it is only relatively recently that Lisbon has embraced food with anything other than solid Portuguese ingredients (even when Portugal's empire was at its height, only the wealthy could afford to cook with the spices which fuelled the Portuguese economy). The ever-popular Chinese restaurants have now been joined by an increasing band of restaurants serving colonial cuisine. The following are some of the best around the city.

PORTUGUESE COLONIAL FOOD

Hua Ta Li
Map 3, I3. Rua dos Bacalhoeiros 119 ℂ218 879 170.
Daily noon–3pm & 6.30–11pm. Inexpensive.
Popular Chinese restaurant, especially at Sunday lunch when it
heaves with people. Seafood features highly; try the squid chop
suey.

Reitiro del Castilho
Map 3, I3. Rua da Padaria 34.
Daily 7am–midnight. No credit cards. Inexpensive.
Budget meals off paper-topped tables in a subterranean vault off
Rua de São Julião. A good lunchtime spot, especially if you like
filling soups.

Rio Coura
Map 3, H1. Rua Augusto Rosa 30.
Daily 8am–midnight. Amex only. Moderate.
A couple of hundred metres up from the Sé, this popular place
offers good-value meals including rough house wine for around
2500$00, served in a traditional tiled dining room.

CASTELO AND MOURARIA

Algures na Mouraria
Map 3, D3. Rua das Farinhas 1.
Tues–Sun noon–3.30pm & 7.30–11.30pm. Inexpensive.
Buried in the earthy Mouraria district, this restaurant offers excellent Angolan dishes such as *moamba de ginguba* (chicken with peanut
sauce), *sarapatel* (kidney, liver and port), *frango à angolana* (chicken in
ginger) and *caril de camarão* (prawn curry).

Arco do Castelo
Map 4, B6. Rua Chão da Feira 25 ℂ218 876 598.
Mon–Sat noon–midnight. Moderate.
Cheerful place just below the entrance to the castle specializing in

Goan dishes such as tempting shrimp curry, Indian sausage and spicy seafood.

Casa do Leão

Map 4, B4. Castelo de São Jorge ℗218 875 962.

Daily 12.30–3.30pm & 8–11pm. Expensive.

Couldn't be better sited, within the castle walls and providing a superb city view from its outside terrace and beautiful tiled interior. Slick service, high but not outrageous prices, and top-rate traditional Portuguese food such as *espetada de lulas com gambas* (squid and prawn kebab). Tourist menu 4500$00.

Costa do Castelo

Map 4, A5. Calç. do Marquês de Tancos 1b ℗218 884 636.

Tues–Sun 8pm–midnight (bar: Tues–Sun 3pm–2am). Moderate.

Boppy bar-restaurant (see p.158) with tasty Mozambiquan dishes such as *almond caril de camarão* (shrimp curry), best enjoyed on the outside terrace with great Baixa views.

Frei Pepinhas

Map 4, E4. Rua de São Tomé 13–21.

Mon–Sat 11am–3.30pm & 6pm–midnight. Inexpensive to moderate.

Long, azulejos-decorated bar-restaurant with wrought-iron chairs and checked blue tablecloths to tempt you in for some moderately priced Portuguese staples. Despite its position, it's mainly the haunt of locals. The *febras* (pork steaks) are always a good bet.

Santo André

Map 4, D3. Costa do Castelo 91.

Daily 10.30am–2am. Inexpensive.

Slightly scruffy place next to the puppet museum, with a small terrace overlooking tram route #12. The attached games room attracts the neighbourhood's young things, while the decent, very reasonably priced food pulls in local diners.

CASTELO AND MOURARIA

São Cristóvão

Map 3, E3. Rua de São Cristóvão 28–30 ©218 885 578.

Daily 10.30am–midnight. Inexpensive.

Titchy Cape Verdean restaurant which crams in tables, a TV and live music on Friday to Sunday evenings, all overseen by motherly owner Mento. Dishes include *catchupa rica* (pork, chicken, maize and beans) and *galinha caboverdiana* (chicken with coconut milk). It's just off Largo de São Cristóvão.

A Tasquinha

Map 4, D6. Largo do Contador Mor 5–7.

Mon–Sat 9am–2am. Moderate.

Considering its position, on the main route up to the castle, this lovely *tasca* (dining room) has remained remarkably unaffected by tourism. The food is good value, too, served either at the few tables in the traditional interior or on a fine outdoor terrace.

ALFAMA

Lautasco

Map 4, G7. Beco do Azinhal 7 ©218 860 173.

Mon–Sat 10am–midnight; closed Dec. Expensive.

Tucked just off the Largo do Chafariz de Dentro in a picturesque Alfama courtyard: by day a shady retreat, by night a magical fairy-lit oasis. Multilingual menus and higher-than-usual prices, but a great spot for dishes such as *borrego* (lamb), *tamboril* (monkfish) and *cataplanas* (stews).

Restaurante Malmequer-Bemmequer

Map 4, E7. Rua de São Miguel 23–25 ©218 876 535.

Mon & Wed–Sat 12.30–3.30pm & 7pm–1am, Tues 7pm–1am; closed last week in Oct. Moderate to expensive.

Cheery, flowery decor, and grilled meat and fish dishes (try the *salmão no carvão* – charcoal-grilled salmon) overseen by a friendly owner. Tourist menu around 2400$00.

ALFAMA

Mestre André

Map 4, G7. Calçadinha de Santo Estevão 4–6.

Mon–Sat noon–2.30am. No credit cards. Moderate.

A fine tavern on steps just off Rua dos Remédios with a bit of traditional colour about it, offering superb pork dishes and a good range of *churrasco* (grilled) dishes. There's an outdoor terrace with seating in summer too.

Rafaelo

Map 4, C9. Rua de São João da Praça 103.

Mon–Tues noon–4pm, Wed–Sat noon–4pm & 8pm–midnight. Expensive.

Attractive, stone-floored bar-restaurant in a tastefully modernized Alfama building. Live music and fado at weekends, and a long menu big on beef dishes as well as a few Brazilian specialities.

Santo António de Alfama

Map 4, F7. Beco de São Miguel 7.

Daily except Tues 8pm–2am. Moderate to expensive.

Restaurants with outdoor seating

Adega do Teixeira	Bairro Alto, p.125
Carvoeiro	Belém, p.134
Casa da Comida	Parque Eduardo VII, p.138
Casa do Leão	Castelo, p.121
Esplanada Santa Marta	Cascais, p.253
João do Grão	Baixa, p.112
Lautasco	Alfama, p.122
Patô Baton	Bairro Alto, p.129
Primoroso	Caparica, p.261
A Tasquinha	Castelo, p.122
York House	Lapa, p.132

RESTAURANTS WITH OUTDOOR SEATING

Restaurant and bar, just off Rua de São Miguel, with a long wine list, tapas and six different beef dishes. The main draw is the vine-covered outdoor terrace overlooking the church of São Miguel, in the heart of Alfama.

CAMPO DE SANTA CLARA AND GRAÇA

Haweli Tandoori

Map 2, G8. Trav. do Monte 14.

Wed–Mon noon–3pm & 7–11.30pm. Inexpensive.

Recommended, budget-priced Indian restaurant near the Miradouro da Graça, with a good range of curries and tandoori dishes. There are also some fine vegetarian options and a take away service. It's on a small alley on the west side of the main Largo da Graça.

Mercado de Santa Clara

Map 4, I3. Mercado de Santa Clara.

Tues–Sat noon–3pm & 7.30–midnight, Sun noon–3pm. Moderate to expensive.

Award-winning cuisine in the upstairs room of wonderful old market building with distant views of the Tejo. Specializes in beef dishes, but also serves fish. Come on Tuesday or Saturday lunchtime to be in the thick of the Feira da Ladra market bustle; it's much quieter at other times.

O Pardieiro

Map 4, F1. Largo da Graça 36.

Mon–Sat 8am–midnight. Moderate.

Good-quality Portuguese food at reasonable prices in a simple restaurant on the edge of Largo da Graça. From the Baixa, it's one stop after São Vicente de Fora on tram #28.

Via Graça

Map 4, E1. Rua Damasceno Monteiro 9b ©218 870 830.

Mon–Fri 12.30–3.30pm & 7.30pm–midnight, Sat 7.30pm–midnight. Moderate to expensive.

Tucked away below the Miradouro da Graça (take a left after Largo da Graça becomes Rua da Graça), this unattractive new building hides an interior offering stunning panoramas of Lisbon. Specialities include *santola* (spider crab) and *pato com moscatel* (duck with moscatel).

BAIRRO ALTO AND RATO

Adega do Teixeira
Map 5, F2. Rua do Teixeira 39.
Mon–Sat 10am–midnight. Moderate.
Down a quiet side street, this makes a good choice if you want a tranquil start to your evening before hitting the bars nearby. It has a smart interior and a lovely leafy terrace, and offers largish meals and some unusual egg dishes.

Água do Bengo
Map 5, F2. Rua do Teixeira 1 ©213 477 516.
Tues–Sat 8pm–1am. Moderate.
Owned by Angolan musician Waldemar Bastos, this African music bar-restaurant has fishing nets on the walls and tropical grilled fish and meat on the menu. If Waldemar is in town and in the mood, he'll grab his guitar and play a tune or two.

Alfaia
Map 5, E3. Trav. da Queimada 18–24.
Tues–Sat noon–3pm & 7–10.30pm, Mon 7–11.30pm. Moderate.
With azulejos on the wall, low ceilings, barrels of wine behind the bar and chattering diners, this is your archetypal Bairro Alto local with reasonably priced Portuguese dishes.

Ali-a-Papa

Map 5, E4. Rua da Atalaia 95 ℗213 474 143.
Daily except Tues 7.30pm–1am. Moderate.
One of Lisbon's few Moroccan restaurants, with an attractive
interior and fashionable clientele. Refreshing mint tea and good-
value couscous and *tajine* dishes.

O Barrigas

Map 5, E3. Trav. da Queimada 31.
Daily noon–2am. No credit cards. Inexpensive to moderate.
Minuscule tavern with friendly service and simple dishes like steaks.
Inexpensive if you settle for the half portions, which should suffice.

Bizarro

Map 5, E3. Rua da Atalaia 131–133.
Tues–Fri & Sun noon–7pm, Sat 7pm–midnight. Moderate.
The prices are not at all bizarre, despite the name, and the *ementa
turística* is a good deal in this friendly, unpretentious place with a
TV in one corner for those who are feeling antisocial.

Bota Alta

Map 5, F3. Trav. da Queimada 37 ℗213 427 959.
Mon–Fri noon–2.30pm & 7pm–midnight, Sat noon–2.30pm.
Moderate.
Attractive old tavern-restaurant decorated with old boots (*botas*) and
eclectic pictures; attracts queues for its vast portions of traditional
Portuguese food – *bacalhau com natas* (cod cooked in cream) among
other things – and jugs of local wine. The tables are crammed in
cheek-by-jowl and it's always packed; try to arrive before 8pm.

O Cantinho do Bem Estar

Map 5, E5. Rua do Norte 46.
Tues–Sun 10am–2am. No credit cards. Inexpensive.
Friendly and authentic tiled Alentejan restaurant where the owner
stuffs so many tables in he could have a second career as a taxider-

mist – get here before 9pm. The good-value tourist menu includes local wine served in ceramic jugs.

Casa Trasmontana

Map 5, G4. Calç. do Duque 39 ℂ213 420 300.

Daily noon–3pm & 7pm–2am. No credit cards. Inexpensive.

A different dish of the day – usually meat-orientated – is on offer in this tiny restaurant specializing in cuisine from the north of Portugal. An interesting and friendly little place, it's on the steps off Largo T. Coelho which head down to Rossio station.

Cataplana

Map 5, E5. Rua do Diário de Notícias 27 ℂ213 422 993.

Daily 10am–3pm & 7pm–midnight. Inexpensive.

Quirky local with bubbling fish tanks, guitars on the walls, a chattering TV and occasional live music. Simple Portuguese food, tasty house specials, and *cataplana* fish stews.

Cervejaria da Trindade

Map 5, G5. Rua Nova da Trindade 20 ℂ213 423 506.

Daily 9am–2am. Inexpensive.

Avoid the dull modern extensions and grab a table in the original huge, vaulted beer hall-restaurant, decorated with some of the city's loveliest azulejos depicting the elements and seasons. Shellfish are the speciality, though other fish and meat dishes are cheaper. There is also a patio garden and – a rarity – children's highchairs can be supplied.

Estibordo

Map 5, G4. Trav. João de Deus 14.

Mon–Fri noon–11.30pm, Sat 5–11.30pm. Inexpensive.

Simple local restaurant with slightly gloomy ship-theme decor. Specialities include prawns or veal in breadcrumbs, served with liberal swathes of mayonnaise. Not for healthy eaters, but very good value.

BAIRRO ALTO

Fidalgo

Map 5, E4. Rua da Barroca 27 ℂ213 422 900.

Mon–Sat 10am–12pm. Moderate.

This has long been a fashionable and cosy hangout for artists and media types, who are rewarded by delicious seafood creations such as *arroz de tamboril com camarão* (monkfish rice with shrimps), plus the odd *leitão* (suckling pig). Bookings recommended.

Hell's Kitchen

Map 5, F2. Rua da Atalaia 176 ℂ213 422 822.

Daily 7pm–2am. Inexpensive.

Fashionable and popular place with an unusual and vaguely inferno-like orange interior and good-value dishes such as falafels and creole salmon. A good late-night option.

Mamma Rosa

Map 5, F3. Rua do Grémio Lusitano 14 ℂ213 465 350.

Daily 8pm–2am. Inexpensive.

Lively, intimate pizzeria, bustling with students, which dishes up uninspiring but inexpensive pasta, pizza and grilled meats. It's also a popular gay hangout.

Massima Culpa

Map 5, E4. Rua da Atalaia 33–37 ℂ213 420 121.

Daily 8pm–2am. Expensive.

Upmarket Italian restaurant, popular with families, offering a fine selection of pasta dishes and friendly, efficient service, though the minimalist decor is somewhat bland.

Pap'Açorda

Map 5, E4. Rua da Atalaia 57–59 ℂ213 464 811.

Mon 8–11pm, Tues–Sat 12.30–2.30pm & 8–11pm. Expensive.

Renowned restaurant which attracts Lisbon's fashionable elite to its chandelier-hung dining room, converted from an old bakery. *Açorda* – a sort of bread stew, seasoned with fresh coriander and a raw egg – is the house speciality. Bookings recommended.

A Paridinha
Map 5, 4E. Rua da Barroca 70 ©213 422 345.
Daily except Tues 8pm–2am. Moderate to expensive.
Highly rated, cool green restaurant with fantastic *catchupa* and other Cape Verdean dishes such as *feijão ervilha* (bean and pea stew), *caril de amendoim* (chicken and peanut curry) and *escabeche de peixe* (Cape Verde dry fish); there's occasional live music too.

Patô Baton
Map 5, E4. Trav. dos Fiéis de Deus 28 ©213 426 372.
Mon 8–11pm, Tues–Sat 12.30–2.30pm & 8–11pm. Expensive.
Jazzy sounds and decor and French-Portuguese cuisine with a modern twist. There are also a few tables on the pedestrianized steps outside.

Sinal Vermelho
Map 5, F4. Rua das Gáveas 89 ©213 461 252.
Daily 12.15–3pm & 7.15–11.30pm. Moderate.
Roomy, split-level *adega* (wine cellar) that's popular with Lisbon's trendies. Specialities include rabbit and liver dishes.

Último Tango
Map 5, E4. Rua do Diário de Notícias 62 ©213 420 341.
Mon–Sat 7.30–11pm. Moderate.
Spotless and welcoming Argentinian restaurant, with wooden tables and a cosy interior. The large steaks are a good bet.

Vá e Volte
Map 5, F4. Rua do Diário de Notícias 100.
Tues–Sun 7pm–midnight. Inexpensive to moderate.
Small bar at the front opens onto a friendly little family diner whose large plates of fried or grilled fish and meat, though nothing special, are reliably filling.

BAIRRO ALTO

PRAÇA DO PRÍNCIPE REAL AND RATO

Comida de Santo
Map 8, C6. Calçada Engenheiro Miguel Pais 39.
Daily 12.30–3.30pm & 7.30pm–1am. Expensive.

Rowdy, late-opening Brazilian restaurant serving cocktails and classic dishes such as *feijoada a brasileira* (bean stew) and *picanha* (thin
slices of beef). It's off Rua da Escola Politécnica, near the Science
and Natural History museums.

Faz Frio
Map 8, E7. Rua Dom Pedro V 96–98 ©213 461 860.
Daily 9am–midnight. Inexpensive.

A beautiful, traditional restaurant, replete with tiles and confession-
al-like cubicles. Huge portions of bacalhau, seafood paella, prawns
in breadcrumbs plus dishes of the day are available, though the service can be patchy.

Real Fábrica
Map 8, B5. Rua da Escola Politécnica 275 ©213 872 918.
Daily 7am–3am. Expensive.

This place – with smart, stone-walled interior decorated with big
mirrors – is also known for its beer, which is brewed in huge barrels in a corner. The curved wooden downstairs bar offers inexpensive lunchtime snacks, while the lovely upstairs dining room sells a
colossal Brazilian buffet which includes *picanha* (thin slices of beef),
turkey with bacon, fried bananas, pineapple, black beans and rice
for around 5000$00 a head. There's also an outdoor terrace.

Tascardoso
Map 5, F1. Rua Dom Pedro V 137 ©213 475 698.
Mon–Fri noon–3pm & 6–9pm. Inexpensive.

Go through the stand-up bar and downstairs to the tiny eating area
for excellent tapas-style meats and cheeses and good-value hot
dishes.

LAPA AND AROUND

Aya

Map 6, G4. Rua das Trinas 67, Lapa.

Tues–Sat 12.30–2pm & 7.30–9.30pm, Sun 7.30–9.30pm.
Expensive.

This very Portuguese building – all tiles – shelters a highly rated Japanese restaurant that keeps the wealthy locals satisfied.

Cantinho da Paz

Map 6, I4. Rua da Paz 4, São Bento ℂ213 969 698.

Tues–Sun 12.30–2.30pm & 7.30–11pm. Moderate.

Simple Goan restaurant favoured by MPs from the local parliament building; shark soup, prawn curry and other Indian specialities including vegetarian options. It's just off tram route #28.

Farah's Tandoori

Map 6, F3. Rua de Santana à Lapa 73, Estrela.

Daily except Tues noon–3pm & 7–10.30pm. Inexpensive to moderate.

Between Lapa and Estrela, this is one of Lisbon's more reliable Indian restaurants, good for vegetarians with dishes such as vegetable tikka masala, Bombay alu and palak paneer. Meat dishes are also fragrant and delicious, and the owners speak English.

Flor da Estrela

Map 6, G3. Rua João de Deus 11, Estrela.

Mon–Sat 8am–midnight. Moderate.

Neighbourhood restaurant around the back of the Estrela basilica, serving all the usual dishes and cheap wine. There are a few outdoor tables, but the interior is more attractive. Try the *feijoada de marisco* (bean stew with seafood).

LAPA AND AROUND

Indo-Africa/Cantinho da Paz II

Map 6, I5. Rua do Poço dos Negros 64, São Bento ©213 908 638.
Daily except Tues 12.30–3.30pm & 7.30–11.30pm.
Moderate.

Sister to restaurant above, only here you can sample a range of
Portuguese colonial cuisine under one roof: Goan, Cape Verdean
and Angolan dishes such as *vitela com açafrão e amêndoa* (veal with
saffron rice and almonds), *carne de vaca com molho de amendoim* (beef
with peanut sauce) and *feijoada indiana*; plus live music at weekends.

Picanha

Map 6, G5. Rua das Janelas Verdes 47, Lapa ©213 975 401.
Mon–Fri 12–3pm & 7.30pm–midnight, Sat & Sun 7.30pm–midnight.
Moderate.

Intimate, ornately tiled interior offers multilingual service and
picanha (thin slices of beef) accompanied by black-eyed beans, salad
and potatoes. Great if this appeals to you, since for a fixed-price
you can eat as much of the stuff as you want; otherwise forget it, as
it's all they do.

Sua Excelência

Map 6, F5. Rua do Conde 34, Lapa ©213 903 614.
Daily except Wed 1–3pm & 8–10.30pm. Expensive.

Small, intimate restaurant in the heart of Lapa specializing in
Mozambiquan tiger prawns. The proprietor's camp digressions as
he talks you through what's on offer will either delight or enrage.
Marvellously inventive Portuguese cooking, though, and worth the
high prices. Reservations advised.

York House

Map 6, G5. Rua das Janelas Verdes 47, Lapa ©213 968 143.
Daily 12.30–2.30pm & 7.30–9.30pm. Moderate to expensive.

Inside this sumptuous hotel is a surprisingly moderately priced
restaurant serving delicious fish, meat, pasta and vegetarian options.
In summer, you can dine in the tranquil courtyard.

ALCÂNTARA

Espalha Brasas
Map 6, B7. Armazém 12, Doca de Santo Amaro ✆213 962 059
Mon–Wed noon–2am. Moderate.
Tapas and superb grilled meats can be enjoyed at outdoor riverside tables, or head for the bright upstairs room which offers great views over the river.

Indochina
Map 6, D6. Rua Cintura do Porto de Lisboa, Doca de Alcântara ✆213 955 875.
Tues–Sun 8pm–1am. Moderate to expensive.
One of the city's more imaginative new developments, this spacious restaurant serves Thai, Vietnamese, Chinese and Japanese dishes in a converted warehouse done up in the style of a 1930s colonial house. From 2am, it becomes a club (see p.169).

Tertúlia do Tejo
Map 6, B7. Pavilhão 4, Doca de Santo Amaro ✆213 955 552.
Daily 12.30–3pm & 7.30–11pm. Expensive.
Upmarket Portuguese restaurant on three floors of a converted warehouse. There are evocative old photos of Portugal in the upstairs room and more intimate seating in the attic room, plus fine river views.

Zeno
Map 6, B7. Doca de Santo Amaro ✆213 973 948.
Mon–Sat 12.30pm–2.30am, Sun 8.30pm–2.30am. Moderate to expensive.
Thriving Brazilian restaurant in a converted warehouse by the

river, with live music most nights. The speciality is *feijoada à brasileira* (Brazilian bean stew), followed by refreshing tropical desserts.

BELÉM

Cápsula ·
Map 7, G5. Rua Vieira Portuense 74.
Daily noon–10pm. No credit cards. Inexpensive.
One of the many places on this pretty row of buildings facing the greenery of Praça do Império. This has a tiled interior, upstairs seating and outside tables catering for tourists tucking into tuna steaks, trout and the like at good-value prices.

Carvoeiro
Map 7, G5. Rua Vieira Portuense 66–68.
Daily noon–3pm & 7–10pm. No credit cards. Inexpensive.
A little *tasca* (dining room), with good-value grilled fish and jugs of wine, outdoor tables and efficient service.

Já Sei
Map 7, F6. Avda de Brasília ©213 015 969.
Mon 12.30–3.30pm, Tues–Sun 12.30–3.30pm & 7.30–10.30pm. Expensive.
Prowling waiters see to your every need in this modern glass edifice with great views over the Discoveries Monument. The international and Portuguese dishes are all of high quality.

São Jerónimo
Map 7, F2. Rua dos Jerónimos 12 ©213 648 797.
Mon–Fri 12.30–2.30pm & 7.30–10.30pm, Sat 7.30–10.30pm. Expensive.
Classic formal dining by the side of the monastery. High prices but worth it, for the excellent fish dishes in particular.

Vela Latina

Map 7, C6. Doca do Bom Sucesso ©213 017 118.
Mon–Sat 12.30–3pm & 8–11.30pm. Expensive.
Trendy option overlooking the docks, with expensive Portuguese
cooking and a bar till 2am. It has a cheaper self-service café round
the corner, too.

AROUND AVENIDA DA LIBERDADE

RUA DAS PORTAS DE SANTO ANTÃO

Andorra

Map 3, A7. Rua das Portas de Santo Antão 82 ©213 426 047.
Mon–Sat noon–midnight. Moderate.
Occupying a raised part of this pedestrianized street, with
well-positioned outdoor tables and a small and cosy interior,
this good-value restaurant specializes in *açorda* (a garlic and bread
sauce) and *arroz de marisco* (seafood rice), plus fresh fish and
steaks.

Bom Jardim/Rei dos Frangos

Map 3, A7. Trav. de Santo Antão 11–18.
Daily noon–11.30pm. Inexpensive.
On both sides of an alleyway connecting Restauradores with Rua
das Portas de Santo Antão, this is *the* place for spit-roast chicken, as
long as you don't mind a high grease content. It's now so popular
that it has spread into three buildings on either side of the road – if
one is full, try another.

Cafreal

Map 3, A7. Rua das Portas de Santo Antão 71.
Daily noon–11pm. Moderate.
Bustling tourist joint where waiters in lime-green jackets keep the
hordes happy with grilled fish and clams in wine sauce. The interi-

or is uninspiring, but there are a few outdoor tables from where you can watch the world go by.

.

Casa do Alentejo

Map 3, A7. Rua das Portas de Santo Antão 58.

Daily noon–2.30pm & 7–11pm. Moderate.

Extravagantly decorated interior which is as much a private club dedicated to Alentejan culture as it is a restaurant. The courtyard is stunning, as is the period furniture. The house also holds assorted exhibits, adding great ambience to sound Portuguese food served in two upstairs dining rooms.

Escorial

Map 3, A7. Rua das Portas de Santo Antão 47 ℂ213 464 429.

Daily noon–4pm & 7pm–1am. Expensive.

Quality restaurant with a darkened interior offering tiger prawns, steak, partridge and Spanish paella, not to mention English translations such as "selfish bisque" and "tarts of the house". There are a few outdoor tables, too.

Gambrinus

Map 3, B7. Rua das Portas de Santo Antão 15 ℂ213 421 466.

Daily noon–2am. Expensive.

Rated one of Lisbon's top seafood restaurants, with a smart, wood-panelled interior. The menu features broiled eel with bacon, lobster, and crepes for dessert.

Solmar

Map 3, A7. Rua das Portas de Santo Antão 108 ℂ213 423 371.

Daily noon–3pm & 7–10pm. Expensive.

A vast and cavernous showpiece seafood restaurant, complete with fountain and marine mosaics, although the emphasis seems to be more on luring customers in than keeping them happy once inside, and dishes can be hit or miss.

AROUND AVENIDA DA LIBERDADE

A Casa de Pompeia

Map 8, E6. Rua da Alegria 23.

Mon–Sat noon–midnight. Moderate.

A hike up the hill towards the Bairro Alto will bring you to this convivial restaurant offering trendy Portuguese food, with good grilled meat dishes and friendly staff.

Centro de Alimentaçao e Saúde Natural

Map 8, D3. Rua Mouzinho da Silveira 25 ©213 150 898.

Mon–Fri 9am–2.30pm & 3.50–6pm. Inexpensive.

Self-service restaurant with light, bright upstairs dining rooms and a summer courtyard offering good and inexpensive vegetarian options such as chickpea stew, pepper rice and natural fruit juices.

Restaurante Estrela

Map 8, F3. Rua Santa Marta 14a.

Mon–Fri 9am–midnight, Sat 9am–6pm. Inexpensive.

Tiny tiled *tasca*, just one of many remarkably inexpensive places on this street to the east of the Avenida da Liberdade, serving Portuguese dishes like *arroz de pato* (duck rice). You'll find it on the walking route described on p.67.

A Gina

Map 8, E5. Parque Mayer, Avda da Liberdade.

Mon–Sat 10am–midnight. No credit cards. Inexpensive.

The small group of minor theatres tucked off Travessa do Salitre also hides a cluster of restaurants which make a good spot for lunch, although by night the area can feel a bit derelict. This one has a fun seaside feel, with outdoor grills, simple tasty food and seating indoors and out.

O Manel

Map 8, E5. Parque Mayer, Avda da Liberdade.

Mon–Sat noon–11pm. Moderate.

Also in the theatre park (see *A Gina* above), this restaurant serves great *feijoada* (bean stew) and bacalhau dishes in a log-cabin-style interior. There's even an open fire in winter.

Restaurante 33

Map 8, D3. Rua Alex. Herculano 33 ©213 546 079.

Mon–Fri 12.30–2pm & 8–10pm, Sat 12.30–2pm. Moderate.

Fine old wood-beamed building in a part of town geared to businesspeople, where you can eat *perdiz com cebolas* (partridge stuffed with onions), duck rice and curried seafood in some style, but at surprisingly reasonable prices.

Os Tibetanos

Map 8, D5. Rua do Salitre 117 ©213 142 038.

Mon–Fri noon–2pm & 7.30–9.30pm. Inexpensive.

Run by a Buddhist Centre, this stripped-pine restaurant has superb and unusual veggie food such as vegetarian paella. It gets full at lunchtimes in particular, so grab a table early.

PARQUE EDUARDO VII AND SALDANHA

Botequim do Rei

Map 9, C7. Esplanade da Parque Eduardo VII.

Tues–Sun 9am–11pm. Moderate.

Fish and meat dishes are fairly average, but the setting, right in the park by a small lake, is particularly tranquil. Take care here, though, after dark.

Casa da Comida

Map 2, D7. Trav. das Amoreiras 1 ©213 885 376.

Mon–Fri 12.30–3.30pm & 8pm–midnight, Sat 8pm–midnight. Expensive.

One of the city's top French-Portuguese restaurants in one of the city's nicest squares, under the aqueduct (see p.78). Superb mansion surroundings, an outdoor patio, and meals costing a good 6000$00 and upwards.

Centro de Arte Moderna

Map 9, C4. Fundação Calouste Gulbenkian.

Daily noon–4pm. No credit cards. Inexpensive.

Join the lunchtime queues at the museum restaurant for good-value hot and cold dishes. There's an excellent choice of salads for vegetarians, which you can eat overlooking the lovely gardens. Get there early though before the smokers fume the place out.

Li Yuan

Map 9, E6. Rua Viriato 23 ©213 577 740.

Daily noon–2.30pm & 9–10.30pm. Moderate.

One of Lisbon's best Chinese restaurants, with delicately cooked dishes in a tasteful modern building behind the towering Sheraton Hotel.

Solar do Morais

Map 9, C6. Rua Augusto dos Santos 3.

Sun–Fri 9am–10.30pm. Inexpensive.

Very much a local, despite its position between the tourist draws of Parque Eduardo VII and the Gulbenkian, on a tiny road joining Avenida António Augusto de Aguiar and Rua de São Sebastião da Pedreira. The cool, arched interior has cabinets of fresh food, bottles lining the walls and a large ham on the bar. Trout and salmon dishes are good bets, and there's a small outdoor terrace.

AROUND AVENIDA ALMIRANTE REIS

Cervejaria Portugália

Map 2, G6. Avda Almirante Reis 117.

Mon–Sat 10pm–1.30am. Moderate.

Busy beer hall-restaurant near metro Arroios where you can either snack and drink at the bar or eat fine *mariscos* or steak in the dining room. A popular family outing and always busy.

Espiral
Map 2, F6. Praça Ilha do Faial 14a (off Largo de Dona Estefânia) ℂ213 573 585.
Daily noon–9.30pm. Inexpensive.
Self-service macrobiotic restaurant downstairs (offering vegetarian, Chinese and fish dishes) with adjacent snack bar, plus upstairs bookshop and noticeboard with information on the city's alternative/green scene. The food isn't that great, but there's often live music at the weekend. Take the metro to either Picoas or Arroios stations to get there.

CAMPO PEQUENO

Restaurante Chimarrão
Map 2, F5. Campo Pequeno 79 ℂ217 939 760.
Daily noon–4pm & 7pm–midnight. Moderate to expensive.
If you're looking for quantity, 3800$00 spent here gets you unlimited stabs at twelve types of barbecued meat and various salads – you'll need to pace yourself. There are also branches at Avda Roma 90, Rua 1º de Dezembro and at Parque das Nações.

Ser-Veja-Ria
Map 2, F5. Avda João XXI 80C.
Daily noon–2am. Moderate.
If you are out around Campo Pequeno, this modern *cervejaria* (hence the pun on its name) is a decent choice with reasonably priced food and drink.

PARQUE DAS NAÇÕES

Os Alentejanos
Cais dos Argonautas ℂ218 956 116.

Tues–Sun 12.30–10pm. Inexpensive to moderate.

Great wooden barrels and hams dangling from the ceiling jolly up an otherwise dull restaurant serving regional food from the Alentejo district – tapas (olives, cheeses, *presunto* ham) and thick red wines are the best bet.

Chimarrão

Doca dos Olivais ℭ218 952 222.

Daily noon–4pm & 7pm–midnight. Moderate to expensive.

In a prime position, with an outdoor terrace right on the waterside of Olivais docks, this Brazilian chain specializes in barbecued meats; if you have a very large appetite, go for the set meals, which are vast. There's also a good salad bar for the less carnivorously inclined.

Oceanario Café

Armazém 204 ℭ218 950 202.

Mon–Thurs & Sun 10am–8pm, Fri & Sat 10am–1am. Inexpensive.

Unpretentious self-service canteen and bar with outdoor tables near the Oceanarium; the buffet food is fresh and good value, with an extensive range of salads, hot dishes of the day and tasty desserts.

For a map of the Parque das Naçoes, see p.81.

Restaurante Panorâmico

Torre Vasco da Gama ℭ218 939 550.

Tues–Sun 11am–3pm & 8–11pm. Expensive.

The top of the old oil refinery tower is now an exclusive restaurant with fantastic views and some pretty decent Portuguese and international food at almost-as-high prices.

Os Sabores da Terra

Pavilhão de Portugal (Council of Ministers) ℭ218 918 617.

Tues–Sat 12.30–3.30pm & 7.30–10.30pm; Sun 12.30–3.30pm. Inexpensive to moderate.

PARQUE DAS NAÇÕES

Small bar with a good range of regional wines and snacks and a few outdoor tables. A good place for lunch.

Restaurante del Uruguay
Cais dos Argonautas ©218 955 445.
Tues–Fri noon–3pm & 7.30–10.30pm; Sat & Sun noon–4pm & 7.30–11.30pm. Moderate.
A chance to sample Uruguayan cuisine in a modern restaurant near the Water Gardens. The *picaña a la parrilla con papa paisana* (thin strips of beef with potatoes, garlic and salsa) is recommended.

Restaurante Viagen dos Sabores
Pavilhão de Portugal (Council of Ministers) ©218 918 617.
Tues–Sat 12.30–3.30pm & 7.30–10.30pm, Sun 12.30–3.30pm. Expensive.
Popular with politicians from the neighbouring Council of Ministers, with attentive service and views over Olivais docks, this is the closest you'll get to a culinary experience in the Parque. The expensive food features dishes such as as *alcatra da terceira* (steak from the Azores) and *espetada de frango com mel e amêndoas* (chicken kebab with honey and almonds).

PARQUE DAS NAÇÕES

Cafés

![drop cap L]Lisbon has literally thousands of **cafés**, ranging from atmospheric turn-of-the-century artists' haunts and Art Deco wonders to those with trendy minimalist interiors frequented by clubbers in designer clothing. Whatever the decor, you're sure to get a decent coffee (*café*) – try a wickedly strong *bica* (espresso) or a milky *galão* – and, as likely as not, a decent range of *bolos* (cakes) and pastries such as *pastéis de nata* (custard-cream tarts). Some of the older cafés and *pastelarias* (cafés specializing in cakes) are particularly good for an inexpensive breakfast, coffee or even a beer during the afternoon. Many open first thing in the morning and don't close till well into the evening, while a few – like *A Brasileira* (see p.146) and *Cerca Moura* (see p.147) – are also on the late-night bar-crawl circuit. The newer, more fashionable venues – such as those in Chiado and the Alcântara docks – double as bar-restaurants, serving a good range of beers, wines and decent Portuguese meals, though prices are correspondingly high.

Cafés with particularly good food have been listed in "Eating" (p.109); those which are best for an alcoholic drink can be found in the "Bars and clubs" (p.153). The following are recommended for a coffee, soft drink or snack.

Our listings are divided into the following areas: Baixa (p.144); Chiado (p.146); Cais do Sodré (p.147); Alfama and Graça (p.147); Bairro Alto (p.149); Lapa (p.149); Alcântara (p.150); Belém (p.151); Around Avenida da Liberdade (p.151); Saldanha (p.152).

BAIXA

Atinel
Map 3, L4. Fluvial, Praça do Comércio.
Mon–Fri 6am–9.30pm, Sat 6am–8.30pm.
A popular tourist spot, right by the ferry terminal. The riverside vista is unbeatable, even if its food is only average.

A Camponeza
Map 3, E6. Rua dos Sapateiros 155–157.
Mon–Sat 7am–10pm.
This *leitaria* (dairy shop) traditionally offers dairy products, but also serves coffees and snacks in a beautiful, tiled building just off Rossio.

Casa Chineza
Map 3, E7. Rua Aurea 274.
Mon–Fri 7am–8pm, Sat 7am–4pm.
Apart from the odd bit of neon lighting, this beautifully decorated old Baixa café hasn't changed for years, and attracts a steady stream of local workers with its pastries and coffee.

Casulo
Map 3, A7. Praça dos Restauradores.
Mon–Sat 6am–2am.

BAIXA

A fairly average café but in a great position, right on the square. There are a few outdoor seats, too, and it's a handy spot for breakfast.

Martinho da Arcada
Map 3, J5. Praça do Comércio 3.
Mon–Sat 7–11pm.

One of Lisbon's most famous and traditional cafés is now divided into a simple stand-up café next to a considerably more expensive restaurant (see p.112). There are outdoor tables under the arches, the perfect spot for a coffee and a *pastel de nata*.

Nicola
Map 3, D7. Rossio 24.
Mon–Fri 9am–7.30pm, Sat 10am–1pm.

Historic coffee house, former haunt of some of Lisbon's great literary figures, with outdoor tables overlooking the bustle of Rossio. Sadly, it lost much of its appeal during a thorough modernization in the 1990s.

Nicola Gourmet
Map 3, D7. Rua 1° de Dezembro 10–14.
Mon–Fri 10am–7.30pm, Sat 10am–1pm.

One wall is taken over by large wooden cabinets full of coffee beans which are ground aromatically in front of you either to take away or to drink at one of the cosy interior tables.

Suíça
Map 3, D6. Rossio
Daily 7am–10pm.

Famous for its cakes and pastries; you'll have a hard job getting an outdoor table here, though there's plenty of room inside. The café stretches through to Praça da Figueira, where you'll find the best alfresco seating.

BAIXA

For cafés with views, see p.148; for cafés with outdoor seating, see p.150.

CHIADO

Bernard
Map 5, F6. Rua Garrett 104.

Mon–Sat 8am–2am.

Often overlooked because of its proximity to *A Brasileira*, this is another old-style café offering superb cakes, ice cream and coffees, and an outdoor terrace on Chiado's most fashionable street.

A Brasileira
Map 5, F6. Rua Garrett 120.

Daily 8am–2am.

Marked by a bronze of the poet Pessoa outside, this is the most famous of Lisbon's old-style coffee houses. The tables on the pedestrianized street get snapped up by tourists, but the real appeal is in its traditional interior. At night the clientele changes to a youthful brigade on the beer.

Museu do Chiado café
Map 5, F7. Rua Serpa Pinto 4–6.

Tues 2–6pm, Wed–Sun 10am–6pm.

With its charming statue-filled patio and outdoor tables, this is a lovely spot to enjoy a coffee or drink. If you're lucky you'll hear opera singers practising in the São Carlos Theatre opposite.

Café No Chiado
Map 5, E6. Largo do Picadeiro 11.

Mon–Fri 10am–2pm & 6pm–2am, Sat noon–2am.

Café at the top end of Rua Duque de Bragança with an

average interior (there's an upstairs Internet room, Ciber Chiado, *info@cnc.pt*, if you need to get on-line) but with lovely outdoor tables in a picturesque square. Tram #28 passes right by.

CAIS DO SODRÉ

Agora Café
Map 5, D9. Avda Ribeira das Naus 2.
Mon–Fri 7am–10pm, Sat & Sun 7am–8.30pm.
Basic fast-food outlet attached to a student resource building: the appeal lies in its riverside location, which means you can enjoy cheapish drinks and snacks on outdoor tables overlooking the Tejo, usually accompanied by very loud (sometimes live) rock music.

Wagons-Lit
Map 5, B9. Estação Fluvial.
Mon–Fri 7am–10pm, Sat & Sun 7am–8.30pm.
A simple and more tranquil spot than the *Agora* next door, offering coffees, drinks and snacks, with outdoor tables right by the river; a great place to while away a few minutes if you have a ferry to catch.

ALFAMA AND GRAÇA

Cerca Moura
Map 4, E6. Largo das Portas do Sol 4.
Mon–Sat 11am–2am, Sun 11am–8pm.
A good place to take a break from climbing up and down the hilly streets, but the main appeal of this slightly pricey café is the stunning view of Alfama from the outdoor seats on the esplanade in front.

Esplanada da Graça
Map 4, E2. Largo da Graça.

Daily 10am–2am.

A tiny kiosk serving coffee, drinks and snacks by the Miradouro da Graça. It's not cheap, but its seats have stunning views over the bridge and Baixa, particularly at sunset, After dark, it cranks up a powerful music system to change the atmosphere from somnambulant to decidedly lively.

Monasterium Café
Map 4, G4. Igreja São Vincente de Fora.

Tues–Sun 10am–6pm.

Surprisingly enterprising café in the São Vicente monastery building, with comfy chairs indoors, tables in a tranquil patio out front, and a small roof terrace with stupendous views over Alfama (including an aerial view of tram #28 squeezing through its narrowest street) and the Tejo.

Pastelaria Estrela da Graça
Map 4, F1. Largo da Graça 98a.

Daily 7am–10pm.

Cafés and bars with views

Round the corner from the Miradouro da Graça on the main square, this local café serves superb home-made cakes, pastries and inexpensive lunches, complete with a toy fire engine outside to keep the kids happy.

BAIRRO ALTO

Académica
Map 3, E8. Largo do Carmo.
Daily 7am–midnight.
The outdoor tables of this café are on one of the city's nicest, quietest squares, outside the ruined Carmo church. As well as the usual coffee it also does light lunches; in summer, the grilled sardines are hard to beat.

Esplanada do Príncipe Real
Map 8, D7. Praça do Príncipe Real.
Daily 7am–midnight.
The outdoor tables under the trees of this attractive square are best, though there are also indoor tables in a glass pavilion. Also a popular gay haunt.

Pastelaria São Roque
Map 8, F7. Rua Dom Pedro V 57c.
Daily 7am–7.30pm.
Relaxed corner café with a wonderfully ornate ceiling, high enough to house a giraffe, where you can have coffee, croissants or fresh bread.

LAPA

O Chão da Lapa
Map 6, F5. Rua do Olival 10.

Daily 9am–8pm.

Plush and sophisticated tearooms serving pastries and drinks to the smart set of Lapa. It's just up the hill from the Museu de Arte Antiga.

Sítio do pica-pau
Map 6, F4. Rua dos Remédios à Lapa 61.

Mon–Fri 8am–8pm.

Tiny café right in the heart of Lapa, with an attractive outdoor wooden platform commanding views over the rooftops and river.

ALCÂNTARA

Zonadoca
Map 6, B7. Pavilhão 7A, Doca de Santo Amaro.

Daily 10.30am–4am.

Worth a visit for its ice creams, though you can also enjoy coffee or alcohol at this friendly, family-oriented café in a converted warehouse. The outdoor seats overlook Lisbon's trendiest dock development, right underneath Ponte 25 de Abril.

Cafés and bars with outdoor tables

Académica	Bairro Alto, p.149
A Brasileira	Chiado, p.146
Martinho da Arcada	Baixa, p.145
Café Nicola	Baixa, p.145
Café No Chiado	Chiado, p.146
Passeio d'Avenida	Avenida da Liberdade, p.151
Caffè Rosso	Chiado, p.156
Suíça	Baixa, p.145
Zonadoca	Alcântara, p.150

BELÉM

Antiga Confeitaria de Belém
Map 9, G4. Rua de Belém 90.
Daily 8am–midnight.
No visit to Belém is complete without a coffee and hot *pastel de nata* liberally sprinkled with *canela* (cinnamon) in this excellent and cavernous tiled pastry shop and café.

Café Quadrante
Map 9, D5. Centro Cultural de Belém.
Daily 10am–10pm.
Part of the Belem Cultural Centre; the best place to enjoy its coffee and snacks is on the outdoor terrace by the roof gardens, overlooking the bridge, river and Discoveries Monument.

AROUND AVENIDA DA LIBERDADE

Bela Ipanema
Map 8, E4. Avenida da Liberdade 169.
Mon–Sat 6am–2am.
Bustling café by the São Jorge cinema, where a steady stream of locals pop in for snacks, beers and coffees at the bar or in its small dining area; outdoor tables face the *avenida*.

Passeio d'Avenida
Map 8, G6. Praça Central, Avenida da Liberdade.
Mon–Sat 9am–1am.
This glass-covered café-restaurant may be a tourist trap, but the outdoor seats on the leafy central swathe of the Avenida da Liberdade make a great place for a coffee or beer.

Pastelaria Anunciada

Map 8, G6. Largo da Anunciada.

Fri–Sun 8am–10pm.

Beautifully tiled *pastelaria*, its windows stuffed full of sweets and bottles of port, at the foot of the Elevador do Lavra. A good place for a light meal or a snack.

SALDANHA

Café Versailles

Map 9, F5. Avda da República 15a.

Daily 7.30am–10pm.

Traditional café full of busy waiters and starched tablecloths. It gets liveliest at around 4pm, when Lisbon's elderly dames gather for a chat beneath the chandeliers.

Bars and clubs

Y ou can get a drink of some sort at almost any time of day or night at one of Lisbon's thousands of **bars** and cafés. These vary from local places where children play around family groups until midnight to modern, designer spaces with happening sounds playing until the small hours. Lisbon's **clubs** are also varied, but rarely get going much before midnight.

At night, the best area to head for is the **Bairro Alto.** This hosts one of Europe's biggest parties, with up to fifty thousand people descending on the maze of streets. You'll be hard pushed to find a bar open late at night in the **Baixa**, though things are picking up further east in **Alfama** and **Graça**, where a growing number of places cater for the crowds leaving the excellent local restaurants. **Cais do Sodré** itself has a growing number of riverside clubs and bars, while committed clubbers, drinkers and lowlife enthusiasts might try one of a dozen places along the nearby Rua Nova do Carvalho, which range from the atmospheric to the downright seedy. Friday and Saturday nights tend to be overcrowded and expensive everywhere, while on Sunday, especially in the Bairro Alto, places often close to recover from weekend excesses. Note that few of the places listed below open much before 10pm unless otherwise stated.

....

Though most cafés in Lisbon sell alcohol, those which are recommended principally for a coffee, soft drink or snack are listed in "Cafés" (see p.143).

....

Since the early 1990s, a number of late-night clubs and bars have opened up along the riverside **Avenida 24 de Julho** – especially around Santos station – and further west in Alcântara. These areas remain highly fashionable, though the current hot spot is the warehouse development opposite **Santa Apolónia station** to the east of the city. For something a little less pretentious, head for the **Alcântara and Santo Amaro docks**, whose tastefully renovated warehouses attract a steady flow of people from families by day to hardened clubbers by night. The general shift towards these riverside areas is partly as a result of the local authority's desire to move clubs out of the residential Bairro Alto (where establishments are obliged to close at 4am or so); in the new areas, clubs can stay open until around 6am.

The competition for custom means there's a high casualty rate among new clubs and bars. Some change hands, names, decor and clientele every other week, so you're almost certain to come across good places that aren't in our listings. **Drinks** are uniformly expensive in all fashionable clubs – from 300–800$00 for a beer – the plus side is that many clubs don't charge **admission**. Generally, where there *is* an admission charge, expect to pay around 3000$00; this usually includes a drink or two. If you're handed a ticket on entry, keep hold of it and present it when you buy your first drink. Some club entrances are extremely low-key, revealing their presence simply by a street light and a slot in the door, like a letter box at eye level. Don't be intimidated by this: just knock and walk in – and straight out again, if you don't like the look of the place.

Our listings are divided into the following areas: Baixa
(p.155); Chiado (p.156); Cais do Sodré (p.157 & 164);
Alfama, Castelo and Graça (p.158); Bairro Alto (p.159
& 165); Lapa and São Bento (p.167); Alcântara (p.162
& 167); Alcântara docks (p.168); Around Avenida 24
de Julho (p.169). For listings of gay and lesbian clubs
and bars, see p.171.

BARS

A Ginginha
Map 3, B6. Largo de São Domingos 8, Rossio.
Daily 9am–10.30pm.
Everyone should try *ginginha* – Portuguese cherry brandy – once.
There's just about room in this microscopic joint to walk in,
down a glassful and stagger outside to see the city in a new light.

Ginginha-Rubi
Map 3, B5. Rua B. Queiroz.
Daily 9am–10.30pm.
Even tinier than *A Ginginha*, offering *ginginha* with or without the
cherry stone (some argue that its presence helps enhance the alco-
holic content), and worth a peer inside for its beautiful azulejos.

A Licorista
Map 3, E6. Rua dos Sapateiros 218.
Mon–Fri 8am–8pm, Sat 8am–1pm.
Attractive, traditional tiled and brick-ceilinged bar, a good local
refreshment stop near the Baixa shops. At lunchtime, tables are
set for inexpensive meals.

Portuguese drinks

Portugal is rightly famed for its excellent wines, and though the locals rarely drink it in bars, you can always get a decent glass of **vinho** (wine) or **porto** (port). Lisboans are more likely to go for **cervejas** (beers) – the two most common brands are Sagres and Superbock, either in *garrafas* (bottles) or draught: a *caneca* is a pint, an *imperial* is a half. Local **spirits** are cheap and the measures more than generous. If you want to be more adventurous, the local brandy – *macieira* – is smooth on the palate (but rough on the head). Even more lethal are the local *aguardente* firewaters such as *Bagaço* and the cherry-based *ginginha,* which seem to fuel certain Lisboan workers from breakfast onwards.

O Pirata
Map 3, A8. Praça dos Restauradores 15.
Mon–Sat 8am–midnight.
Tiny bar on the west side of the *praça* for serious drinkers who want to sample the unique house drink, Pirata, a spirit whose recipe is jealously guarded. There are other inexpensive drinks for the less adventurous.

CHIADO

Caffè Rosso
Map 3, G8. Galerias Garrett, Rua Ivens 53–61, entrance on Rua Garrett.
Daily 9am–2am.
Relaxed courtyard bar in renovated shop galleries, with seats under huge square canopies. It serves coffee and snacks too, and there's a spacious downstairs room with modernist seats and lighting.

British Bar

Map 5, C8. Rua Bernardino Costa 52.

Mon–Sat noon–1am.

Wonderful Anglo-Portuguese hybrid stuck in a 1930s time warp, featuring ceiling fans, marble counter and dark wooden shelves stacked with wines and spirits. There's also Guinness on tap and regulars who look as if they've been coming here since it opened.

California

Map 5, C8. Rua Bernardino Costa 39.

Tues–Sun 1pm–4am.

A good late-night option as, despite its officially posted closing time, it never actually seems to shut. Pricey drinks, with 1980s decor and sounds.

Casa Cid

Map 5, B7. Rua de Ribeira Nova 32.

Daily 4am–9pm.

Something of an institution, serving food and drinks to market workers and down-at-heel nightlife stop-outs in one of Lisbon's most characterful streets, though it's slightly seedy at night.

Irish Pub O'Gilins

Map 5, C8. Rua dos Remolares 8–10.

Daily 11am–2am.

The oldest of Lisbon's popular, if rather expensive, Irish bars, with a pleasant, light wooden interior. There's live music from Thursday to Saturday, and pub quizzes for expats on Sunday.

Poisa Copos

Map 5, A9. Cais da Ribeira.

Tues–Sat 6am–4am.

Popular with students, this small bar by the river in a converted

warehouse has such long opening hours it need hardly bother
to close. Handy for a pick-me-up at six in the morning.

Bar do Rio
Map 5, A9. Armazém 7, Cais do Sodré.
Mon–Sat 10pm–4am.
Old riverside warehouse now decked out as a hip esplanade-bar,
part of the up-and-coming area just round the back of the station.

ALFAMA, CASTELO AND GRAÇA

Chapitô
Map 4, A5. Costa do Castelo 1–7 ©218 878 225.
Mon–Fri 9am–9pm, Sat–Sun 10pm–1.30am.
Multi-purpose venue incorporating a theatre, a circus school
and a lively bar with a marvellous river view. It's youthful and
fashion-conscious and there's no charge for admission; the only
trouble is the notoriously fickle opening times; phone ahead to
check before you trek up the hill.

Costa do Castelo
Map 4, A5. Calç. do Marquês de Tancos 1b ©218 884 636.
Tues–Sun 3pm–2am.
Beautifully positioned sunny terrace-café with Baixa views, a
long list of cocktails and a restaurant serving mid-price
Mozambiquan dishes (see p.121). There's live (usually Brazilian
or jazz) music on Thursday and Friday nights, and poetry read-
ings on others.

Bar da Graça
Map 4, F1. Trav. da Pereira 43.
Mon–Sat 9pm–4am.
Off the east side of Largo da Graça, this friendly bar mixes live
music and art exhibitions, and serves a mean range of cocktails
and good snacks.

Apollo XIII
Map 5, F2. Trav. da Cara 8.
Mon–Sat 10pm–3.30am.
A young, boisterous student crowd stuffs itself into this hard-to-spot aluminium sweatbox most nights.

Arroz Doce
Map 5, E3. Rua da Atalaia 117–119.
Mon–Sat 6pm–2am.
Nice, unpretentious bar in the middle of the frenetic Bairro Alto nightlife, with friendly owners; try "Auntie's" sangria, poured from a jug the size of a house.

Bar Ártis
Map 5, F3. Rua do Diário de Notícias 95.
Tues–Fri 8pm–2am, Sat & Sun 8pm–4am.
A relaxed, mildly sophisticated bar with good wines and a fine range of snacks like chicken toasties. It's popular with creative types, who wallow in the jazzy decor and music.

Cafédiário
Map 5, E5. Rua do Diário de Notícias 3.
Daily 2pm–2am.
One of the district's more popular and fashionable spots, this offers jazz and laid-back dance music in a basic bar that also attracts a gay presence.

Café Targus
Map 5, E4. Rua do Diário de Notícias 40.
Daily noon–2am.
A popular pre-clubbing bar; people flood in at midnight before moving on to the discos. Sounds usually include a good mix of soul, funk and jazz

Catacombas Jazz Bar

Map 5, E3. Trav. da Água da Flor 43.

Tues–Sat noon–midnight.

Once a secretive and fashionable drinking den, this was renovated in the 1990s and, though now less hip, is still a pleasant spot for a drink, with live jazz at weekends.

Foxtrot

Map 5, A1. Trav. de Santa Teresa.

Mon–Thurs 6pm–2am, Fri–Sat 6.30pm–2am, Sun 9pm–2am.

Relaxed bar on the São Bento side of the Bairro Alto, with comfy sofas and snooker tables, plus an outdoor patio, snacks and a long list of cocktails. From Praça do Prínçipe Real head down Rua Jasmine and bear right into Trav. de Santa Teresa.

Harry's Bar

Map 5, F2. Rua de São Pedro de Alcântara 57–61.

Mon–Sat 10pm–4am.

A tiny little front-room bar, with waiter service, bar snacks and an eclectic clientele – popular later on with slightly older drama queens from the nearby gay discos. Ring bell for admission.

Independente

Map 5, F3. Trav. de Água da Flor 40.

Mon–Sat 8pm–2am.

Polished, metal-and-wood bar with loud but usually catchy rock music and friendly, English-speaking staff. You may end up staying longer than you planned.

Instituto do Vinho do Porto

Map 5, G2. Rua de São Pedro de Alcântara 45.

Mon–Fri 10am–11.30pm, Sat 11am–10.30pm.

Firmly on the tourist circuit, the *Instituto* lures in visitors with over three hundred types of port, starting at around 200$00 a glass, served at low tables in a comfortable old mansion. Waiters are notoriously snooty and the cheaper ports never seem to be in stock, but it's still a good place to kick off an evening.

Lisbona
Map 5, F2. Rua da Atalaia 196,
Mon–Sat 7pm–2am.
Earthy local bar with its share of characterful regulars, but its chequerboard tiles covered in soccer memorabilia, old film posters and graffiti also lure in the Bairro Alto trendies. Catchy music and good beer too.

Pavilhão Chinês
Map 5, G1. Rua Dom Pedro V 89.
Mon–Sat 6pm–2am, Sun 9pm–2am.
Quirky bar, completely lined with mirrored cabinets containing ludicrous and bizarre tableaux of artefacts from around the world, with one room devoted entirely to war helmets. Drinks include a long list of renowned speciality cocktails.

Portas Largas
Map 5, E3. Rua da Atalaia 105.
Daily 8pm–2am.
The bar's usually wide open *portas largas* (big doors) lend an alfresco ambience to this friendly and atmospheric black-and-white tiled *adega* (wine cellar), with cheapish drinks, music from fado to pop and a young, partly gay clientele who spill onto the streets on warm evenings before hitting the club *Frágil* opposite (see p.166).

São Martinho
Map 5, F2. Rua da Atalaia 156.
Tues–Sun noon–midnight.
A rare, authentically crusty bar in this part of town, which has avoided its neighbours' pretensions. Grab a low stool and enjoy cheapish beer in a bar tiled like a public toilet; a games room is attached.

BARS: BAIRRO ALTO

Sem Nom Bar

Map 5, F3. Rua do Diário de Notícias 132.

Daily 10pm–4am.

Popular rock and pop sounds and reasonably priced drinks make for a great atmosphere at weekends; in the week, when it's quieter, get a seat by the door and watch the world go by.

Snob

Map 5, D1. Rua do Século 178.

Daily 4.30pm–3.30am.

Upmarket bar-restaurant on the way towards Praça do Prínçipe Real, full of media types enjoying cocktails in a smart English pub-like atmosphere. A good late-night eating option for steaks or light snacks.

O Tacão Grande

Map 5, F2. Trav. da Cara 3.

Daily 9.30pm–4am.

For those into raw rock, free peanuts, inexpensive beer and lots of youthful company, this barn-like place is for you.

Tertúlia

Map 5, E4. Rua do Diário de Notícias 60.

Mon–Thurs 8.30pm–3am, Fri & Sat 8.30pm–4am.

Laid-back café-bar with inexpensive drinks, newspapers, jazz in the background and varied fortnightly exhibitions. There's a piano for customers too, if you've the urge to play.

ALCÂNTARA

Alcântara Café

Map 6, B5. Rua Maria Luísa Holstein 15.

Daily 8pm–3am.

Stunning designer bar-restaurant successfully blending industrial and modern decor. A place to be seen before moving onto neighbouring clubs, hence the high prices.

Café da Ponte
Map 6, B7. Doca de Santo Amaro.
Daily 7.30pm–4am.
This bills itself as Lisbon's craziest café, serving everything from croissants to cocktails and dinner until 11.30pm. The lively atmosphere is abetted by riverside seating, Sunday karaoke nights and live music on Thursdays.

Cais de Alcântara
Map 6, D6. Doca de Alcântara ©213 958 661.
Mon–Wed 4pm–2am, Thurs–Sat 4pm–4am.
Pick of the row of bar-restaurants on boats in the docks, this one offers moderately priced food, a pool table and lively music. A good spot by day or night.

Cais S
Map 6, B7. Doca de Santo Amaro.
Daily 11am–4am.
Minimalist bar decorated with giant metal insects, where you can dance till late, drink by the river or visit the surf shop.

The docks are best reached by train from Cais do Sodré to Alcântara Mar station. Trains run until around 2am, after which a taxi back to town will cost approximately 1500$00.

Doca 6
Map 6, B7. Doca de Santo Amaro ©213 957 905.
Tues–Sun 12.30pm–2am.
Rated one of the best bars in the docks with a lively atmosphere and good if pricey food like bouillabaisse and French-

influenced dishes. Restaurant tables get snapped up so it's best
to reserve one if you want to eat.

Doca de Santo
Map 6, B6. Doca de Santo Amaro.
Tues–Thurs noon–3am, Fri & Sat noon–4am, Sun noon–midnight.
The first prominent building you come across approaching
from Alcântara Mar station, this large palm-fringed club, bar
and restaurant was one of the first places in the docks to attract
– and keep – a late-night clientele. The cocktail bar on the
esplanade is the latest attraction.

Metalúrgica
Map 6, G6. Avda 24 de Julho 110.
Daily 10pm–4am.
Unpretentious and fun bar with cheaper-than-usual drinks,
which dishes out pop, blues and soul to a happy, mixed
crowd.

A Última Ceia
Map 6, G6. Avda 24 de Julho 96.
Tues–Sun 11pm–4am.
Rock and pop restaurant-bar. Thursday to Sunday nights are
karaoke nights with a vengeance. All the fun starts after midnight.

CLUBS

CAIS DO SODRÉ

Absoluto
Map 5, A7. Rua D. Luís I 5.
Mon–Sat 8am–2am (disco: Thurs midnight–5am, Fri & Sat
midnight–6am).
Restaurant, bar and disco complex playing everything from the

latest hits to Júlio Iglesias, with occasional live bands too. There are even a few outdoor tables.

Armazém F.
Map 2, E9. Armazém 65, Rua da Cintura da Porto de Lisboa.
Daily 8pm–4am.
Huge converted *armazém* (warehouse), west along the river-front from Cais do Sodré, with room for a bar, restaurant and club playing mainstream pop and rock. Arrive early to avoid the queues which form at around 1.30am. Thursday night is – bizarrely – ballroom-dancing night.

Jamaica
Map 5, C8. Rua Nova do Carvalho 8.
Mon–Sat 10.30pm–4am.
Well-established, characterful club on a somewhat seedy road full of tacky nightlife venues. This is definitely the best one, attracting a mixed bag of sailors, students, expats and trendies. Music is predominantly retro, with reggae on Tuesday nights.

Tokio
Map 5, C8. Rua Nova do Carvalho 12.
Mon–Sat 10.30pm–4am.
Seedier version of *Jamaica* (see above), with rock and pop sounds – you may even hear a Portuguese disc or two – although the place can feel a bit sad when the crowds aren't in, which is quite often.

BAIRRO ALTO

Cena de Copos
Map 5, E4. Rua da Barroca 103–105.
Mon–Fri 9.30pm–2am, Sat & Sun 10pm–4am.
Not a club to frequent unless you're under 25 and bursting with energy, though the cheap cocktails may help you roll back

the years. Don't turn up till after midnight for the full atmosphere.

Frágil

Map 5, E3. Rua da Atalaia 126.

Tues–Sun 11pm–4am.

An icon of cool for years before its owner opened *Lux*, it remains a great place, particularly from Thursday to Saturday. Partly gay, definitely pretentious. The old building is awash with house and soul till late; it's best after 1am. Ring to get in.

Keops

Map 5, E3. Rua da Rosa 157–159.

Tues–Sun 11pm–3.30am.

Small, friendly spot with a tiny dance floor if you want to get to grips with the soul, funk and a bit of jazz played by different DJs nightly. Cheap sangria is another draw.

Bar Nova

Map 5, F1. Rua da Rosa 261.

Daily 10pm–2am.

Distinctively black-fronted club with three rooms and a terrace; it hasn't become too pretentious – so far. Hip rock and pop are the mainstays, with revival sounds on Sundays and Mondays.

Sudoeste

Map 5, E3. Rua da Barroca 135.

Sat & Sun 6pm–4am.

No longer considered hip, this friendly, small and intimate place has areas for chatting and a dance floor. Ring for admission. Happy hour is 10pm–1am – that's quite an hour.

Os Três Pastorinhos

Map 5, E4. Rua da Barroca 111.

Tues–Sun 11pm–4am.
One of the city's "in" places since the 1980s, and still gets busy after midnight: music treads the line between dance and easy listening, with funk and soul. There's a minute dance floor at the back.

SÃO BENTO AND LAPA

Incógnito
Map 6, I5. Rua dos Poiais de São Bento 37, São Bento.
Mon–Sat 10.30pm–4am.
Appropriately named – the only giveaway from the outside is a pair of large metallic doors. Once within, you'll find the low-lit dance floor downstairs booming with varied sounds. Tuesdays feature club classics; Thursday is big beat night.

Stones
Map 6, F5. Rua do Olival 1, Lapa.
Tues–Sun 10pm–4am.
Retro rocking and an endless if pricey list of drinks. It's just up from the Museu de Arte Antiga. Ring to enter.

ALCÂNTARA

Alcântara-Mar
Map 6, B5. Rua Cozinha Económica 11–15.
Daily 11.30pm–6am.
Wonderful big and glitzy spot for house and techno, attracting soccer stars, gays, executives and trendies amid the chandeliers, candelabras and country-house furnishings. Always great fun.

Benzina
Map 6, B5. Trav. Teixeira Júnior 6.
Mon–Thurs & Sun midnight–4am, Fri & Sat midnight–6am.

Smart chrome-and-wood interior. Tuesdays is disco and funk night, slipping into underground sounds on Wednesdays and Thursdays. Popular with the Bairro Alto crowd, who like ending a night here.

Paradise Garage
Map 6 C4. Rua João de Oliveira Miguens 38–48.
Mon–Sat 10pm–4am.
Large, ultra-trendy club on a tiny side road off Rua da Cruz à Alcântara offering various sounds from disco and soul to techno. There's rock on Wednesday nights and it's becoming a major venue for visiting bands too.

Pillon
Map 6, B4. Rua do Alvito 10.
Daily 10pm–4am.
Catchy and rhythmic Cape Verdean and African disco sounds for a relaxed crowd. The liveliest night is usually Tuesday.

ALCÂNTARA DOCKS

Blues Café
Map 6, D6. Rua da Cintura do Porto de Lisboa ©213 957 085.
Mon–Sat 8.30pm–4am (restaurant 8pm–1am).
Attractively converted dockside warehouse with Cajun food in the restaurant and dancing till late in what is claimed to be Lisbon's only blues club. Live music on Wednesdays.

Docks Club
Map 6, D6. Doca de Alcântara.
Mon–Sat 10pm–6am (restaurant 8.30pm–1am).
Another thriving warehouse conversion, part bar, part restaurant, but mainly a dance temple for Lisbon's monied set.

Indochina

Map 6, D6. Rua Cintura do Porto de Lisboa.
Mon–Sat 10pm–6am (restaurant 8.30pm–1am).

Another of nightclub mogul Pedro Luz's offerings, this is a large, colonial-style Asian restaurant in a converted warehouse which becomes a club from around midnight. Thursday nights are the liveliest, with soul, jungle, Latin and classics spinning till the small hours.

Kings and Queens

Map 6, D6. Rua Cintura do Porto de Lisboa, Armázem H Naves A–B.
Mon–Sat 11pm–6am.

Pedro Luz launched this club as a "high-tech gay disco", but it has since successfully attracted a large following of beautiful people of all sexual persuasions. It's a huge, pulsating place which can hold 2500 people; the kings and queens tend to turn up after 4am.

Salsa Latina

Map 6, B7. Gare Marítima de Alcântara, Doca de Santo Amaro.
Daily 12.30pm–3am.

A bar-restaurant and club just outside the docks in a fantastic 1940s maritime station, offering salsa Thursday to Saturday (midnight–3am) with live music (see p.182), and salsa lessons Monday to Wednesday. Alternatively, just come and admire the terrace views. Food is moderate, but there's a minimum consumption at the bar of 5000$00.

AROUND AVENIDA 24 DE JULHO

Indústria

Map 6, I6. Rua do Instituto Indústrial 6, Santos.
Tues–Sat midnight–6am.

Increasingly popular club in a converted factory with three bars and dance floors echoing to house and dance sounds. It attracts a varied crowd and is liveliest after 3am.

CLUBS: AROUND AVENIDA 24 DE JULHO

Kapital

Map 6, G6. Avda 24 de Julho 68, Santos.

Tues–Sat 10.30pm–6am, Sun–Mon 10.30pm–4am.

Well-established (so some say passé) venue, with three sleekly designed floors full of bright young things buying expensive drinks and dancing to techno, but it's hard work getting past the style police on the door. There's a great rooftop terrace. Wednesday night is rock night.

Kremlin

Map 6, G6. Escadinhas da Praia 5, Santos.

Tues–Sat midnight–7am.

Its tough door policy, based on its reputation as one of the city's most fashionable nightspots, has put off good-time clubbers, though it's still packed with flash, young, raving Lisboans. Best after 2am.

Plateau

Map 6, G6. Escadinhas da Praia 3–7, Santos.

Tues–Sat midnight–6am.

This was one of the very first fashionable clubs along the Avenida 24 de Julho, well designed by nightclub mogul Pedro Luz. Sounds are largely stuck in the 1980s and 1990s, which at least means the admission policy is more relaxed. A good place if you like pop and mainstream sounds. Wednesday is usually the liveliest night.

Gay Lisbon

L isbon's **gay and lesbian** scene is becoming more open in a city which was until quite recently fairly conservative. The Associação ILGA Portugal, Rua de São Lazaro 88 (Map 8, I5; ℂ218 873 918; Mon–Sat 4–8pm) organizes gay events and can help with information and medical advice – check their Web site (in English and Portuguese) at *www.ilga-portugal.org*. Nightlife focuses on the Bairro Alto and Praça do Prínçipe Real, where a generally laid-back group of clubs and bars attracts gay people of all ages. As at other clubs, the best nights are from Thursday to Saturday, with the action kicking off at 9pm and ending well after sunrise. Hangovers are eased on gay beaches such as the one south of Caparica at toy-train stop #18 (see p.259), or further south at Praia do Meco. One of the main annual events is the Gay Film Festival, held at various cinemas in September.

The following bars and clubs are pretty much gay and lesbian only; places which attract a mixed gay and straight crowd are listed in "Bars & clubs" on p.153.

BARS AND CLUBS

106

Map 8, D7. Rua São Marçal 106.

Daily 9pm–2am.

Ring on the doorbell and you'll be given a quick look-over before being allowed into this friendly if sparse bar, which makes a good place to start the evening.

Água no Bico
Map 8, D7. Rua de São Marçal 170.

Daily 9pm–2am.

Welcoming gay bar with tables packed in cheek-by-jowl to promote intimate conversation.

Bric-a-Bar
Map 8, D7. Rua Cecílio de Sousa 82–84 ©213 428 971.

Daily 9pm–4am.

On a steep road beyond Praça do Príncipe Real, this cruisy disco has a large dance floor, "dark room" and various bars.

Finalmente
Map 8, D7. Rua da Palmeira 38.

Daily 10.30pm–4.30am.

A well-known and very busy place, with a first-class disco and lashings of kitsch. Weekend drag shows (2am) feature skimpily dressed young *senhoritas* camping it up to high-tech sounds. Entry's free, but there's a minimum drinks consumption of 1000$00.

Katedral
Map 8, C7. Rua de Manuel Bernardes 22.

Mon–Thurs & Sun 7pm–2am; Fri & Sat 8pm–4am.

Intimate, relaxed snooker bar attracting a lesbian crowd; one of the city's better places for gay women.

Memorial
Map 8, D6. Rua Gustavo Matos Sequeira 42.

Tues–Sat 11pm–4am, Sun 4pm–8pm.

One of the few lesbian clubs, with floor shows some nights; otherwise it's low key, with disco and "romantic" sounds.

Sétimo Ceu
Map 5, E5. Trav. da Espera 54.
Mon–Sat 10pm–2am.
A real success story of recent years; now an obligatory stop for gays and lesbians, who imbibe beers and *caipirinhas* served by Brazilian owner. Great atmosphere spilling onto the street.

Sinal Vermelho
Map 5, F4. Rua das Gáveas 89 ℂ213 431 281.
Daily 8pm–1am.
The "Red Sign" (*sinal vermelho*) is a large, bright bar with Portuguese nosh and a loud, uncruisy gay crowd.

Trumps
Map 8, C6. Rua da Imprensa Nacional 104b ℂ213 971 059.
Daily 10pm–6am.
Popular gay disco with a reasonably relaxed door policy. It's a bit cruisy during the middle of the week, and gets packed from Thursday to Saturday, when there's also a good lesbian turnout. Drag shows are held on Wednesdays and Sundays. Admission free, though there's sometimes a mimimum consumption of 2000$00 if the doorman has the hump.

Live music

Although tourist brochures tend to suggest that **live music** in Lisbon begins and ends with **fado**, the city's traditional music, there's no reason to miss out on other forms. **Brazilian** and **African** music from the former colonies are very popular, while Portuguese **jazz** can be good (there are big international jazz festivals in the summer: see p.214), and **rock and pop** can occasionally – and pleasantly – surprise. Classical music also has a keen following, with performances in churches, historic buildings and cultural centres throughout the city.

It's worth checking the listings magazines (see p.9) and posters around the city to see what's on. In addition, many of the venues reviewed in "Bars and clubs" have live music on certain nights – see p.153 for details. There's an **admission charge** of around 500–600$00 or more depending on performer and venue to get into most music clubs, which usually covers your first drink, and most stay open until around 4am or later. There's often a crossover between music styles at many of the places listed below. In addition, top American and British rock bands and visiting Brazilian singers play at the major venues listed on p.185; you can usually get advance tickets for these from the Agencia de Bilhetes para Espectaculos Publicos (ABEP) kiosk (℡213 475 823) at the corner of Praça dos Restauradores, near the post office, which also has ticket and programme details for all the city's cinemas and theatres. For performances by top artists, expect to pay something in the region of 5000–8000$00.

Our music listings are divided as follows: fado (p.175); African (p.179); Brazilian (p.180); rock and pop (p.182); jazz (p.184); classical (p.185).

Most major cultural events in the city – including just about every classical music concert – are sponsored either by the Fundação Calouste Gulbenkian (p.68) or the Centro Cultural de Belém (p.57); both publish full seasonal programmes which are available from the centres themselves, large hotels and tourist offices. In addition, many of Lisbon's **festivals** feature performances of fado, classical and jazz music – see p.212 for a full listing.

FADO

Fado (literally "fate") is often described as a kind of working-class blues – something like a flamenco Billie Holiday sung to a Portuguese guitar and viola accompaniment. Fado songs inevitably evoke the characteristically Portuguese emotion of *saudade*, a yearning for something lost or missed. Its origins are believed to be a fusion of rural folk quatrains with a lascivious song and dance – *fofa* and *lundum* – popular with the African and Brazilian immigrants who settled in Alfama in the early nineteenth century. One of the first known fado stars was Maria Severa, an Alfama singer whose tumultuous relationship with the Count of Vimiosa scandalized Lisbon society in the 1830s; fortunately her music attracted as much publicity as the affair. Today's biggest fado star is Amália Rodrigues, the daughter of an Alfama orange-seller, whose voice and stunning looks have made her one of Portugal's most successsful artists.

Along with Coimbra (which has its own distinct tradition), Lisbon is still the best place to hear fado. There are thirty or so fado clubs in the Bairro Alto, Alfama and elsewhere, usually called either a *casa de fado* or an *adega típica*. There's no real distinction between these places: all are small, all serve food (though you don't always have to eat), and all open around 9–10pm, get going towards midnight, and stay open until 3–4am. In the more formal clubs you'll be expected to remain quiet during performances, though emotions let rip once the artists have finished.

The drawbacks of fado clubs are inflated minimum charges – these days rarely below 3000$00 – and, in the more touristy places, extreme tackiness. Uniformed bouncers are fast becoming the norm, as are warm-up singers crooning Beatles songs and photographers snapping you at your table. We've selected the most authentic places.

ALFAMA

Clube do Fado
Map 4, C9. Rua de São João da Praça 92–94 ℂ218 882 694.
Daily 9pm–2am.
Intimate and homely place with stone pillars, an old well and a mainly local clientele. Attracts small-time performers, up-and-coming talent and the occasional big names.

Parreirinha d'Alfama
Map 4, G7. Beco do Espírito Santo 1 ℂ218 868 209.
Tues–Sun 8pm–2am.
A reasonably authentic venue just off Largo do Chafariz de Dentro, with music by renowned singers and food at moderate prices.

Taverna do Embuçado
Map 4, F8. Beco dos Cortumes 10 ℂ218 865 078.

Mon–Sat 8.30pm–2.30am.

Well-established if pricey Alfama *adega* with a homely feel, and attracts some big-name artists too.

Tradicional

Map 4, B9. Rua Afonso de Albuquerque 4.

Fri & Sat 10pm–3am.

Small place that's really little more than a bar, with live folk, viola playing, and fado on Fridays and Saturdays.

BAIRRO ALTO

Adega do Machado

Map 5, F4. Rua do Norte 91 ℗213 224 640.

Tues–Sun 8.30pm–2am.

One of the longest-established Bairro Alto joints, as the faded photos on the wall show, presenting several styles of fado from Lisbon and Coimbra. Minimum consumption of 3000$00 builds to around 6000$00 a head if you sample the fine Portuguese cooking.

Adega Mesquita

Map 5, F3. Rua do Diário de Notícias 107 ℗213 462 077.

Daily 8pm–3.30am.

Another of the big Bairro Alto names, with better-than-average music, air conditioning and traditional dancing and singing. Packs in the tourists, although the meals are poor.

Adega do Ribatejo

Map 5, F3. Rua do Diário de Notícias 23 ℗213 468 343.

Great little *adega*, still popular with the locals, with one of the lowest minimum charges (around 2000$00) and enjoyable food. Regulars describe the fado here as "pure emotion". The singers include a couple of professionals, the manager and – best of all – the cooks.

FADO

Arcadas do Faia
Map 5, E4. Rua da Barroca 54 ☏213 426 742.
Mon–Sat 8pm–3am.
A growing number of big names play here, though it's definitely geared to tourists.

Café Luso
Map 5, F3. Trav. da Queimada 10 ☏213 422 281.
Mon–Sat 9.30pm–2am (restaurant 8pm–2am).
Another pricey option, with local food and some interesting sounds in a rather dark place with kitsch decor. Portuguese folk dancing is also a feature, as is jazz on Thursdays and Fridays from 11pm.

NoNo
Map 5, E5. Rua do Norte 47 ☏213 429 989.
Daily 8pm–3.30am.
Small, attractively tiled fado and guitar restaurant. The fado gets going at 9.15pm. Prices are moderate, with a minimum consumption of around 2000$00.

A Severa
Map 5, F5. Rua das Gáveas 55 ☏213 464 006.
Daily except Thurs 8pm–2am.
A city institution, named after the nineteenth-century gypsy singer Maria Severa, with big fado names and equally big prices.

LAPA AND ALCÂNTARA

O Senhor Vinho
Map 6, G4. Rua do Meio à Lapa 18, Lapa ☏213 977 456.
Mon–Sat 8.30pm–2.30am.
Famous club sporting some of the best singers in Portugal, which makes the 4000$00 minimum charge (rising to around 8000$00 after a meal) pretty reasonable. Good decor and relaxed atmosphere.

FADO

Timpanas

Map 6, C5. Rua Gilberto Rola 24, Alcântara ©213 972 431.

Daily except Wed 8.30pm–2am.

One of Lisbon's most authentic options, and handy if you fancy moving on to some of the local clubs afterwards.

AFRICAN

Many African musicians settled in Lisbon after the colonial wars and independence, particularly from Cape Verde, as well as from Guinea-Bissau, Angola and Mozambique. In recent years, Lisboans have embraced their musical styles with vigour, perhaps because the lively African beat is in such complete contrast to the nostalgic tradition of fado. The big Cape Verdean star to listen out for is Cesária Evora, a world-famous ballad (*morna*) singer, who performs barefoot, while the blend of Latin and African sounds that typifies the music of Guinea-Bissau is best represented by the likes of Justino Delgado, Africa Libre, Jetu Katem and the guitarist Naka.

B.leza

Map 6, I5. Largo do Conde Barão 50, Santos.

Tues–Sun 11pm–4am.

Live music most nights in this wonderful sixteenth-century building, with space to dance in, tables to relax at, and food too.

Keyanda

Map 6, B5. Rua Maria Luísa Holstein 11, Alcântara.

Tues–Sun midnight–6am.

Fairly smart African club in converted warehouse near Alcântara Café (see p.162), this gets packed at weekends for dance music, but has live music on Thursdays and Tuesdays, when it's more bearable.

Kudissanga

Map 2, E5. Rua Carlos Reis 51, Sete Rios.

Tues–Sun 10.30pm–4am.

A bit out of the way, near the zoo, but considered one of Lisbon's best African music venues and attracting big-name stars.

Kussunguila

Map 6, B4. Rua dos Lusíadas 5, Alcântara ✆213 633 590.

Daily 11pm–6am.

Over-the-top African club with live bands on Monday and Thursday nights, plus discos, African karaoke and other extravaganzas the rest of the time.

Lontra

Map 6, I3. Rua de São Bento 157, São Bento ✆213 691 083.

Tues–Sun 11pm–4am.

You'll be hard pushed not to join in the dancing at this intimate African club, which has live music most nights; come after midnight.

Ritz Club

Map 8, F6. Rua da Glória 57 ✆213 425 140.

Tues–Sat 10.30pm–4am (restaurant 8pm–3am).

Lisbon's largest African club occupies the premises of an old brothel-cum-music hall one block west of Avenida da Liberdade. It's a great place, with a resident Cape Verdean band, plus occasional big-name performers. If you fancy a break from the music there are quiet rooms with wicker chairs for a drink and a chat.

BRAZILIAN

Although Brazilians are no longer allowed into Portugal without a work permit or visa, there is still a thriving Brazilian community in Lisbon. The demand for Brazilian music is also partly the result of Brazilian soap operas, which are immensely popular on TV.

Bipi-Bipi

Map 2, F5. Rua Oliveira Martins 6, Campo Pequeno ©217 978 924.
Tues–Sun 10.30pm–2am.

Uptown venue for Brazilian bands, exotic cocktails and dirty dancing. Particularly riotous at weekends after midnight. To get there go to metro Campo Pequeno, then head along Avda João XXI – Rua Oliveira Martins is the third on the left.

Chafarica

Map 4, G4. Calçada de São Vicente 81, Alfama ©218 867 449.
Mon–Sat 10pm–3am.

Tiny, long-established Brazilian bar with live music till late most nights. Best after midnight, especially after a few *caipirinhas*, the lethal Brazilian concoction of rum, lime, sugar and ice.

Havana

Map 6, B7. Doca de Santo Amaro, Alcântara ©213 979 893.
Daily noon–6am.

Cuban-themed bar-restaurant with wicker chairs, a distinctive stairway, and live Brazilian sounds on Friday nights.

Pé Sujo

Map 4, C8. Largo de São Martinho 6–7, Alfama ©218 865 629.
Tues–Sun 10pm–2am.

The "Dirty Foot" is five minutes' walk from the Sé, at the point where Rua A. Rosa becomes Rua do Limoeiro, with a large wooden terrace outside. Hit a good night and there'll be massive audience participation and table-banging samba sessions in the tiny room, though less lively if the house band misses the mark.

BRAZILIAN

Pintaí

Map 5, F3. Largo Trindade Coelho 22.

Mon–Sat 10pm–3am.

Small, popular "tropical" bar across the road from São Roque church, with live, bouncy Brazilian music most nights aided by a long list of cocktails.

Salsa Latina

Map 6, B7. Gare Marítima de Alcântara.

Daily 12.30pm–3am.

Set in the superb 1940s maritime station by Doca de Santa Amaro (see p.54), this is part bar-restaurant, part salsa club, with riotous dancing to live bands serving up Brazilian rhythms, jazz, Dixieland and other infectious sounds.

ROCK AND POP

Lisbon's clubs and bars are quick to catch onto the latest international rock and pop sounds, though in recent years there's been a boom in the popularity of local bands. Pedro Abrunhosa's jazzy rap sounds are worth listening out for, while mainstream pop bands Delfins, Rio Grande and Santos e Pecadores are also big. Another recent phenomenon has been *Música Pimba*, a fashionably tacky mixture of traditional sounds and modern satirical lyrics. The main names to catch in this genre are Marco Paulo and Quim Barreiros.

Álcool Puro

Map 6, H5. Avda Dom Carlos I 59, Santos ©213 967 467.

Mon–Sat 11pm–4am.

Different bands every night in this fashionable rock bar whose name translates as "pure alcohol". A good place to check out up-and-coming Portuguese rock bands.

Anos Sessenta

Map 4, C1. Largo do Terreirinho 21, Mouraria ℂ218 873 444.

Tues–Sun 10pm–4am.

This small club, "the Sixties", has different rock bands on Fridays and Saturdays; the music is retro, as its name suggests. It's a few minutes' walk uphill from Largo Martim Moniz, near the castle.

Paradise Garage

Map 6, C4. Rua João de Oliveira Miguens 38, Alcântara ℂ213 955 977.

Mon–Sat 10pm–4am.

Big on the club scene (see p.168), this venue also hosts regular gigs, including foreign bands. It's on a tiny side road off Rua da Cruz à Alcântara.

Rock City

Map 2, E9. Armazém 225, Rua da Cintura do Porto de Lisboa, Cais do Santos. ℂ213 428 640.

Mon–Fri 1pm–3am, Sat & Sun 9pm–3am.

Flash, American-themed bar-restaurant just down river from Cais do Sodré station – just head for the palm trees. There's live mainstream rock music most nights.

Rock Line

Map 6, B5. Rua das Fontaínhas 86.

Tues–Sun 10pm–6am.

Loud bar which pulls in a young crowd, with raw live rock bands thrashing their guitars most nights.

Sua Excelência O Marquês

Map 4, C9. Largo Marquês do Lavradio 1. ℂ885 07 86.

Mon–Sat 10pm–4am.

Dark rock bar with live music most nights, hidden away in a little square behind the Sé (from the Sé it's to the right of Rua de São João). A surprisingly trendy place for this neck of the woods.

JAZZ

Jazz has a loyal and committed following in Lisbon – you'll hear it in many bars, and it also features prominently in several of Lisbon's summer festivals (see p.212) – so it's somewhat surprising that there are so few clubs specifically dedicated to it. Touring jazz stars sometimes play at the following venues, and also appear at the large music venues listed in the box on p.185.

Café Luso
Map 5, F3. Trav. da Queimada 10, Bairro Alto ©213 422 281.
Mon–Sat 8pm–3am.
Touristy but welcoming fado joint (see p.178) which also features regular Thursday and Friday jazz sessions from 11pm, sometimes with big names.

Hot Clube de Portugal
Map 8, F6. Praça da Alegria 39 ©213 467 369.
Tues–Sat 10pm–1am.
The city's best jazz venue, in a tiny basement club hosting local and visiting artists. It's appropriately named, as it can get very steamy in summer, but there's a tiny courtyard to escape to if things get too hot.

Speakeasy
Map 6, F7. Armazém 115, Cais das Oficinas, Doca de Alcântara, Alcântara ©213 957 308.
Mon–Sat noon–3pm & 6pm–4am.
Newish docklands jazz bar and restaurant with some big and up-and-coming names nightly after 11pm.

Large music venues

Atlantic Pavilion (Map p.81), Parque das Naçoes ℂ218 918 409. Portugal's largest indoor venue, which hosts big-name stars and holds up to 17,000 spectators.

Aula Magna (Map 2, D3), Reitoria da Universidade de Lisboa, Alamada da Universidade ℂ217 967 624. Right opposite metro Cidade Universitária, this student-union venue attracts some big names, but it's all seated, which can detract from the atmosphere.

Coliseu dos Recreios (Map 8, H6), Rua das Portas de Santo Antão, Baixa ℂ213 461 997 or 213 431 697. A lovely old domed building originally built as a circus ring, this is now the main city-centre indoor rock and pop venue.

Estádio José Alvalade (Map 2, E2), Alvalade ℂ217 589 021. The Sporting Lisbon soccer stadium stages concerts by huge international stars. Highly atmospheric when it's full.

Estádio do Restelo (Map 7, E1), Restelo, Belém ℂ213 010 461. Belenenses' soccer stadium plays host to smaller rock and pop bands.

Sony Plaza (Map p.81), Parque das Naçoes ℂ218 918 409. The Parque's main outdoor venue, holds up to ten thousand people for summer concerts and New Year's Eve extravaganzas.

CLASSICAL

Classical music has an avid following in Lisbon. The Gulbenkian has its own respected orchestra, while visiting orchestras, musicians and opera stars frequently appear at the main venues listed in the box above. There are three concert halls at the **Fundação Calouste Gulbenkian** (see p.68; ℂ217 935 131), including a beautifully positioned open-air amphitheatre, which has alfresco classical and jazz performances in the summer. It's also worth checking out performances at the auditoriums at the **Centro Cultural de Belém** (see p.57; ℭ213 612 400) and in the enormous, modern **Culturgest** arts complex at Avenida João XXI 63 (Map 2, F5; ℭ217 905 454) near metro Campo Pequeno. In addition, regular classical concerts take place at the Teatro Nacional de São Carlos, Rua Serpa Pinto 9, Chiado (Map 3, H9; ℭ213 465 914); the Teatro Municipal de São Luís, Rua António Maria Cardoso 40, Baixa (Map 5, E7; ℭ213 421 772); the Coliseu dos Recreios, Rua das Portas de Santo Antão, Baixa (Map 3, A7; ℭ213 461 997); and the Jules Verne Auditorium, Parque das Nações (Map p.81, ℭ218 918 409). There are also frequent **free concerts and recitals** at the São Roque church, the Sé, the Basílica da Estrela, São Vicente de Fora and the Igreja dos Mártires (see index for details of venues). Look out too for classical music performances during the Sintra Music Festival (see p.214). The **opera** season runs from September to June at the Teatro Nacional de São Carlos, Rua Serpa Pinto 9, Chiado (Map 5, E7; ℭ213 465 914).

CLASSICAL

Cinema and theatre

Lisbon and its environs have dozens of **cinemas**, virtually all of them showing original-language films with Portuguese subtitles, though sadly most of Lisbon's lovely Art Nouveau and Art Deco palaces have now either been closed down or replaced by bland multiplexes. The tourist office should be able to tell you what's on, or consult the listings outside the ABEP kiosk (daily 8am–8pm) at the southeast corner of Restauradores (though remember that film titles are often totally different in Portuguese and may not be direct translations). Most cinemas are open from around midday, with last performances at around 11pm. Tickets cost around 800$00, and are even cheaper on Mondays.

The four-screen Quarteto, Rua das Flores Lima 16 (Map 2, F4; ©217 971 378; metro Entre Campos or Roma), off Avenida dos Estados Unídos da América, specializes in **arthouse movies**; in June, it acts as the Lisbon venue for the Troia International Film Festival, which showcases movies from countries which produce fewer than 21 films per year, subtitled in Portuguese. The Instituto da Cinemateca Portuguesa, Rua Barata Salgueiro (Map 8, D4; ©213 546 279; metro Avenida 39), the national film theatre, has twice-daily shows, ranging from contemporary Portuguese films to silent classics.

Mainstream movies can be seen most centrally at the São Jorge, Avenida da Liberdade 174 (Map 8, E4; ☏213 579 144), and the Xenon, Praça dos Restauradores (Map 8, G7; ☏213 468 446). There are ten screens at the Amoreiras complex, Avenida Eng. Duarte Pacheco (Map 2, C7; ☏213 831 275), though all are modest in size. Another multiplex is the Monumental, Edifício Monumental, Avenida Praia da Vitória 71, Saldanha (Map 9, G6; ☏213 531 859), which has no fewer that fourteen screens and is only a short walk from both the city youth hostel and main bus station. Further afield, there are ten screens in the vast Colombo shopping centre (Map 2, A3; ☏217 113 200) at Avenida Lusíada Letras, opposite metro Colégio Militar-Luz. Finally, if you find yourself in Cascais on a rainy day, you can escape to the seven-screen Warner-Lusomundo at the massive and well-signed shopping mall, Cascais Shopping (☏214 600 420).

Lisbon has several beautiful old **theatres**, which present a diverse range of plays from experimental contemporary works to Shakespeare and the Greek classics. You could try the performances of Portuguese and foreign plays – usually in Portuguese, but occasionally in English – at the Teatro Nacional de Dona Maria II on Rossio (Map 3, B7; ☏213 472 246), set up at the end of the nineteenth century by playwright Almeida Garrett. You may also want to check out performances by The Lisbon Players, an amateur English-speaking theatrical group consisting largely of expat actors. Performances and readings – which can be hit or miss – take place at Rua da Estrela 10, Lapa (Map 6, G2; ☏213 961 946).

CINEMA AND THEATRE

Sport and outdoor activities

Portugal's national game is **football**, and during the football season from September to June Lisbon men who aren't at the game tend to have transistors clamped to their ears on match days. Despite this football mania, matches in Lisbon are surprisingly family-orientated and relaxed, and it's definitely worth a trip to those held at either of Lisbon's giants: Benfica and Sporting.

Another sport with a loyal (if smaller) following is **bull-fighting**, and summer spectacles in Lisbon and Cascais are undeniably impressive. The influence of the Atlantic gives Lisbon an ideal climate for **golf**, and some of the country's top courses are in the Lisbon area. The hefty Atlantic breakers also attract **surfers** to Lisbon's beaches, while the greater city area has good facilities for those into sailing, tennis or horse-riding. Annual spectator events to look out for include the nearby world **windsurfing** championships, the Lisbon **marathon** and – if the circuit's safety problems get sorted out – Estoril's **Formula One Grand Prix**.

BULLFIGHTING

From April to September, **bullfights** take place most Thursday evenings at the Praça de Touros do Campo Pequeno (Map 9, G2; ℰ217 932 093; metro Campo Pequeno), an impressive Moorish-style bullring built in 1892. Tickets cost 3000–12,000$00, depending on where you sit, and performances start at 10pm. Portuguese bull-fights differ from Spanish ones in that the bulls are not killed in the rings, but they can still be bloody affairs. First the *cavaleiro* (horse-rider) performs with the bull, avoiding its advances and sticking it with a lance, after which the animal is encouraged to charge at the *forcados* (stoppers), a row of eight men; the man at the front leaps onto its padded horns while the rest of the group try to wrestle the bull to the ground. There are less frequent fights at Cascais in summer (see p.248); look out for posters round town or contact the Cascais tourist board for details.

FOOTBALL

Football is the biggest game in Lisbon, a city which boasts two European giants, Benfica and Sporting, and one other First Division team, Belenenses of Belém (though they occasionally drop out of the top division). Regular league fixtures take place on Sunday afternoons, or Sunday evenings for big matches. The daily soccer tabloid *Bola,* available from any newsagent or newspaper kiosk, has fix-tures, match reports and news. To buy advance tickets – which cost between 600$00 and 6000$00 – go to the ABEP kiosk in Praça dos Restauradores (for a small com-mission), or at kiosks (not the turnstiles) at the grounds on the night. Obtaining tickets isn't usually a problem unless it's a big European tie or a championship crunch game involving Sporting, Benfica or Porto.

International matches are held at the Estádio Nacional (National Stadium), Praça da Maratona, Cruz Quebrada (bus #6 from Algés or train to Cruz Quebrada from Cais do Sodré). The stadium holds up to 55,000 but is pretty run-down and soulless – it's not among the eight stadiums selected as venues for the 2004 European Football Championships, to be held in Portugal. However, the Portuguese **Cup Final** is also held here in June; if any of the top sides are involved, forget trying to get a ticket.

Benfica (officially called Sport Lisboa e Benfica), Lisbon's most famous football team, have a glorious past. They have won both the Portuguese championship and the Portuguese cup over twenty times, and were European champions in 1961–62, beating arch Iberian rivals Real Madrid 5–3 in a classic final in which the great Eusébio was the hero. They were European Cup finalists again in 1968 (when they lost another classic to Manchester United), and runners-up again in 1988 and 1990. Recent years have been difficult for the great club. Despite winning the Portuguese championship in 1994 and cup in 1993 and 1996, the club was rocked by financial irregularities: in 1997, the board of directors allegedly spent £15,000 on cigars and issued 140 mobile phones to "club officials" in an eighteen month spell. This was accompanied by the team's alarming loss of form, which reached its nadir in the 1998-99 season, when former Liverpool player Graham Souness shipped in various ageing players from the English Premiership, a disastrous move which led to Benfica finishing not only below great rivals Porto, but even behind the northern city's second club, Boavista. A change of leadership and the start of a new century can only lead to better things.

Games take place at the huge, 92,000-capacity Estádio da Luz, Avenida Gen. Norton Matos (Map 2, B3; ©217 266 129), to the north of the city centre – facilities are currently being upgraded in preparation for the 2004 European Championsips, for which this will be the main venue. The

FOOTBALL

best way to get to matches is on the metro – Colégio Militar-Luz is a short walk from the stadium. If you want to learn something about the club's history, drop into the Club Museum (Mon–Fri 9.30am–1pm & 2–6pm, Sat 9.30am–1pm; 250$00), up the stairs by the main entrance.

Benfica's traditional rivals, Sporting Club de Portugal – usually known as **Sporting Lisbon** – play at the 75,000-capacity Estádio José Alvalade, Rua Francisco Stromp (Map 2, E2; ✆217 589 021) – metro Campo Grande or bus #1 or #36; they are due to move to a new state-of-the-art stadium next door in 2003 (which will be Lisbon's other venue for the Euro 2004). Though historically less successful than Benfica, the team have still won fifteen league titles and in recent years have pushed Benfica hard as the main challengers to northern rivals, Porto. However, their last league title was in 1982 under the leadership of eccentric Englishman Malcolm Allison.

Belenenses are comparative lightweights, having won just one league title, back in 1964 (though this is an impressive enough feat when you consider that no other team has won the league other than themselves, Sporting, Benfica and Porto). Their attractively sited Estádio do Restelo (Map 9, E1; ✆213 010 461), round the back of Belém's Mosteiro dos Jerónimos, offers such picturesque views over the river that the soccer action is almost insignificant; nevertheless, top teams frequently visit.

FORMULA ONE MOTOR RACING

The Portuguese **Grand Prix** at Estoril has traditionally been one of the main races in the Formula One season. However, the Autodromo do Estoril at Alcabideche, on the EN9 from Estoril to Sintra, has fallen into disrepute, and races were cancelled in the late 1990s because the course was considered too potholed. If sufficient funds are forthcoming, the Grand Prix should be back on the menu for the 2000 or 2001 season.

GOLF

Portugal is famous for its **golf courses**, and there are several highly rated examples in the Lisbon area. Many of the best ones are between Estoril and Sintra. Perhaps the most famous is the upmarket Caesar Park Penha Longa Golf Club (Estrada da Lagoa Azul-Linho, off the EN9 from Estoril to Sintra; ℂ219 249 022), in a former monastic estate, which has hosted the Portuguese Open. Try also the Estoril Golf Club, Avenida da República (ℂ214 680 176), right on the A5 motorway from Lisbon to Cascais. The main hotels in Estoril and the golf courses themselves can supply golf passes for these courses, at a price (around 34,000$00 for five rounds), as well as renting out equipment. Late October or early November welcomes golfers to Estoril's major courses for its International **Golf Week**. Other top courses include the Marinha Golf Club, Quinta da Marinha, Cascais (ℂ214 869 881), off the Cascais-Guincho road; and Lisbon Sports Club, Casal da Carregueira, Belas, near Queluz (ℂ214 310 077). Prices are around 10,000$00, often more at weekends.

HORSE-RIDING

Penha Longa Country Club (ℂ219 249 033), near Sintra, rents out horses and can arrange riding lessons. The Quinta da Marinha Riding School near Cascais hires out horses for around 4000$00 per hour (ℂ214 869 084); the tourist office in Cascais (see p.248) can give details of other stables in the area.

LISBON MARATHON

Portugal has produced some world-class long-distance runners in recent years, most notably marathon runner Rosa Mota, who in 1988 became the first Portuguese woman to win an Olympic gold medal. Top names can often be seen performing at the **Discoveries Marathon** in November, which usually starts at the Ponte 25 de Abril and finishes at Belém's Mosteiro dos Jerónimos. There's also a half-marathon in the city in March.

SURFING AND WINDSURFING

Sections of the **World Windsurfing Championships** are usually held at Praia da Ribeira d'Ilhas, a small resort 3km north of Ericeira (itself an hour's bus ride north of Lisbon or Sintra). Praia do Guincho (see p.251), north of Cascais, also holds Windsurfing and Surfing Championships, usually in August.

If you want to **surf**, head for Caparica (see p.259) or Praia Grande (see p.236), though be careful not to get in the way of the local surfers, who have very strict codes of conduct. Ericeira is another good base; you can rent surfing equipment here from Ultimar at Rua 5 de Outubro 37 (©261 862 371). Windsurfing is best in the calmer waters round Cascais, where you can rent equipment from the John Davies bar on Praia da Duquesa (©214 830 455), the next bay round from Praia da Conceição (summer only). Carcavelos (see p.246) also has a windsurfing school, Mistral (Windsurf Café, Avda Marginal 2775 ©214 578 965), though be warned that the sea here is even dirtier than at Cascais, itself badly polluted.

SWIMMING

The best beaches close to Lisbon are at Cascais (though the water quality here is poor), Guincho (see p.251) and Caparica (see p.259); at the last two, watch out for dangerous currents. In Lisbon, the most central swimming pool is in the Atheneum club on Rua das Portas de Santo Antão, next to the Coliseu (Mon–Fri 1–4.30pm & 9–10pm, 500$00; Sat 3.30–7pm, 800$00) – head through the cavernous union building and upstairs to the pool, once open air but now sadly glassed in.

TENNIS

As well as relatively inexpensive municipal courts at Jardim do Campo Grande (metro Campo Grande, see p.75), you can also find private courts at the Clube VII, Parque Eduardo VII (𝄐213 865 818); Quinta do Junqueiro (Carcavelos); Estoril Tennis Club, Avenida Conde de Barcelona, Estoril (𝄐214 662 770) and Quinta da Marinha, Cascais (𝄐214 869 084). Courts must be reserved in advance, and non-club members have to pay through the nose for the privilege (around 1000$00 per player for an hour), but facilities are first rate.

The best place to catch international tennis stars is at the **Estoril Open**, held at the Estádio Nacional in Cruz Quebrada (also the venue for the football cup final, see p.191), usually in early April.

Shopping

Lisbon may not be the first city that springs to mind for those with the shop-till-you drop mentality, but if you are used to the characterless shopping malls of most European city centres, you'll find the **Baixa's** traditional and specialist shops a pleasurable experience. For more cutting-edge outlets, head to the **Bairro Alto**, fast becoming a centre for alternative designer clothes and furniture.

For those seeking traditional local goods, **fado cassettes**, **azulejos ceramics** and **textiles** can be found at various outlets around the city; we've listed those which offer the best value or quality. Other than these, perhaps the most Portuguese of items to take home is a bottle of **wine** or **port**: check out the vintages at the *Instituto do Vinho do Porto* (see p.160), and then buy from one of the specialist shops listed or from any deli or supermarket.

....

Our listings are divided as follows:
arts and crafts (p.197); books, cards and magazines (p.198);
clothes (p.199); food and drink (p.202); markets (p.204);
music (p.205); supermarkets (p.207).

....

Traditionally, **shopping hours** are Monday to Friday 9am–1pm and 3–7pm or 8pm, Saturday 9am–1am, though many of the larger, international stores stay open until late on Saturday and some open on Sunday. Many of the Bairro Alto shops are open afternoons and evenings only, usually 2–9pm, while shops in the Amoreiras complex stay open 9am–midnight (11pm on Sundays). Credit cards are widely accepted.

ARTS AND CRAFTS

Cheapish **arts and crafts** shops are concentrated along Rua do Alecrim in Chiado, Rua Dom Pedro V in the Bairro Alto and Rua de São Bento between São Bento and Rato; none is particularly outstanding, but most make for some good browsing. Other interesting shops include the following.

Fábrica Sant'ana
Map 5, E6. Rua do Alecrim 95, Chiado.
Mon–Fri 9.30am–7pm, Sat 10am–2pm.
If you're interested in Portuguese azulejos, check out this factory shop, founded in 1741, which sells copies of traditional designs and a great range of pots and ceramics.

Fábrica Viúva Lamego
Map 2, F8. Largo do Intendente 25, Intendente.
Mon–Fri 9am–1pm & 3–7pm, Sat 9am–1pm; closed Sat July & Aug.
Highly rated azulejos factory shop near metro Intendente producing made-to-order hand-painted designs. You can also order reproduction antiques.

Madeira House
Map 3, G6. Rua Augusta 133, Baixa.
Mon–Fri 9am–1pm & 3–7pm, Sat 9am–1pm.
Touristy shop in the heart of this pedestrianized street. Along with a scattering of tacky souvenirs there are some attractively crafted azulejos, lace tablecloths and pottery, most of it from Madeira.

ARTS AND CRAFTS

Olaria do Desterro
Map 8, I4. Rua Nova do Desterro 14, Intendente.
Mon–Fri 8am–noon & 1–7pm, Sat 9am–1pm.

Old family firm which has been turning out excellent and colourful Portuguese pottery for over 150 years – most of it by the owner who is now in his nineties. Prices are reasonable, too. From metro Intendente, head south down Avenida Almirante Reis and it's on the second street to the right.

Ratton Cerâmicas.
Map 5, B2. Rua da Academia das Ciências 2c, São Bento.
Mon–Fri 10am–noon & 2.30–7pm.

Art gallery that also displays and sells some of the country's leading Portuguese ceramics and tiles; prices accordingly high.

BOOKS, CARDS AND MAGAZINES

FNAC
Map 2, A3. Loja 103a, Colombo Shopping Centre.
Daily 10am–midnight.

Branch of the international chain offering a good range of English-language books, along with an extensive music department and audiovisual equipment; the only problem is finding it in this vast shopping centre.

Foto Galeria
Map 4, A5. Costa do Castelo 12a, Alfama.
Mon–Fri 9.30am–1.30pm & 3–7pm.

Photographic gallery selling some fine arty black-and-white postcards which give a different and interesting perspective on a city known for its quality of light.

Livraria Bertrand
Map 3, G7. Rua Garrett 73, Chiado.

Mon–Fri 9am–8pm, Sat 9am–10pm, Sun 2–7pm.

One of Lisbon's oldest and best-known general bookshops, with novels in English and a range of foreign magazines. A good place to find English translations of Portuguese writers such as Pessoa.

Livraria Britânica

Map 8, C6. Rua Luís Fernandes 14, Praça do Príncipe Real.
Mon–Fri 9.30am–7pm, Sat 9.30am–1pm.

Just up from the Praça do Príncipe Real (it's on a small side road off Rua de São Marçal), this exclusively English-language bookshop caters mainly for the nearby British Council – pricey but well stocked.

Livraria Buchholz

Map 8, D2. Rua Duque de Palmela 4, Avda da Liberdade.
Mon–Fri 9am–6pm, Sat 9am–1pm.

Just off the top end of Avenida da Liberdade, this has a good range of English-language novels and books on Portugal, plus helpful and efficient staff.

Livraria Portugal

Map 3, F7. Rua do Carmo 70–74, Chiado.
Mon–Fri 9am–12.30pm & 2.30–7pm, Sat 9am–1pm.

Excellent and well laid-out bookshop with a good range of novels and non-fiction in Portuguese and English. It sells many of the books listed on pp.275–280.

CLOTHES AND ACCESSORIES

The main shopping area for clothes is in the modern city, from metro Roma down Avenida de Roma to Praça de Londres (Map 2, F4–F5). International designers have outlets at the top end of Avenida da Liberdade, while Portuguese designers' shops can be found in Amoreiras shopping centre and in various fashionable stores in Chiado and the Bairro Alto. Despite its reputation for good shoes, Lisbon's shoe shops tend to have limited styles and very small sizes. Recommended shops include:

Ana Salazar
Map 3, F7. Rua do Carmo 87, Chiado.
Mon–Fri 10am–7pm, Sat 10am–1pm.
One of Lisbon's best-known shops for designer women's clothes, though its reputation is based more on style than on materials used. There's another branch at Avenida da Roma 16.

Atalaia 31
Map 5, D4. Rua da Atalaia 31, Bairro Alto.
Mon–Sat 11am–8.30pm.
This shop is typical of the fashionable stores that have been moving into the Bairro Alto recently, with expensive designer men's clothes, sunglasses and brand-name cosmetics.

Azevedo Rua
Map 3, C6. Rossio 73.
Mon–Sat 9am–1pm & 3–10pm.
Long-established, traditional shop selling good, old-fashioned hats and umbrellas; the latter in particular can be useful outside the summer months.

Eldorado
Map 5, E5. Rua do Norte 23–25, Bairro Alto.
Mon–Thurs 1–8pm, Fri 1–9pm, Sat 4–9pm.
An interesting mixture of clubbing clothes, secondhand cast-offs and old records and CDs aimed at Lisbon's young groovers. A good place to head for if you need a new wardrobe for a night out without breaking the bank.

José António Tenente
Map 5, G5. Trav. do Carmo 8, Bairro Alto.

Mon–Sat 10.30am–7.30pm.

Famous – and currently very popular – designer clothes for men and women, with distinctly out-of-the-ordinary creations. Good if you want to buy something unusual, but they don't come cheap.

Lena Ayres

Map 5, E3. Rua da Atalaia 96, Bairro Alto.
Mon–Fri noon–8.30pm, Sat 3–8pm.

Local shops in the Bairro Alto used to be good for bacalhau and fruit, now you can get designer clothes at every turn. This shop offers wacky dresses and some imaginative clothes for women.

Luvaria Ulisses

Map 3, F7. Rua do Carmo 87A, Chiado.
Mon–Fri noon–8.30pm, Sat 3–8pm.

Superb ornate doorway gives onto minuscule glove shop with handware to suit all tastes tucked into rows of boxes; even if it's boiling outside, think ahead and consider getting next winter's gloves here.

Mala Miss

Map 3, C5. Rua de B. Queiroz 5, Baixa.
Mon–Fri 9.30pm–7pm, Sat 9.30am–1.30pm.

Aptly translates as "Miss Bag", with wide range of inexpensive leather handbags, briefcases and belts – there are lots of other shops selling shoes and leather goods on this road too.

Manuel Alves & José Manuel Gonçalves

Map 5, E3. Rua da Rosa 39 & 85–87, Bairro Alto.
Mon–Fri 2–8pm, Sat 10am–1pm.

Well-known and established Portuguese designers selling quality products at high prices. You can find menswear at the first shop, women's clothing at the second.

Nuno Gama

Map 5, D4. Trav. dos Fiéis de Deus 74, Bairro Alto.

Mon–Fri 11am–9pm, Sat noon–5pm.

Currently one of Lisbon's most fashionable clothes shops, catering for men and women. The clothes aren't cheap, but the quality's good.

Printemps

Map 3, F7. Rue do Carmo 28, Chiado.

Mon–Sat 10am–8pm.

Wonderfully reconstructed building risen from the ashes of the old burnt-out Grandella shop, this French department store stocks ladies, men's and children's fashion, bags, perfumes and more.

Zara

Map 3, H6. Rua Augusta 71, Baixa.

Mon–Sat 9.30am–7.30pm.

Stylish Spanish store selling a wide range of colourful and summery clothing for men, women and children. The fact that it is nearly always packed testifies to its popularity. There's another branch at Rua Garrett 1–11 in Chiado.

FOOD AND DRINK

Casa Pereira da Conceição

Map 3, H6. Rua Augusta 102–104, Baixa.

Mon–Fri 9am–7pm, Sat 9am–1pm & 3–7pm.

Fine 1930s Art Deco shop on the Baixa's main pedestrianized street, selling tempting coffee beans, teas, chocolates, cafetieres, fans and china. The aroma alone makes it worth a visit.

Confeitaria Nacional

Map 3, D5. Praça da Figueira 18, Baixa.

Mon–Fri 8am–8.30pm, Sat 8am–1.30pm.

On the corner with Rua dos Correeiros, this wonderful traditional nineteenth-century confectioner's offers a superb range of pastries, cakes and sweets.

Conserveira de Lisboa
Map 4, A9. Rua dos Bacalhoeiras 34, Baixa.
Mon–Fri 10am–6pm, Sat 9am–1pm.
Wall-to-wall tin cans make this colourful shop a bizarre but intriguing place to stock up on tinned sardines, squid, and just about any other canable beastie.

....

**For general food supplies, see "Supermarkets" (p.207).
A couple of the markets listed on p.204 are also good
places to stock up on provisions.**

....

Ferreira & Silva
Map 4, C9. Rua de São João da Praça 118, Alfama.
Mon–Fri 9am–1pm & 4–7pm; Sat 9am–1pm.
The line of international flags outside shows it's geared to tourists, and though not cheap, it does stock a good range of wines and ports, with knowledgeable staff to advise.

Londrina
Map 3, A7. Rua das Portas de Santo Antão 55, Baixa.
Mon–Fri 9am–7pm, Sat 9am–1pm.
The best of several shops on this street at which to stock up on food supplies. Barely bigger than a bottle itself, it somehow crams in enough inexpensive wine and port to sink a battleship, not to mention a fine array of cheeses, bacalhau and hams.

Manuel Tavares
Map 3, D5. Rua da Betesga 1a, Baixa.
Mon–Fri 9am–7.30pm, Sat 9am–1pm.
Small, century-old treasure trove with a great selection of nuts,

FOOD AND DRINK

chocolate and national cheeses, and a basement stuffed with vintage wines and ports, some dating from the turn of the century.

Napoleão

Map 3, H4. Rua dos Fanqueiros 70, Baixa.
Mon–Sat 10am–2pm & 4–7pm.

If you want some quality local produce to take home with you, this stocks a great range of port and wine, with knowledgeable, English-speaking staff to help you with your choices. It's at the junction with Rua da Conceição.

MARKETS

Mercado 31 de Janeiro

Map 9, F7. Rua Eng. Vieira de Silva, Saldanha.
Mon–Sat 7am–2pm.

Once an outdoor affair, this is now housed in a smart new block on two floors which feature everything from fresh fish and flowers to traditional arts and crafts.

See p.37 and p.246 for details of the Feira da Ladra, Lisbon's main flea market, and the Thursday market in Carcavelos.

Mercado da Ribeira

Map 5, A7. Avda 24 de Julho, Cais do Sodré.
Mon–Sat 6am–2pm.

One of Lisbon's most atmospheric covered markets, just a short walk from Cais do Sodré; the fish hall is fascinating, revealing some of the Atlantic's huge diversity of creatures.

Feira Numismática

Map 3, J5. Praça do Comércio, Baixa.

Sun morning.

A good Sunday outing if you're interested in the country's past, selling old coins and notes from Portugal and its former colonies, with stalls spilling out from under the arches of the arcades.

Rotunda do Aeroporto

Map 2, H3. Rotunda do Aeroporto.

Sun morning.

Many of Europe's brand-name clothes are made in Portugal, and a large quantity of these seem to end up as seconds in Lisbon's markets. This is the main rag-trade market, with complete wardrobes of clothing for a few thousand escudos. Take an airport bus, get off just before the airport and follow the crowds.

MUSIC

Discoteca Amália

Map 3, E7. Rua Aurea 274, Baixa.

Mon–Fri 9.30am–7pm, Sat 9.30am–1pm.

A small but well-stocked shop with a good collection of the latest sounds. If you want to get a fado CD or cassette, the staff are usually happy to provide some recommendations.

A Loja da Música

Map 3, A7. Rua das Portas de Santo Antão 92.

Mon–Sat 10am–8pm, Sun 10am–7pm.

Large shop with a big collection of everything from indie labels to fado, tucked into the side of the Coliseu, one of Lisbon's main live-music venues.

Virgin Megastore

Map 3, A9. Restauradores 18.

Mon–Sat 10am–10pm, Sun 2–8pm.

Occupying the grand former Eden Theatre, this dominates one side of Restauradores, with three floors offering all kinds of music from the Spice Girls to fado performer Amália Rodrigues.

SHOPPING CENTRES

Lisbon's shopping centres are phenomenally popular, especially at weekends when whole families visit for a day out. The kids' amusements, restaurants, cafés, cinemas and a whole range of international and local shops make the appeal at least partly understandable.

For details of Amoreiras shopping centre, see p.78.

Centro Comércial Mouraria

Map 3, B3. Largo Martim Moniz, Mouraria.

Lisbon's tackiest and most run-down shopping centre, but sufficiently atmospheric to warrant a look round its six levels (three of them underground). Hundreds of small, family-run stores selling Indian fabrics, oriental and African produce, including an aromatic collection of cafés on level 3 – a real slice of Lisbon's ethnic community.

Colombo Shopping Centre

Map 2, B3. Avda Colégio Militar-Luz, Luz.

Iberia's largest shopping complex, opposite metro Colégio Militar-Luz, boasts over four hundred shops including leading international stores, ten cinema screens, 63 restaurants, a bowling alley and kids' entertainment areas.

Libersil

Map 8, G5. Avda da Liberdade 38.

Small, central shopping centre with range of mostly Portuguese stores.

Monumental

Map 9, F6. Praça Duque de Saldanha, Saldanha.

By metro Saldanha, this is a relatively new shopping centre with cinemas, good cafés, and a reasonable selection of shops.

SUPERMARKETS

For general supplies, there's a huge Pão d'Açúcar super-market in the Amoreiras centre (daily 9am–midnight); this Brazilian chain has other branches throughout the city, such as at Rua Luís de Camões 133, Bairro Alto – most stay open until around 8pm. On a smaller scale, try the more central Mercado da Figueira, Praça da Figueira 10 (Mon–Fri 8am–8pm, Sat 8am–7pm), or the branches of Mini Preço or Pingo Doce which are dotted around the city.

Kids' Lisbon

There are plenty of activities to keep kids entertained in the Lisbon area. The tourist office and the city's listings magazines (see p.9) can provide **information** about events specifically for children – *Lisboa em*, in particular, has a good section on child-friendly events.

Most **hotels** and *pensões* will happily provide extra beds or cots for children if notified in advance. There is usually no charge for children under 6 who share their parents' room, while discounts of up to fifty percent on accommodation for 6- to 8-year-olds are not uncommon. On **public transport**, under-5s can go free while 5- to 12-year-olds travel half price on trains but pay full fare on metros and buses.

> **Should you hit a spell of bad weather, your best bet is to head for Belém, which has several interesting museums suitable for older children.**

Parents with prams or **pushchairs** will find Lisbon's steep streets hard work, with pavements notoriously potholed and often blocked by parked cars. Cars are the main worry for parents: always keep a look-out for vehicles which cut corners and don't observe pedestrian crossings.

CAFÉS AND RESTAURANTS

Children will be welcomed in most **cafés and restaurants** at any time of the day. Indeed, waiters often go out of their way to spend a few minutes entertaining restless children; toddlers may even find themselves being carried off for a quick tour of the kitchens while parents finish their meals in peace. However, **changing facilities** in restaurants, cafés and public toilets are non-existent, and high-chairs and menus specifically for children are scarce. In addition, restaurants rarely open much before 8pm, so kids will need to adjust to Portuguese hours; local kids are still up at midnight.

> For those with babies, fresh milk is sold in larger shops and supermarkets; smaller shops and cafés usually stock UHT milk only. Nappies are widely available in supermarkets and chemists; the latter also sell formula milk, babies' bottles and jars of baby food.

MUSEUMS

The **Museu da Marioneta** (Puppet Museum) in Alfama (see p.35) may interest older children, especially at those times when the weekend puppet shows are running. Puppet shows – in Portuguese – are also held at the nearby **Teatro Taborda**, Costa do Castelo 75 (Map 4, C3) on Fridays, Saturdays and Sundays.

In Belém, the **Museu de Arte Popular** (Folk Art Museum), the **Museu dos Coches** (Coach Museum) and the **Museu da Marinha** (Maritime Museum) are all good bets for older children (see p.61); the latter even has its own children's section, the **Museu das Crianças**, with interactive and hands-on displays designed to raise children's awareness of other children's feelings. There's also an underwhelming **planetarium** (Planetário Calouste Gulbenkian, Praça do Império, Belém ©213 620 002). Finally, in Sintra, **the Museu do Brinquedo** is a well-laid out toy museum (see p.230).

PARKS AND PLAY AREAS

Lisbon has several parks and squares with children's **play areas**, though loose bolts on some of the equipment can be alarming. Parque Eduardo VII contains an impressive mock-galleon in a play area just south of the *estufas* (see p.68), and there's also a small children's playground in the attractive Praça Prínçipe Real (see p.44). Slightly further out is a similar, excellent playground in the Estrela gardens (see p.48). The gardens at the Fundação Gulbenkian are often awash with uniformed children from the local **crèche**, the Centro Artístico Infantil (entrance just off Rua Marquês de Sá da Bandeira), well-stocked with toys and offering free childcare sessions for 4- to 12-year-olds between 9.30am and 5.30pm.

> Even if you don't approve of the caged animals, the Lisbon Zoo (see p.77) is set in a lovely park, and there's an enjoyable cable-car ride too.

In **Sintra**, the Castelo dos Mouros, the gardens around the Palácio da Pena and the gardens of Monserrate are all great places for kids to let off steam.

SHOPPING

The **Colombo shopping centre** by metro Colégio Militar-Luz is the largest shopping centre in Iberia, with whole zones set aside to keep restless kids happy while their parents shop; there's even a roller-coaster.

The Parque das Nações at Olivais (see p.80) has several attractions suitable for kids, notably the cable-car ride, water gardens, the Virtual Reality Pavilion and the huge Oceanarium.

SWIMMING AND BEACHES

Sea-swimming can be dangerous in the Lisbon area; the **beaches** at Cascais (see p.248) are relatively calm but pollution levels are questionable, while the cleaner, blue-flag water at Caparica (see p.259) can be accompanied by dangerous undertows. However, the latter has supervised areas and the waves are superb for older kids into boogie-boarding or body-surfing, while the toy train up the beach is always a big hit for kids of all ages.

TRANSPORT AND FUN RIDES

Taking rides on Lisbon's **trams, funicular railways and ferries** can provide hours of endless fun. There is also a quaint fairground offering **fun rides** at the Feira Popular, by Entrecampos metro (see p.75). In Sintra you can take a pricey **horse and carriage ride** round town, or a tram from nearby Ribeira da Sintra to the beach at Praia das Maçãs (see p.236).

Festivals

The Portuguese have a reputation for being somewhat reserved, at least in comparison with their Spanish neighbours, but they know how to have a good time when it comes to **festivals**. This is especially so during the celebrations for the **santos populares** (popular saints) when parts of Lisbon become one big street party. The arts are also highly valued in Lisbon, and the year is punctuated with **cultural events** which are definitely worth checking out.

SPRING

Carnaval
Late February or early March Muted city carnival, with festivities in most local districts, although most people prefer to watch the Rio carnival on TV instead.

Moda Lisboa (Lisbon Fashion)
April The luvvies of the fashion world come to Lisbon's bi-annual fashion show (the other one is usually in November), when mainly Portuguese designers get the chance to parade their wears on the catwalk.

Public holidays

Lisbon has a generous helping of **public holidays** when most of the city shuts down; don't attempt to travel in or out of the city at either end of these holidays. The fixed dates below fall on different days each year. If they fall on a Sunday, the holiday is lost; if the holiday falls on a Thursday or Tuesday, many people don't bother working on the Friday or Monday. Official holidays are: January 1 (New Year's Day); February/March (Carnival; see p.212); mid-April (Good Friday); April 25 (celebrating the 1974 revolution); May 1 (Labour Day); June 10 (Portugal Day and Camões Day); June 13 (Santo António); August 15 (Feast of the Assumption); October 5 (Republic Day); November 1 (All Saints' Day); December 1 (Independence Day, celebrating independence from Spain in 1640); December 8 (Immaculate Conception); December 24–25 (Christmas).

SUMMER

Santos Populares (Popular Saints)
June Lisbon's main popular festivals, featuring fireworks, fairground rides and street-partying to celebrate the *santos populares* – saints António (June 13), João (June 24), and Pedro (June 29). Celebrations for each begin on the evening before the actual day. The festival of Santo António is the largest; there are festivals in each district and the whole city is decked out in coloured ribbons. The street party is best in Alfama, with food and drinks stalls taking over just about every square. In Sintra, the main *festa* is for São Pedro.

Festas da Lisboa
June A series of city-sponsored cultural and other events, many

promoted by the Gulbenkian Foundation, including free concerts, exhibitions and culinary contests at various venues round the city. There's also an increasingly popular Gay Pride event.

Sintra Music Festival

Late June, **July and August** Adventurous performances by international orchestras, musicians and dance groups in and around Sintra, Estoril and Cascais. Concerts are held in parks, gardens and palaces, including the fantastic Palácio de Queluz. An offshoot of the festival are the **Noites de Bailado** at Seteais Palace, a series of ballet, dance and operatic performances, again with top international names, mostly performed in the gardens during July and August. Tickets and programmes for all performances are available from the Gabinete do Sintra-Festival, Praça da República 23, Sintra ℭ219 243 518.

For details of Lisbon's major sporting events,
see p.189.

International Jazz Festival

July or August Big annual jazz festival at the Gulbenkian; the events in the open-air amphitheatre are particularly attractive, and there are usually appearances by international bands and performers.

Feira Internacional Artesanato (Handicrafts Fair)

July State-run handicrafts fair held in Estoril on the Avenida de Portugal, near the Casino. A similar event occurs during the same period at FIL, the main exhibition hall at the Parque das Nações, when crafts from every region of the country are displayed and offered for sale.

Tbe Music Festival of Capuchos

August and September Innovative performances of classical music, opera and ballet at the Convent of Capuchos, just outside Caparica, as well as other venues along the coast.

AUTUMN

Festa das Vindimas (Wine Harvest Festival)

First or second weekend of September Held in the hilltop town of Palmela – around an hour by bus from Praça de Espanha – in the heart of some fine vineyards, this event includes the chance to taste the local produce and enjoy parades, bull-running, folk music and fireworks.

Festival de Cinema Gay e Lésbico (Gay and Lesbian Film Festival)

September Increasingly respected film festival with radical and mainstream movies and talks by directors, usually at the Instituto da Cinemateca Portuguesa (see p.187) and other venues.

Encontros ACARTE

September A cultural programme organized by – and partly held at – the Gulbenkian Foundation, promoting up-and-coming local and international talent, with shows around the city featuring music, art, the performing arts and animation.

Seixal Jazz

October and early November The industrial suburb of Seixal (a short ferry ride over the Tejo from Estação Fluvial by Praça de Comércio) hosts big names from the Portuguese and international jazz world at the Fórum Cultural do Seixal (©212 226 413).

All Saints' Day and São Martinho

November 1 and 11 Candles are lit for the dead on All Saints' Day (Nov 1), while November 11 sees the more earthy São

Martinho, when the saint's day is traditionally celebrated by eating chestnuts and *agua pé* – the first of the year's wine harvest.

WINTER

Christmas
December The build-up to December 25 begins in early December with lights decorating central shopping streets and a huge Christmas tree filling the centre of Praça da Figueira. The bullring at Campo Pequeno (see p.190) usually hosts a travelling circus at this time. Distinctive hooped *bolo-rei* (dried fruit "king cake") appears in shops and *pastelarias*. Christmas Day itself remains a family affair, with traditional midnight Mass on December 24, followed by a meal of bacalhau.

New Year's Eve
December 31 The best place to head for on New Year's Eve is Praça do Comércio, when fireworks light up the riverfront and there's a party which usually continues well into the next morning. There are also similar events at Cascais and the Parque das Nações.

Directory

AIRLINES Air.France, Avda 5 de Outubro 206 ©217 900 202; Alitalia, Praça Marquês de Pombal 1–5° ©213 536 141; British Airways, Avda da Liberdade 36-2° ©213 217 900; Go ©0808 204 204; Iberia, Rua Rosa Araújo 2 ©213 558 119; KLM, Campo Grande 220B ©217 955 018; Lufthansa, Avda da Liberdade 192 ©213 573 722; Sabena, Avda da Liberdade 144 ©213 465 572; Swissair, Avda da Liberdade 38 ©213 226 000; TAP, Praça Marquês de Pombal·3 ©213 179 100; Varig, Praça Marquês de Pombal 1 ©213 136 830.

AIRPORT INFORMATION ©218 413 700.

AMERICAN EXPRESS The local agent is Top Tours, Avda Duque de Loulé 108 ©213 155 885 (Mon–Fri 9.30am–1pm & 2.30–6.30pm; metro Marquês de Pombal).

BANKS Most main branches are in the Baixa; standard banking hours are Monday to Friday 8.30am to 3pm. If you have a credit or debit card, ATMs (usually with the option of English-language instructions) can be found throughout Lisbon, and are the easiest way of obtaining escudos.

BUSES The main terminal is at Avda João Crisóstomo (metro Saldanha; ©213 545 775 or 213 545 439), which serves international and most domestic departures, including express services to the Algarve. Other bus services leave from Praça de Espanha (metro Praça de Espanha) and Avda 5 de Outubro 75 (metro Saldanha; ©217 262 740) for Transportes Sul do Tejo departures to Caparica, Sesimbra and places south of the Tejo; Campo Pequeno (metro Campo Pequeno) for AVIC services (©217 910 579) to the northwest coast; and SolexPresso (©217 963 620) to the Alentejo and Algarve; Campo das Cebolas, at the end of Rua dos Bacalhoeiros, east of Praça do Comércio, for Renex services (©218 874 871) to the Minho and Algarve; and Campo Grande 5 (metro Campo Grande) or Rua Fernandes da Fonseca (metro Martim Moniz; ©217 951 447), northeast of Rossio, for Empresa Barraqueiro services to Mafra and Ericeira. You can buy advance bus tickets at most major travel agents – see p.221 for a list. Fares and timetables for Portugal's main national coach service can be found on *www.rede-expressos.pt*

CAR RENTAL Alamo/Guerin: Avda Alvares Cabral 45b ©213 882 724; Auto Jardim: airport ©218 463 187; Avis: Avda Praia da Vitória 12c ©213 561 176, airport ©218 499 947; Budget: Rua Castilho 167b ©213 860 516, airport ©218 478 803; Eurodollar: airport ©218 478 748; Europcar: Santa Apolónia station ©218 875 472, airport ©218 401 176; Hertz: Rua Castilho 72 ©213 812 430, airport ©218 492 722; Nova Rent: Largo Monterroio Mascarenhas 9 ©213 870 808.

CONTRACEPTION See "Pharmacies and contraception".

CRIME Pickpocketing is very common, especially on public transport and in crowded tourist areas; keep valuables out of sight. Car break-ins are also frequent. Muggings do occur and Lisbon does have a drugs problem, but the city is relatively safe and serious crime against tourists is rare.

CURRENCY EXCHANGE There's a currency exchange office at the airport (open 24hr) and at Santa

Apolónia station (daily 8.30am–8.30pm).

DISABLED TRAVELLERS Lisbon airport offers a service for wheelchair users if advance notice is given (℡213 632 044), while the Orange Badge symbol is recognized for disabled car parking. The main public transport company, Carris, offer an inexpensive dial-a-ride minibus service, O Serviço Especial de Transporte de Deficientes (Mon–Fri 6.30am–11pm, Sat 7am–10pm, Sun 8am-10pm; ℡217 585 676, *www.carris.pt*), though advance notice is required. The following museums have disabled access: Museu de Arqueologia; Museu de Arte Popular; Museu do Chiado; Museu dos Coches; Museu Nacional de Arte Antiga. For a list of hotels with disabled access, see p.90.

EMAIL You can send email from the otherwise sterile *Web Café*, Rua do Diário de Notícias 12 (Map 5, E4, daily 4pm–2am; ℡213 421 181, *web1@mail.esoterica.pt*) or at *Ciber Chiado*, above the *Café No Chiado* (see p.146), Largo do Picadeiro 11 at the top end of Rua dos D. de Bragança (Map 5, E6; Mon–Fri 11am–1am, Sat 2pm–midnight; ℡213 466 722, *info@cnc.pt*). Larger outlets, which charge for sending email, include Espaço Agora (Map 5, E9; daily 3pm–2am; see p.147), a student resource at Pavilhão 2, Avda Ribeira das Naus by Cais do Sodré ferry terminal; and the Forum Telecom building (Map 7, E7; Mon–Fri 9am–5pm), Avda Fontes Pereira de Melo 38, by metro Picoas.

EMBASSIES Ireland: Rua da Imprensa à Estrela 1-4° (℡213 929 440; tram #28 to Estrela); Netherlands: Avda Infante Santo 43–5° (℡213 961 163; tram #28 to Estrela); South Africa: Avda Luís Bivar 10 (℡213 525 618; metro São Sebastião or Saldanha); UK: Rua São Bernardo 33 (℡213 961 191; tram #28 to Estrela); USA: Avda das Forças Armadas (℡217 273 300; metro Jardim Zoológico).

EMERGENCIES ℡115.

HOSPITAL British Hospital, Rua Saraiva de Carvalho 49 (℃213 955 067 or 213 976 329), has English-speaking staff. For an ambulance, call ℃213 017 777.

LAUNDRY Lavandaria Saus Ana, in the Centro Comércial da Mouraria, Largo Martim Moniz 9 (metro Socorro), does service washes for 1000$00 (Mon–Sat 9.30am–8pm), or try Lava Neve, Rua da Alegria 37, Bairro Alto.

LEFT LUGGAGE There are 24hr lockers at the airport (in level 1 of car park 1); at Rossio, Cais do Sodré and Santa Apolónia stations (all 6am–2am), and a left-luggage office at the bus terminal on Avda João Crisóstomo (Mon–Fri 6.30am–8pm, Sat & Sun 9am–1pm & 2–6pm).

LOST PROPERTY The police lost property office is at Rua dos Anjos 56a (metro Anjos). The metro office is at Restauradores metro (℃213 427 707); the Carris office is at Rua de Santa Justa 11, Baixa (℃213 427 944; metro Rossio).

NEWSPAPERS There are several newsstands around Rossio and Restauradores, such as the one attached to the ABEP ticket kiosk, which sell foreign-language papers, as do the lobbies of many of the larger hotels.

PHARMACIES AND CONTRACEPTION Pharmacies are open Mon–Fri 9am–1pm & 3–7pm, Sat 9am–1pm. Local papers carry information about 24hr pharmacies and the details are posted on every pharmacy door. Condoms – and even, in some areas, hyperdermic syringes – are available from automatic vending machines outside pharmacies.

POLICE There's a 24hr office at Rua Capelo 13 (℃213 466 141), west of the Baixa near the Teatro de São Carlos. If you've had anything stolen, come here for a report in order to make a claim on your travel insurance.

POST OFFICE The main post office is at Praça dos Restauradores 58 (Mon–Fri 8am–10pm, Sat & Sun 9am–6pm), from where you can send airmail and *correio azul* (express mail – the fastest service). There's a 24hr post office at the airport. Stamps can also be purchased from some – but not all – newsagents.

SWIMMING POOLS The most central option is the pool in the Atheneum club on Rua das Portas de Santo Antão, next to the Coliseu (Mon–Fri 3.30–4.30pm & 9–10pm, Sat 3.30–7pm; Mon–Fri 500\$00, Sat 650\$00).

TELEPHONES For international calls there's a telephone office next to the post office in Praça dos Restauradores (see above). There's a second office on the corner of Rossio (no. 65; 8am–11pm). You can also make international calls from any phone booth. Phonecards, available in denominations of 650\$00, 1300\$00 or 1900\$00 from any post office, make calls from cabins a lot easier.

TIME Lisbon time is the same as Greenwich Mean Time (GMT). Clocks go forward an hour in late March and back to GMT in late October.

TIPPING Service charges are added to hotel and restaurant bills. It's usual to round-up restaurant bills to the nearest 100\$00 or so; other than this, tips are not expected. Hotel porters, toilet attendants and cinema ushers expect tips of at least 100\$00.

TOILETS There are very few public toilets in the streets, although they can be found in nearly all museums and main tourist sights (signed variously as *casa de banho*, *retrete*, *banheiro*, *lavabos* or WC), and it is not difficult to sneak into a café or restaurant if need be. Gents are usually marked H (*homens*) or C (*cabalheiros*), and ladies M (*mulheres*) or S (*senhoras*).

TRAVEL AGENTS Marcus & Harting (Map 3, C6),

Rossio 45–50 (℗213 46 92 71) is a good, central option for bus tickets and general travel information. The well-informed Top Tours (Map 9, E8) is at Avda Duque de Loulé 108 (℗315 58 85), near metro Marquês de Pombal. They also act as American Express agents. Tagus Travel (Map 9, D9), Rua Camilo Castelo Branco 20 (℗352 59 86), specializes in discounted student tickets and sells ISIC cards.

BEYOND THE CITY

BEYOND THE CITY

Sintra, Queluz and Mafra

f you make just one day-trip during your stay in Lisbon the beautiful hilltop town of **Sintra** is the one to choose. Served by regular trains from Rossio station, this is the most popular excursion from Lisbon and ideally deserves several days' exploration. Home to two of Portugal's most extraordinary palaces, the town also boasts a semi-tropical garden, a Moorish castle with breathtaking views over Lisbon, and one of the best modern art museums in the Iberian peninsula.

The eighteenth-century Rococo **Palácio de Queluz**, on the same train line as Sintra, is worth a brief break in your journey to or from Lisbon. Finally, north of Sintra, about ninety minutes by bus from Lisbon, lies **Mafra** – an uninspiring town made famous by its extravagant **Palácio-Convento de Mafra**, the building of which virtually bankrupted the nation.

SINTRA

Map 1, C4. Trains every 15min from Rossio station (200$00; 50min); Sintra's train station is actually in Estefânia, a 15min walk

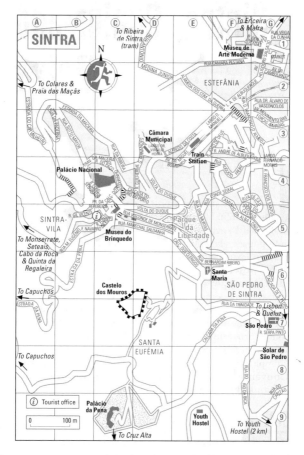

from the centre of Sintra-Vila, or take bus #434. There are also regular buses from Estoril, Cascais, Cabo da Roca and Mafra; these stop opposite the railway station.

Summer residence of the kings of Portugal, and of the Moorish lords of Lisbon before them, **Sintra**'s verdant charms have long been celebrated. British travellers of the eighteenth and nineteenth centuries found a new Arcadia in the town's cool, wooded heights, recording with satisfaction the old Spanish proverb: "To see the world and leave out Sintra is to go blind about". Byron stayed here in 1809 and began *Childe Harold*, his great mock-epic poem, in which the "horrid crags" of "Cintra's glorious Eden" form a first location. Writing home, in a letter to his mother, he proclaimed the village:

> *perhaps in every aspect the most delightful in Europe; it contains beauties of every description natural and artificial. Palaces and gardens rising in the midst of rocks, cataracts and precipices; convents on stupendous heights, a distant view of the sea and the Tagus . . . it unites in itself all the wildness of the Western Highlands with the verdure of the South of France.*

That the young Byron had seen neither the Western Highlands nor the South of France is irrelevant: his description of Sintra's romantic appeal is still exact.

Sintra loops around a series of green and wooded ravines, a confusing place in which to get your bearings. Basically, it consists of three distinct and separate villages: the drab **Estefânia** (around the train station), **Sintra-Vila** (the attractive main town) and, 2km to the east, the functional **São Pedro de Sintra**. It's fifteen minutes' walk between the station and Sintra-Vila, passing en route the fantastical Câmara Municipal (town hall); and around twenty minutes from Sintra-Vila to São Pedro. Sintra-Vila's **turismo** (daily: June–Sept 9am–8pm; Oct–May 9am–7pm; ℂ219 231 157) is just off the central Praça da República, where you'll find a post office and bank too. If you want to stay, the *turismo* can help you in times when accommodation is scarce, such as during the village's annual *festa* in honour of Saint Peter (June 28–29), and in July, during Sintra's music festival. The end of July also sees the Feira Grande in São Pedro, with crafts, antiques and cheeses on sale.

The old town, Sintra-Vila, with its narrow streets and lively bars and restaurants, is dominated by the **Palácio Nacional**, the former summer residence of Portuguese royalty and now an unmissable museum. The lush wooded hills around shelter some of the area's grandest treasures, in particular the ruined Moorish castle – the **Castelo dos Mouros** – with its stunning views; and the ludicrously extravagant nineteenth-century **Palácio da Pena** palace. The **Palácio de Seteais**, now a hotel, and the **Quinta da Regaleira**, both just outside Sintra, are worth a visit for even more opulence, while further afield lie the luxurious gardens of **Monserrate**, one-time haunt of English author William Beckford. An antidote to the area's extravagance is the **Convento dos Capuchos**, a spartan former hermitage in a stunning woodside location, while for a complete contrast, there is a string of low-key beach resorts to the west, as well as bus connections to Europe's most westerly point at **Cabo da Roca**.

The useful **bus #434** takes a circular route from Sintra station to the outlying sights, passing Sintra-Vila and the Castelo dos Mouros (daily every hour from around 10am to 5pm). Tickets can be purchased on board and cost 500$00 for the round trip – you can get on and off as often as you like (see p.248 for details of day or weekly passes). Alternatively, there are taxis outside the train station and in Praça da República, near the palace; the trip one-way to Monserrate, for example, costs roughly 1500$00. Agree the price first – meters aren't always used and overcharging is common.

The Museu de Arte Moderna

Map p.226, G1. Tues 2–6pm, Wed–Sun 10am–6pm; 600$00.

Before heading into Sintra-Vila, a worthwhile point of call in Estefânia just five minutes' walk from the station (turn right out of the station; the museum is in Avenida Heliodoro Salgado) is the **Museu de Arte Moderna**, a collection amassed by Madeiran tobacco magnate Joe Barardo which art critics have compared favourably to the Guggenheim in Bilbao. Built in Sintra's former casino, the 1920s building spreads over three floors, chronologically displaying the main modern movements, including pop art, minimalism, kinetic art and conceptual art.

Exhibits on the ground floor include a Jackson Pollock, but for the real highlights head to the first floor past the giant Gilbert and George panels, *March 1986*, for works by, amongst others, David Hockney, Lichtenstein and Warhol, including his Campbell's soup tins and Brillo boxes and a wonderful portrait of Judy Garland. Lovers of kitsch will enjoy Jeff Koons' sculpture of a poodle and Bobtail the sheepdog.

The top floor contains a café and restaurant, with an out-door terrace offering great views towards the Palácio da Pena.

Palácio Nacional

Map p.226, C4. Mon, Tues & Thurs–Sun 10am–12.30pm & 2–4.30pm; 400$00, free Sun 10am–12.30pm.

The extraordinary **Palácio Nacional** or Paço Real was probably already in existence under the Moors. It takes its present form, however, from the rebuilding of Dom João I (1385–1433) and his fortunate successor, Dom Manuel, the chief royal beneficiary of Vasco da Gama's explorations. Its style, as you might expect, is an amalgam of Gothic – with impressive roofline battlements – and the latter king's Manueline additions, with their characteristically extravagant twisted and animate forms. Inside, the Gothic-Manueline modes are tempered by a good deal of Moorish influence, adapted over the centuries by a succession of royal occupants. The last royal to live here, in the 1880s, was Maria Pia, grandmother of the country's last reigning monarch – Manuel II, "The Unfortunate".

Today the palace is a museum, and is best seen early or late in the day to avoid the crowds. You first pass the kitchens, their roofs tapering into the giant chimneys that are the palace's distinguishing features, and then go to the upper floor. First stop here is a gallery above the palace chapel, perhaps built on the old mosque. In a room alongside, the deranged Afonso VI was confined for six years by his brother Pedro II; he eventually died here in 1683, listening to Mass through a grid, Pedro having seized "his throne, his liberty and his queen". Beyond the gallery, a succession of state rooms climaxes in the Sala das Armas, its domed and coffered ceiling emblazoned with the arms of 72 noble families.

Highlights on the lower floor include the Manueline Sala dos Cisnes, so called for the swans (*cisnes*) on its ceiling, and the Sala das Pegas, which takes its name from the flock of magpies (*pegas*) painted on the frieze and ceiling, holding in their beaks the legend *por bem* (in honour) – reputedly the response of João I, caught by his queen, Philippa (of Lancaster), in the act of kissing a lady-in-waiting. He had the room decorated with as many magpies as there were women at court in order to satirize and put a stop to their gossip.

The Museu do Brinquedo

Map p.226, C5. Tues–Sun 10am–6pm; 600$00.

Just south of the palace, the **Museu do Brinquedo** – the fascinating private toy collection of João Arbués Moreira – is housed in a former fire station on Rua Visconde de Monserrate, imaginatively converted into a high-tech museum complete with internal glass lifts, a café and videos. The huge array of toys exhibited over three floors are somewhat confusingly labelled, but look out for the 3000-year-old stone Egyptian toys on the first floor; the 1930s Hornby trains, and some of the first ever toy cars, produced in Germany in the early 1900s. There are cases of toy soldiers numerous enough to scare a real army, wooden toys from Senegal, wire bikes from Zimbabwe and a top floor stuffed with dolls and doll's house furniture. Perhaps the most interesting section is that on early Portuguese toys, containing old cars made from papier-mâché, tin-plate animals, wooden trams and trains, as well as a selection of 1930s beach toys, including beautifully painted buckets and the metal fish that appears on the museum brochure. There's also a small play area for young children.

Castelo dos Mouros

Map p.226, C6–D7. Daily: June–Sept 10am–7pm; Oct–May 10am–5pm; free; bus #434 from Sintra station.

From Calçada dos Clérigos, near the church of **Santa Maria**, a stone pathway leads up to the ruined ramparts of the Castelo dos Mouros. Taken by Afonso Henriques with the aid of Scandinavian Crusaders, the Moorish castle spans two rocky pinnacles, with the remains of a mosque spread midway between the fortifications. The views from here are extraordinary: south beyond Lisbon's Ponte 25 de Abril bridge to the Serra da Arrábida, west to Cascais and Cabo da Roca (mainland Europe's westernmost point), and north to Peniche and the Berlenga islands.

Palácio da Pena

Map p.226, C9. Tues–Sun: July–Oct 10am–6pm; Nov–June
10am–5pm; 400$00; free Sunday 10am–2pm.

The upper gate of the castle gives on to the road up to
Pena, opposite the lower entrance to **Pena park** (daily:
June–Sept 9am–7pm; Oct–May 10am–5pm; free), a stretch
of rambling woodland with a scattering of lakes and follies,
ideal for a picnic. At the top of the park, about twenty
minutes' walk, looms the fabulous **Palácio da Pena**, a wild
fantasy of domes, towers, ramparts and walkways,
approached through mock-Manueline gateways and a draw-
bridge that does not draw. A compelling riot of kitsch built
in the 1840s to the specifications of Ferdinand of Saxe-
Coburg-Gotha, husband of Queen Maria II, it bears comparison with the mock-medieval castles of Ludwig of
Bavaria. The architect, the German Baron Eschwege,
immortalized himself in the guise of a warrior-knight in a
huge statue that guards the palace from a neighbouring
crag. The interior is no less bizarre, preserved exactly as it
was left by the royal family when they fled Portugal in
1910. The result is fascinating: rooms of stone decorated to
look like wood, turbaned Moors nonchalantly holding
electric chandeliers – it's all here. Of an original convent,
founded to celebrate the first sight of Vasco da Gama's
returning fleet, a chapel and genuine Manueline cloister
have been retained.

Above Pena, past the statue of Eschwege, a marked foot-
path climbs to the **Cruz Alta**, highest point of the Serra de
Sintra.

Quinta da Regaleira

Daily: June–Sept 10am–7.30pm; Oct–May 10am–5.30pm; 90min
tours (must be booked in advance on ©219 106 650); 2000$00,

Quinta da Regaleira, a UNESCO World Heritage site, is one of Sintra's most elaborate private estates, lying just five minutes' walk west out of town on the Seteais-Monserrate road. The estate was designed by Italian architect and theatrical set designer Luigi Manini for wealthy landowner António Augusto Carvalho Monteiro at the turn of the century. The Italian's sense of the dramatic is obvious: a mish-mash of Gothic, Renaissance and Manueline palaces, chapels and houses in dense woodland. The principal building, the mock-Manueline Palácio dos Milhões, sprouts turrets and towers with superb views over the area. The surrounding gardens shelter fountains, terraces, lakes and grottoes; the highlight is the Initiation Well, inspired by the initiation practices of the Knight Templars and Freemasons. A moss-covered spiral stairway descends inside the well to an underground warren of grottoes, which eventually resurface at the edge of a lake.

Palácio de Seteais

Beyond Quinta da Regaleira, the **Palácio de Seteais** ("Seven Sighs") stands just to the right of the Monseratte road on Rua Barbosa du Bocage 8, fifteen minutes' walk from the centre of Sintra-Vila. It is one of the most elegant palaces in Portugal, completed in the last years of the eighteenth century and entered through a majestic Neoclassical arch. It is maintained today as an immensely luxurious hotel (℃219 233 200, fax 219 234 277) offering some of the most expensive accommodation in the country – doubles start at around 46,000$00. With more modest money to blow, make for the bar and terrace – downstairs to the left, past a distinctly unwelcoming reception; its teas are also worth a splurge. Look out, too, for the summer concerts that are held here as part of the Sintra Music Festival.

Monserrate

Daily: June–Sept 10am–6pm; Oct–May 10am–5pm; 200$00.

Beyond Seteais, the road leads past a series of beautiful private *quintas* (manors or estates) to **Monserrate** – about forty minutes' walk. A Victorian folly-like mansion set in a vast botanical park of exotic trees and subtropical shrubs and plants, Monserrate is one of the most romantic sights in Portugal, its charm immeasurably enhanced by the fact that it's only partially maintained, and it would be easy to spend a day wandering around the paths laid out through the woods here.

The name most associated with Monserrate is that of **William Beckford**, author of the Gothic novel *Vathek* and the wealthiest untitled Englishman of his age. He hired Monserrate from 1793 to 1799, having been forced to flee Britain because of homosexual scandal, buggery then being a hanging offence. Setting about improving this "beautiful Claude-like place", he landscaped a waterfall and even imported a flock of sheep from his estate at Fonthill. In this Xanadu-esque dreamland he whiled away his days in summer pavilions, entertained by "bevys of delicate warblers and musicians" posted around the grounds.

Half a century later, a second immensely rich Englishman, **Sir Francis Cook**, bought the estate. His fantasies were scarcely less ambitious, involving the construction of a great Victorian house inspired by Brighton Pavilion. Cook also spared no expense in developing the grounds, importing the head gardener from Kew to lay out succulents and water plants, tropical ferns and palms, and just about every known conifer. Fernando II, who was building the Pena palace at the time, was suitably impressed, conferring a viscountcy on Cook for his efforts.

The house is closed but you can still admire the exterior, with its mix of Moorish and Italian decoration (the dome is modelled on the Duomo in Florence), and peer into a splendid series of empty salons.

Convento dos Capuchos

Daily: June–Sept 10am–6pm; Oct–May 10am–5pm; 200$00.

One of the best long walks in the Sintra area is to the **Convento dos Capuchos**, an extraordinary hermitage with tiny, dwarf-like cells cut from the rock and lined in cork – hence its popular name of the "Cork Convent". Philip II, King of Spain and Portugal, pronounced it the poorest convent of his kingdom, and Byron, visiting a cave where one monk had spent thirty-six years in seclusion, mocked in *Childe Harold*:

> *Deep in yon cave Honorius long did dwell,*
> *In hope to merit Heaven by making earth a Hell.*

Coming upon the place after a walk through the woods, however, it's hard not to be moved by its simplicity and seclusion. It was occupied for three hundred years until being finally abandoned in 1834 by its seven remaining monks, who must have found the gloomy warren of rooms and corridors too much to maintain. Some rooms – the penitents' cells – can only be entered by crawling through 70cm-high doors; here, and on every other ceiling, doorframe and lintel, are attached panels of cork, taken from the surrounding woods. Elsewhere, you'll come across a washroom, kitchen, refectory, tiny chapels, and even a bread oven set apart from the main complex.

There's no public transport to the hermitage. By foot, the most straightforward approach is by the ridge road from Pena (9km). There are other indistinct paths through the woods from Monserrate and elsewhere in the region, but without local advice and a good map you'll be hard pushed

CONVENTO DOS CAPUCHOS

to find your way. Whichever route you take, the surroundings are startling: the minor road between Sintra, the convent and Cabo da Roca sports some of the country's most alarming natural rock formations, with boulders as big as houses looming out of the trees.

THE SINTRA COAST

Map 1, A4.

From Sintra, bus #441 services the string of low-key **beach resorts** which spread along the coast to west – though note that all the beaches can have dangerous currents. **Cabo da Roca** (bus #403 from Sintra or Cascais train stations), a rocky cape with a lighthouse, is notable mainly for being the most westerly point in Europe – there's also a tourist office, where you can buy a certificate to prove you've been.

Heading north brings you first to **Praia da Adraga** (no public transport; by car, follow the signs from the village of Almoçageme), an unspoilt, cliff-backed sandy bay with just one beach restaurant. Beyond here, **Praia Grande** is perhaps the best and safest beach on this section of coast, with a row of handy cafés and restaurants spreading up towards the cliffs, while **Praia das Maçãs** (also served by summer trams from Colares and Ribeira de Sintra, just west of Estefânia) has a big, wide stretch of beach, and is one of the liveliest resorts hereabouts. **Azenhas do Mar**, a kilometre further up the coast, is a pretty fishing village tumbling down the cliff-face above a small beach.

Accommodation

Hotel Central (Map p.226, C4), Largo Rainha D. Amélia 35, Sintra-Vila ©219 230 963.
Comfortable nineteenth-century hotel, opposite the Palácio

Nacional, with polished wood and tiles throughout. Triple rooms available, too, and good off-season discounts. Breakfast included. ③

Pensão Económica (Map p.226, G2), Pátio de Olivença 6, Sintra-Vila ✆219 230 229.

Interesting old building with a cheerful owner and handy for the station; clean, basic and friendly accommodation. Just off Avenida Heliodoro Salgado. ②

Casa de Hóspedes Adelaide (Map p.226, D4), Rua Guilherme Gomes Fernandes 11, Sintra-Vila ✆219 230 873.

Welcoming and inexpensive, located midway between the train station and Sintra-Vila. A good location for the price. ②

Casa Miradouro (Map p.226, B3), Rua Sotto Mayor 55, Sintra-Vila ✆219 235 900, fax 219 241 836.

Renovated turn-of-the-century mansion 500m beyond the Palácio Nacional, with terrific views of coast and castle. Five rooms with bath, terraced garden and good breakfast included. ⑥

....

For an explanation of the accommodation price codes, see p.92.

....

Pensão Nova Sintra (Map p.226, F2), Largo Afonso d'Albuquerque 25, Estefânia ✆ & fax 219 230 220.

Decent rooms and a handy situation on the square by the train station. Some rooms have fine views, though ones at the front can be noisy. ④

Hotel Palácio de Seteais (see also p.233).

One of the most luxurious and expensive hotels in Portugal, set in a superb eighteenth-century building, surrounded by elegant gardens and with antique furnishings at every turn. ⑨

Piela's (Map p.226, F3), Rua João de Deus 70–72, Estefânia ✆219 241 691.

ACCOMMODATION

237

On the street behind the train station, this café-*pastelaria* has six
simple but spotless double rooms, presided over by a welcoming
and informative proprietor. Meals are served, and there's a games
room. Extremely popular, so book well ahead – though the owner
claims he can find alternative rooms if he's full. ③

Pousada de Juventude de Sintra (Map p.226, E9), Santa
Eufémia, São Pedro de Sintra ©219 241 210, fax 219 241 210.
The comfortable hostel is a five-kilometre walk from the train station;
it's best if you first catch a local bus to São Pedro. Meals are
served if you can't face the hike down into town and back.
Closed noon–6pm. Dorm rooms from 1500$00.

Quinta da Paderna (Map p.226, B3), Rua da Paderna 4, Sintra-
Vila ©219 235 053.
Highly attractive accommodation in a lovely old house, with en-suite
bathrooms, just north of Sintra-Vila. A good choice at this price
range. Price does not include breakfast. ⑤

Residencial Sintra (Map p.226, G6), Travessa dos Alvares, São
Pedro ©219 230 738, fax 219 230 738.
Big, rambling old pension with a garden and swimming pool and
friendly multilingual owners. You'll need to book ahead in
summer. ⑤

Hotel Tivoli (Map p.226, C4), Praça da República, Sintra-Vila
©219 233 505, fax 219 231 572, htsintra@mail.telepac.pt.
Sintra's largest, most central hotel – smack next to the palace – with
fine views and comfortable rooms with bath. Rates drop in winter. ⑦

Eating and drinking

Alcobaça (Map p.226, C5), Rua das Padarias 7–11, Sintra-Vila
©219 231 651. Daily noon–4.30pm & 7pm–midnight. Inexpensive
to moderate.
The best central choice for a decent, straightforward Portuguese

meal. Plain tiled dining room with friendly service and large servings of grilled chicken, *arroz de marisco*, clams and steak for around 2500$00 a head. Tourist menu 1600$00.

Casa da Piriquita (Map p.226, C5), Rua das Padarias 1. Daily except Wed 9am–midnight.

Cosy tea-room and bakery, which can get pretty smoky when it's busy with locals queueing to buy *queijadas da Sintra* (sweet cheesecakes) and other pastries.

O Chico (Map p.226, C5), Rua Arco do Teixeira 8, Sintra-Vila. Daily noon–midnight (bar open until 2am). Expensive.

Standard Sintra prices – fairly high – for standard food, but come on Thursdays in summer for the fado and it's good-value entertainment. It's off Rua das Padarias and has attractive outdoor tables on the cobbles. Fish *cataplana* for two people is a good bet at around 5000$00.

Cintrália (Map p.226, G2), Largo Afonso de Albuquerque 1, Estefânia ©219 242 200. Daily noon–midnight. Moderate to expensive.

Attractively renovated *marisqueira* where you can try the specialities of *arroz de lagosta* (lobster rice) and the like under sparkling chandeliers. Service is welcoming.

Marquês de Sintra (Map p.226, D5), Parque das Castanheiros, Sintra-Vila. Daily 10am–8pm.

Snack bar with plastic chairs on outdoor terrace in this small park with great views over the Palácio Nacional.

....

For an explanation of the restaurant price codes, see p.111.

....

Opera Prima (Map p.226, B5), Rua Consiglieri Pedroso 2A, Sintra-Vila ©219 244 518. Daily 11am–2am; closed Mon Nov–April. Moderate.

EATING AND DRINKING

Belgian-owned cellar bar-restaurant with international food and laid-back sounds. There's live music most Thursdays, varying from pop to jazz.

Orixás (Map p.226, F1), Avda Adriano Coelho 7, Estefânia. Tues–Sun noon–3pm & 8–11pm. Expensive.

Brazilian bar, restaurant, music venue and art gallery in a lovely building complete with waterfalls and outdoor terrace, on the road behind the Museu de Arte Moderna. Go for the buffet to sample its range of Brazilian specialities; it costs around 5000$00, but can last all night. With live Brazilian music thrown in, that's not bad value.

Café Paris (Map p.226, C4), Largo Rainha D. Amélia, Sintra-Vila ©219 232 375. Daily: café 8am–midnight; restaurant noon–10pm. Expensive.

The highest-profile café in town, opposite the Palácio Nacional, which means steep prices for underwhelming food, although it's a great place to sit and nurse a drink in the sun.

Pastelaria Vila Velha (Map p.226, C5), Rua das Padarias 8, Sintra-Vila. Tues–Sun 8am–midnight.

Good alternative to *Casa da Piriquita* – less busy, and with a good range of pastries and coffee.

Toca do Javali (Map p.226, G7), Rua 1º Dezembro 18, São Pedro de Sintra ©219 233 503. Daily except Wed noon–midnight. Expensive.

Outdoor tables in summer in a lovely terraced garden, combined with superb cooking at any time of year. Wild boar (*javali*) is the house speciality. Prices are fairly steep, around 4000$00 a head, though the set lunch is a great deal at around 2800$00.

Tulhas (Map p.226, B5), Rua Gil Vicente 4, Sintra-Vila ©219 232 378. Daily noon–3.30pm & 7–10pm. Moderate.

Imaginative cooking in a fine building, converted from old grain silos. The speciality is veal with Madeira at a reasonable 2000$00 or so. Recommended. Book in advance.

PALÁCIO-CONVENTO DE MAFRA

Map 1, D2. Feb–Nov Mon & Wed–Sun 10am–4.30pm; 400$00.
Buses hourly from metro Campo Grande in Lisbon or from Sintra
station.

The town of **Mafra** is distinguished – and utterly dominated – by just one building: the vast **Palácio-Convento** built in emulation of Madrid's Escorial by João V, the wealthiest and most extravagant of all Portuguese monarchs. Arrive at least an hour before closing time to be sure of getting a guardian to show you round (tours take around an hour).

Begun in 1717 to honour a vow made on the birth of a royal heir, **Mafra Convent** was initially intended for just thirteen Franciscan friars. But as gold and diamonds poured in from Brazil, João and his German court architect, Frederico Ludovice, amplified their plans to build a massive basilica, two royal wings and monastic quarters for 300 monks and 150 novices. The result, completed in thirteen years, is quite extraordinary and – on its own bizarre terms – extremely impressive.

In style the building is a fusion of Baroque and Italianate Neoclassicism, but it is the sheer magnitude of the edifice that distinguishes it. There are 5200 doorways, 2500 windows and two immense bell towers each containing over fifty bells; in the last stages of construction more than 45,000 labourers were employed, while throughout the years of building there was a daily average of nearly 15,000. An apocryphal story records the astonishment of the Flemish bellmakers at the size of this order: on their querying it, and asking for payment in advance, Dom João retorted by doubling their price and his original requirement.

Parts of the convent are used by the military, but you'll be shown around a sizeable enough portion. The **royal apartments** are a mix of the tedious and the shocking: the latter most obviously in the **Sala dos Troféus**, with its furniture (even chandeliers) constructed of antlers and upholstered in deerskin. Beyond are the **monastic quarters**, including cells, a pharmacy and a curious infirmary with beds positioned so the ailing monks could see Mass performed. The highlight, however, is the magnificent Rococo **library**, containing some 35,000 volumes. The **basilica** itself, which can be seen separately to the main palace, is no less imposing, with the multicoloured marble designs of its floor mirrored in the ceiling decoration. The **Tapada de Mafra**, the palace's extensive hunting grounds, are also open to the public on Saturdays, Sundays and public holidays (guided visits at 10am and 3.15pm only; 1200$00).

Accommodation

Hotel Castelão, Avda 25 de Abril, Mafra ©261 812 050, fax 061 814 698.
Up by the tourist office, this is a modern and unexciting place, but one of the few options in the area. ④

PALÁCIO DE QUELUZ

Map 1, E5. Daily except Tues 10am–1pm & 2–5pm; 500$00, free Sun 10am–1pm. Train (every 15min) from Rossio or Sintra to Queluz-Belas (180$00).

En route to Sintra, it's worth a stopover to have a look at the royal **Palácio de Queluz**, an elegant, restrained structure regarded as the country's finest example of Rococo architecture. Its low, pink-washed wings enclose a series of public and private rooms and suites, as well as rambling eighteenth-century formal gardens. Although preserved as a museum, it doesn't quite feel like one, retaining instead a strong sense of its past royal owners. In fact, the palace is still pressed into service for accommodating state guests and dignitaries.

To reach the palace, follow the signs from Queluz-Belas train station through the unremarkable town of Queluz until you reach a vast cobbled square, the Largo do Palácio, with the palace walls reaching out around one side – a fifteen-minute walk. The square also holds the local **turismo** (10am–12.30pm & 2pm–7pm; closed Thurs; ☏214 350 039).

You can still eat a meal in the original kitchen, the *Cozinha Velha* **(daily 12.30–3pm & 7.30–10pm; ☏214 350 232), although the food doesn't always live up to its setting and you're looking at around 5000$00 a head for a full meal. There is, however, a cheaper café in the main body of the palace.**

The palace was built by Dom Pedro III, husband and regent to his niece, **Queen Maria I.** Maria lived here throughout her 39-year reign (1777–1816), for the last 27 years of which she was quite mad, following the death of her eldest son, José. William Beckford visited when the Queen's wits were dwindling, and ran races in the gardens with the Princess of Brazil's ladies-in-waiting; at other times firework displays were held above the ornamental canal and bullfights in the courtyards.

Visitors first enter the **Throne Room**, which is lined with mirrors surmounted by paintings and golden flourishes. Beyond is the more restrained **Music Chamber** with its portrait of Queen Maria above a French grand piano. Smaller quarters include bed- and sitting rooms, a tiny oratory overwhelmed with red velvet, and the **Sculpture Room**, whose only exhibit is an earthenware bust of Maria. Another wing comprises an elegant suite of **public rooms** – smoking, coffee and dining rooms – all intimate in scale and surprisingly tastefully decorated. The **Ambassador's Chamber** – where diplomats and foreign ministers were received during the nineteenth century –

PALÁCIO DE QUELUZ

243

echoes the Throne Room in style, with one side lined with porcelain chinoiserie. In the end, though, perhaps one of the most pleasing rooms is the simple **Dressing Room**, with its geometric inlaid wooden floor and spider's-web ceiling.

Entry to the formal **gardens** is included in the ticket price. Low box hedges and elaborate (if weatherworn) statues spread out from the protection of the palace wings, while small pools and fountains, steps and terracing form a harmonious background to the building. From May to October there's a display of Portuguese horsemanship here every Wednesday at 11am (100$00).

Accommodation

Pousada Dona Maria I (Map 1, E5), Largo do Palácio, Palácio de Queluz, Queluz ©214 356 158, fax 214 356 189, *enatur@mail.telepac.pt*.

A *pousada* (government-run inn) which gives you the chance to stay in an annexe of one of Lisbon's grandest palaces. Its 26 rooms come equipped with satellite TV, and there's disabled access. ⑨

Estoril and Cascais

The most straightforward escape from Lisbon is to the string of beach resorts along the coast west of Belém. From the city centre, the appealing **Linha de Cascais** (Cascais Line) train from Cais do Sodré station wends up the Tejo estuary – at times so close to the water that waves almost break over the tracks – and along the coast past a string of sprawling seaside suburbs, of which **Oeiras** and **Carcavelos** have most to offer, before ending at the popular resorts of **Estoril** and **Cascais**. Sadly, the water along this stretch has suffered badly from pollution, and though steps are being taken to clean it up, it remains something of a health hazard. Nonetheless, the coast retains its attractions and Cascais, in particular, has a very relaxed atmosphere.

Trains leave every twenty minutes or so (5.30am–2.30am; 200$00) from Cais do Sodré station, stopping at Belém and Estoril en route to Cascais. Fast trains bypass Belém and stop only at Alcântara, Oeiras and stations beyond.

OEIRAS AND CARCAVELOS

Map 1, D6.

Roughly halfway up the line to Cascais, **Oeiras** marks the spot where the Tejo officially meets the sea. The youth hostel here (see p.96) makes a good alternative base to Lisbon if you fancy being by the water, and the beach and riverside walks are attractive enough, although swimming remains safest in the Ocean Pool next to the beach. The only other sight of note is the **Palácio do Marquês de Pombal**, former home of the rebuilder of Lisbon, now an adult education centre.

The next stop, **Carcavelos**, has the most extensive sandy beach on this part of the coast. Swimmers chance the waters in high summer, and at other times it's a lively spot for beach soccer, surfing and blowy winter walks. Try to visit Carcavelos on Thursday morning, when the town hosts a huge **market**; turn right out of the station and follow the signs. Street upon street is taken over by stalls selling cheap clothes (many with brand-name labels), ceramics and general tat.

ESTORIL

Map 1, C6.

Estoril's train station is next to Avenida Marginal, the coast road which, along with the railway, separates the beach from the town; the two sides are connected by an underpass. Directly opposite the underpass you'll find the very helpful **turismo** (Mon–Sat 9am–7pm, Sun 10am–6pm; ©214 680 113), which offers sound advice on the area, with maps and help with accommodation.

Estoril gained a postwar reputation as a haunt of exiled royalty and the idle rich, and it continues to maintain its pretensions towards being a "Portuguese Riviera", with grandiose villas and luxury hotels. The town's tourism revolves around exclusive golf courses (see p.193) and a **casino** (3pm–3am; free). The latter requires some semblance of formal attire to enter; once inside, you have the choice of roulette, cards, slot machines, restaurants, shops, live shows at 11pm and even an art gallery. It sits at the far end the Parque do Estoril, a lovely stretch of fountains and exotic trees, surrounded by Estoril's nicest bars and restaurants. For a leisurely tour of Estoril, a **toy train** departs from the eastern end of the park (daily every 30min 10am–7pm; 500$00).

Estoril's fine sandy beach is backed by a seafront promenade that stretches all the way to Cascais. A stroll between the two towns is recommended, drifting from beach to bar; the walk takes around twenty minutes.

Accommodation

Pensão-Residencial Smart, Rua José Viana 3 ℂ & fax 214 682 164.
One of the best options in Estoril, with pleasant rooms and breakfast included. It's east of the park – turn right out of the station, then left when you reach Avenida Bombeiros Voluntários. ③

Eating and drinking

English Bar, Avda Sabóia 9 ℂ214 680 413. Daily 12.30–4pm & 7.30–11pm. Expensive.
A pricey bar-restaurant with attractive sea views, just over the main road from Monte Estoril train station. It has a good local reputation, but don't expect any resemblance to an English pub.

Frolic, Avda Clotilde 2765, Estoril. Mon–Thurs & Sun 8am–2am, Fri & Sat 9am–2am.
Restaurant, *pastelaria* and nightclub; the outdoor seats facing the square are a good spot for a late drink.

Jonas Bar, Paredão do Estoril, Monte Estoril. Daily 10am–2am.
Right on the seafront between Cascais and Estoril, this is a fun spot day or night, selling cocktails, juices and snacks.

Pintos, Arcadas do Parque 18b. Daily 8am–2am. Moderate.
Multi-faceted place which quadruples as a restaurant, *marisqueira*, *pastelaria* and pizzeria; the main draw is the outdoor seating facing the square.

ACCOMMODATION, EATING AND DRINKING

CHAPTER TWENTY-THREE

CASCAIS

Map 1, B6.

At the end of the line, Cascais's train station is a short walk north from the town's main street, Rua Frederico Arouca; buses to Guincho, Cabo da Roca and Sintra leave from the stands outside the station. Walk right down Rua Frederico Arouca and cross Avenida C. da Grande Guerra for the **turismo** (Map p.249, D3; Mon–Sat 9am–7pm, Sun 10am–6pm; ©214 868 204), on Rua Visconde da Luz, set in an old mansion, which has maps and information about local events.

Stagecoach bus passes (one-day passes 1200$00; seven-day passes 3000$00; one-month passes 7300$00) represent good value if you want to explore the surrounding area. Bus services link Cascais with Cabo da Roca (p.236), Sintra (p.225) and its beaches (p.236). Passes are also valid on Stagecoach buses to Lisbon airport.

With three fair beaches along its esplanade and a modern marina, **Cascais** is a major resort, positively bursting at the seams in high season, which nowadays lasts from around May to early October. At these times, the commercialism can be trying, though it's not too large or difficult to get around and has a much younger and less exclusive feel than Estoril. Go out of season and the whole place becomes delightful, even retaining a few elements of its previous existence as a fishing village. As well as the **fish market** (Mon–Sat) just south of Rua Frederico Arouca, there's a lively **Wednesday market** on Rua do Mercado – head up Alameda C. da Grande Guerra, bear left at the roundabout and it's on the right. It's also worth catching the Sunday evening **bullfights** from April to September in the Praça de

Touros, Avenida Pedro Alvares Cabral in the west of town, that draw a largely local crowd but rarely attact big-name stars.

You'll find the main concentration of bars and nightlife on Rua Frederico Arouca, the main pedestrian thoroughfare. East of here is Cascais's largest beach, **Praia da Conceição**; the smaller beaches of Praia da Rainha and Praia da Ribeira are in the middle of town. For a wander away from the crowds, stroll up beyond Largo 5 de Outubro (behind the town hall) into the old and surprisingly pretty west side of town, which is at its most delightful in the streets around the graceful **Igreja da Assunção**, worth a look inside for its azulejos, which predate the earthquake of 1755.

Beyond the church lies the pleasant **Parque Municipal da Gandarinha** (daily 10am–5pm), in whose southern reaches stands the mansion of the counts of Guimarães, preserved complete with its nineteenth-century fittings as the **Museu Biblioteca Conde Castro Guimarães** (Tues–Sun 10am–5pm; 400$00); most days, there's someone around to give you a guided tour of the furniture, paintings and archeological finds housed here; even if these don't grab you, the mansion alone is worth a visit. On the north side of the park, opposite the Pavilhão de Cascais, signs direct you to the modern **Museu do Mar** (Tues–Sun 10am–5pm; 400$00), an engaging little collection of model boats, sea-related artefacts, old costumes and pictures.

West from Cascais

Back on the coastal road, the dull walls of the mostly seventeenth-century Fort now guard the entrance to Cascais's new **marina**, an enclave of wealthy yachts serviced by restaurants, bars and boutiques. Keeping to the coastal road, it's about twenty minutes' walk west of the park to the **Boca do Inferno** – the "Mouth of Hell" – where waves crash against caves in the cliff face. The viewpoints above are always packed with tourists (as is the very tacky market on the roadside), although the whole affair is rather unimpressive except in stormy weather. Boca do Inferno is also served by a **toy train** (daily 10am-7pm, every 30min; 500$00), which trundles through town from Cascais train station. En route, look out for the little beach of **Praia de Santa Marta**, with a nice café on a terrace above.

There are hourly buses (Mon–Sat 7.45am–7.45pm, Sun 9am–7.15pm; 320$00) from outside Cascais train station which run the 6km west to **Praia do Guincho**, a great sweeping field of beach with body-crashing Atlantic rollers. It's a superb place to surf or windsurf – World Windsurfing Championships are usually held here in August – but also a dangerous one. The water is clean but the undertow is notoriously strong and people are drowned almost every year. The beach has become increasingly popular in recent times and the coastal approach road is flanked by half a dozen large terrace-restaurants, and a couple of hotels, all with varying views of the breaking rollers and standard, fish-dominated menus. There is also a well-equipped campsite just back from the beach.

Accommodation

Adega do Gonçalves (Map p.249, C3), Rua Afonso Sanches 54, Cascais ℭ214 831 519.
Basic rooms above a reasonable restaurant (see p.252). The situation is good, though it is fairly guaranteed to be noisy if you hope for an early night. ②

Hotel Albatroz (Map p.249, F2), Rua Frederico Arouca 100, Cascais ℭ214 832 821, fax 214 844 827, *albatroz@mail.telepac.pt*
Seaside hotels don't come much grander than this – one of the best in the region, with glorious views from rooms and restaurant, and top-of-the-range facilities. Around 45,000$00 at the height of the summer, half that in winter, but even more if you want a sea view. ⑨

ACCOMMODATION

251

Hotel Baía (Map p.249, E4), Avda Com. Grande Guerra, Cascais ℗214 831 033, fax 214 831 095, *hotelbaia@mail.telepac.pt*.
In-your-face, modern seafront hotel with impressive balconies overlooking the beach and harbour. Rooms are very good value out of season, and not bad in summer; it's worth booking ahead for one with a sea view. ⑥

Estalagem O Muchaxo, Guincho ℗214 870 221, fax 214 870 044.
Slightly shabby at the edges and showing signs of age, this nevertheless remains an attractive place, with stone-flagged bar and picture windows looking across the beach in the restaurant (see p.254), rated as one of the best in the Lisbon area. ⑤

Hotel do Guincho, Guincho ℗214 870 491, fax 214 870 431.
Luxurious hotel overlooking the crashing rollers on one of the coast's most dramatic beaches. ⑧

Solar Dom Carlos (Map p.249, C4), Rua Latina Coelho 8, Cascais ℗214 828 115, fax 214 865 155.
Sixteenth-century mansion on a quiet backstreet in the pretty west side of town. Dom Carlos once stayed here, hence the Royal Chapel; there are cool tiles throughout, attractive rooms, a garden, and the price includes breakfast. Recommended. ④

For an explanation of the accommodation and restaurant price codes, see p.92 and p.111 respectively.

Eating

Adega do Gonçalves (Map p.249, C3), Rua Afonso Sanches 54, Cascais. Daily noon–11pm. No credit cards. Inexpensive.
Traditional *adega* (wine cellar) not yet overwhelmed by tourists, serving huge portions of good food. The locally caught grilled fish is always a good bet.

A Tasca (Map p.249, C3), Rua Afonso Sanches 61, Cascais. Daily noon–3pm & 7–11pm. No credit cards. Inexpensive.
Basic little tavern with friendly, English-speaking owner who turns out decent, budget-priced meals (including *arroz de marisco*) to locals and tourists. If you can manage dessert, try the bizarrely named *baba de camelo* (camel drool) – liquid caramel.

Dom Manolo's (Map p.249, D3), Avda Com. Grande Guerra 13, Cascais. Daily 10am–midnight. No credit cards. Inexpensive.
Busy grillhouse just down from the *turismo*, where the alley runs through to Largo Luís de Camões. Superb chicken and chips; add a salad, local wine and home-made dessert and you'll pay around 2000$00.

Esplanada Santa Marta (Map p.249, C8), Praia de Santa Marta, Cascais. Mon–Sat 7am–2am, Sun 7am–10pm. No credit cards. Moderate.
One of the best places to enjoy charcoal-grilled fish, which is served on a tiny terrace overlooking the sea and little beach on the road out to the Boca do Inferno.

Jardim dos Frangos (Map p.249, D3), Avda Com. Grande Guerra 66, Cascais. Daily 10am–midnight. No credit cards. Inexpensive.
Permanently buzzing with people and sizzling with the speciality, grilled chicken, which is devoured by the plateload at indoor and outdoor tables.

Mar e Mar (Map p.249, G2), Praia da Conceição, Cascais. Daily 8am–2am. Moderate.
Little more than a kiosk on the seafront promenade, but nevertheless turns out surprisingly good quality and reasonably priced seafood, such as squid kebabs. Outdoor tables overlook the attractive beach.

O Marégrafo (Map p.249, F5), Passeio Dona Maria Pia, Cascais ℗214 842 104. Daily except Tues 12.30–3pm & 7.30–11pm. Expensive.

EATING

Fantastic position below the fort, with terrace overlooking the town, harbour and marina. Grilled tiger prawns and mixed seafood kebabs don't come cheap, but the tourist menu at 3500$00 isn't bad value.

O Muchaxo, Praia da Guincho, Guincho ©214 870 221. Daily noon–3.30pm & 7.30–10.30pm. Expensive.

This restaurant, overlooking the crashing waves, is rated one of the best in the Lisbon area. A meal will set you back around 4500$00 a head, but that's not bad value for some delicious Portuguese fish and meat delicacies.

O Pescador (Map p.249 F3), Rua das Flores 18, Cascais ©214 832 054. Mon–Sat 12.30–3pm & 7.30–11pm. Expensive.

One of several close to the fish market, this offers superior fish meals. Good food, smart decor and efficient service.

Bars and clubs

Chequers (Map p.249, D3), Largo Luís de Camões 7, Cascais. Daily 10.30am–2am.

Not quite as "legendary" as it would have you believe, but lively enough English-style pub, especially once the pumping rock music strengthens its grip.

Coconuts (Map p.249, A8), Avda Rei Humberto II de Itália 7, Cascais. Daily 11pm–4am; closed Sun in winter.

Disco about 1km along the road to Boca do Inferno, an odd mix of trendy locals and raving tourists, with an outdoor dance floor overlooking the sea. Theme nights include male strippers on Wednesdays and karaoke.

John Bull (Map p.249, D3), Praça Costa Pinto 31, Cascais. Daily 10.30am–2am.

Backing onto Cascais's most attractive square – an extension of Largo Luís de Camões – this is another English-style pub which fills up early with a good-time crowd; serves meals, too.

Music Bar (Map p.249, F3), Largo da Praia da Rainha, Cascais. Tues–Sun 10am–10pm

One of the few café-bars in Cascais with decent sea views. Although it's a fine spot to have a sunset beer, the outside tables on the patio above the beach are packed throughout the day with tourists drinking coffees and rehydrating with an *água com gás* (fizzy water).

News, Estrada da Malveira da Serra, Cascais. Daily 11pm–4am.

One of the area's "in" discos, with a terrace and a lively night guaranteed, on Fridays especially, when there are live shows. It's around 4km north of Cascais on the road to Malveira; take Avenida 25 de Abril past the market and head right along Avenida Eng. Adelino Amaro da Costa.

Van Gogo (Map p.249, B3), Trav. da Alfarrubeira 9, Cascais. Daily 11pm–4am.

Small, friendly and unpretentious disco attracting a mixed crowd of locals and visitors. Best at weekends. It's on a small side road off Rua Poço Novo.

South of the Tejo

As late as the nineteenth century, the **southern bank of the Tejo estuary** was an underpopulated area used as a quarantine station for foreign visitors; the neighbouring village of Trafaria was so lawless that police only patrolled the area when accompanied by members of the army. The development of Lisbon's port and its related industries in the twentieth century gave the bank a more industrial hue, but it was not until the huge Ponte 25 de Abril suspension bridge – inaugurated as the "Salazar Bridge" in 1966 and renamed after the 1974 revolution – that this separation between town and country was finally ended.

Since then, over a million people have settled over the river in a string of grim and largely industrial suburbs that spread east of the bridge in and around the district of Almada. Almada's port area, **Cacilhas**, a blustery ferry ride south of Lisbon, makes a pleasant excursion, with its excellent seafood restaurants and views back over the estuary. East of here, **Caparica** was before 1966 a remote fishing village, but now the fine expanse of Atlantic beach on the **Costa da Caparica** to the south has led to its transformation into a high-rise resort, and Lisbon's favourite seaside escape.

CACILHAS

Map 1, F7. Cacilhas is a short ferry ride from Fluvial station by Praça do Comércio (every 10–20min, last returning at around 10.30pm; 9.30pm at weekends; 105$00), or take the ferry from Cais do Sodré (every 20–30min during the day, every 40–50min throughout the night; 105$00).

Despite the bridge, **Cacilhas** remains dependent mainly on the little orange ferries that connect it to the capital, and the port is a popular evening and weekend destination for Lisboans seeking good seafood. It's around the ferry terminal and Rua Cândido dos Reis that Cacilhas's fish restaurants – most with great views back over to Lisbon – are to be found. If you feel the urge to walk off your meal, head along the waterfront road, Cais do Ginjal, towards the bridge. The road takes you past atmospherically decaying warehouses and patient fishermen, with exhilarating views over the Tejo. After ten minutes or so, you'll reach a couple of smart restaurants in converted warehouses, *Atira-te ao Rio*, and *Ponto Final* (see p.258). Take the steps up the cliff behind *Ponto Final*; these wind up to the remains of Almada castle, from which there are stunning views over the river.

Beyond Almada castle – best reached by bus #101 from Cacilhas – stands the **Cristo-Rei** (daily: June–Sept 9am–7.30pm; Oct–May 9am–6pm; 250$00), a church and a relatively modest version of Rio de Janeiro's Christ statue, built in 1959. A lift at the statue shuttles you up the plinth above the church, via a souvenir shop, to a dramatic viewing platform, 80m up in the air. From here on a clear day you can catch a glimpse of the glistening roof of the Pena palace at Sintra in the distance. Back on ground level, there's a new **visitor centre** which runs occasional exhibitions and has a handy bar.

CHAPTER TWENTY-FOUR

Eating

Atira-te ao Rio, Cais do Ginjal 69–70 ℗212 751 380. Tues–Fri 8pm–midnight, Sat & Sun 1–4pm & 8pm–midnight. Expensive.
Considering how many of Lisbon's warehouses have been turned into bars and restaurants, it's surprising that this is one of only two restaurants in similar conversions south of the Tejo. The views over to Lisbon are hard to beat and there are superior Brazilian dishes such as *feijoada* (bean stew) and a few outdoor tables, too. To reach it, turn right from the ferry and keep walking along the quay for ten minutes.

Cervejaria Farol, Alfredo Dinis Alex 1–3 (on the right along the quayside as you leave the ferry) ℗212 765 248. Mon, Tues & Thurs–Sun 9am–midnight. Moderate.
The most high-profile seafood restaurant in Cacilhas, but the views across the Tejo make it worthwhile. If you feel extravagant, it's hard to beat the lobsters. Azulejos on the wall show the old *farol* (lighthouse) that once stood here.

Escondidinho de Cacilhas, on the right of the square as you leave the ferry. Mon–Wed & Fri–Sun 8am–midnight. No credit cards. Inexpensive.
The tourist menu is 2000$00, and the speciality is, of course, fish and seafood. You don't get a river view, but this is a genuine, cosy port restaurant visited mainly by locals.

Ponto Final, Rua do Ginjal 72 ℗212 760 743. Daily except Tues noon–midnight. Moderate to expensive.
Next to *Atira-te ao Rio*, this has superbly positioned outdoor tables, though the menu of Portuguese dishes is somewhat limited.

For an explanation of the price codes used in this chapter, see "Eating" p.111 and "Accommodation" p.92.

EATING

COSTA DA CAPARICA

Map 1, E7. Regular express or slower local buses from Cacilhas (daily 7am–9pm, every 15–30min), or from Lisbon's Praça de Espanha (daily 7am–12.45am, every 30min). It's 30min from Cacilhas, around 40min from Praça de Espanha. Regular buses also link Caparica with Trafaria, which has ferry connections to Belém.

Lisbon's main seaside resort, **Caparica** is high-rise, tacky and packed at weekends in summer, but don't let that put you off: its family atmosphere, restaurants and beachside cafés full of tanned surfers make it a thoroughly enjoyable day out. During the summer (roughly May–early Oct), buses stop at the bus park near the beginning of the sands. In winter – when the beaches are dotted with fishermen casting into the exhilarating surf – buses go to the station in Praça Padre Manuel Bernardes, in which case it's best to get off at the first stop in Caparica, on the edge of the leafy square, Praça da Liberdade, five minutes from the beach. If you arrive here, walk diagonally across the square, turn right and at Avenida da Liberdade 18 you'll find the **turismo** (Mon–Sat 9.30am–1pm & 2.30–6pm; ©212 900 071), which can supply information on accommodation. If you want to stay overnight, the options listed below are recommended, but be warned that there's little space available in July and August. Book ahead if you can; if you can't find anywhere, the last bus back to Lisbon departs at around 9pm.

The town's southern edges still service teams of fishermen, whose tractors haul in drift-nets once a day, but the reason for the crowds is Caparica's **beach**, a huge sandy expanse freshened by Atlantic breakers. A narrow-gauge mini-railway (June–Sept; 580$00) runs south along 8km or so of dunes to Fonte da Telha, a scattered resort of beach huts, cafés and restaurants. Ring the bell to jump off at any one of the twenty stops en route. Earlier stops tend to be family-oriented, while later ones are, on the whole, younger and more trendy, with nudity (though officially illegal) more or less obligatory. This is especially true around stops 18 and 19, a predominantly gay area. If you're after solitude you'll need to ride to Fonte da Telha and walk south, though always take care while swimming, especially in unsupervised areas. Fonte da Telha also has bus links with Cacilhas; the roundabout and infrequent service leaves from the top of the hill roughly every one or two hours.

Accommodation

Hotel Costa da Caparica, Avda Gen. Delgado 47 ✆212 910 310, fax 212 910 687.

Large, modern seafront hotel with its own restaurant and pool. Not cheap, but with over 350 rooms it usually has space. ⑤

Orbitur, Avda Afonso de Albuquerque, Quinta de St António, Monte de Caparica ✆212 901 366, fax 212 900 661, *info@orbitur.pt*.

From Praça da Liberdade, walk 5–10min north along the main road towards Trafaria to this campsite, pleasantly situated among pine trees. It comes complete with café and tennis courts, and is generally packed. Though there's a long line of campsites in Caparica, this is one of the few where camping club membership is not required.

Pensão Real, Rua Mestre Manuel 18, Caparica ✆212 901 713, fax 212 901 701.

One of the more reasonable central options in Caparica, a few minutes' walk back from the beach and just off Rua das Pescadores, the main pedestrianized road through town. Not exactly a bargain for plain rooms, but better value than many in this resort. ④

For an explanation of the price codes used
in this chapter, see "Eating" p.111 and
"Accommodation" p.92.

Eating

O Barbas, Praia da Costa ©212 900 163. Mon & Wed–Sun
noon–2am. Moderate.

With window seats looking out over the sands and bubbling fish
tanks inside, *O Barbas* (The Beard) is an atmospheric beach
restaurant with fish to die for. You'll probably see the owner – he's
the one with the huge amounts of facial hair. From Rua das
Pescadores, head north up the esplanade; the restaurant is on
your right.

Bar Terminal, Fonte da Telha. Tues–Sun 10am–10pm (weekends
only in winter). Inexpensive.

Doubles as the terminal for the mini-railway, this is an idyllic little
bar-restaurant on a wooden platform raised above the beach.
Perfect spot for a beer; also serves snacks and the ubiquitous
grilled sardine.

Primoroso, Caparica. Tues–Sun noon–midnight. Moderate.

Continuing north past *O Barbas* along the seafront esplanade,
Primoroso sits on the right. There are plenty of freshly caught fish
to choose from, but if in doubt, try the *cataplana*. The outdoor
tables facing the beach are the perfect spot from which to watch
the sun go down.

CONTEXTS

History

Beginnings

The tourist board likes to promote the romantic idea that Lisbon was founded by Ulysses, though there's little evidence to support either this claim or the theory that the word "Lisboa" is a corruption of his name. It is far more likely that the the true founders of the city were the **Phoenicians**, who called the place Allis Ubbo – "calm harbour" – which later became Olisipo. They established an outpost here around 900 BC and were subsequently succeeded by the Greeks and then the Carthaginians, though neither had much effect on the development of the city.

The city's prosperity grew with the **Romans**, who entered the Iberian peninsula in around 210 BC; Olisipo (Lisbon) became administrative capital of Lusitania, the western part of Iberia, under Julius Caesar in 60 BC. The city's wealth was increased by its fish-preserving industries – fittingly enough, in a city whose favourite dish remains dried cod – and the remains of a Roman fish-preserving factory can still be seen in the Baixa (see p.20). Other remains include the scant ruins of a Roman theatre near Rua Augusto Rosa (see p.32), just above Alfama; there was probably also a Roman fort on the site of today's castle.

Christianity reached Portugal at the end of the first century AD, and within two hundred years there was a bishopric in Lisbon. As the Roman Empire declined, a wave of barbarian invaders moved in. First came the Suevi, followed by the Visigoths, though neither made any sort of lasting impact on Lisbon. At the end of the seventh century, one quarrelling faction of Visigoths appealed for aid from Muslim North Africa, and in 711 a force of Moors crossed over to Spain and swept up into Portugal, establishing a new, Moorish kingdom.

BEGINNINGS

Moorish rule

In contrast to the Visigoths, the Moors were tolerant and productive rulers. **Moorish** Lishbuna thrived on its wide links with the Arab world, Roman irrigation techniques were improved and crop-rotation introduced, exploiting the rich territories of the south. Urban life prospered too, and Lisbon became a major town. The Alcáçova – a Muslim palace – was constructed on the site of today's castle. The Moors named the grandest part of their settlement *alhama* (hot springs) because of the waters that rose to the surface there; over the years, the name changed to Alfama.

Moorish advances were halted in the north, and in the eleventh century, a tiny Roman Catholic kingdom called Portucale was established between the Douro and Minho rivers under Afonso VI. In 1086, pressure exerted by a new wave of Muslim invaders from North Africa forced Afonso to turn to European Crusaders for assistance. His successor, Afonso Henriques, extended his kingdom southwards, and by 1147 had pushed the Moors back almost as far as Lisbon. In the same year, the king persuaded other European Crusaders to help him in the **siege of Lisbon** (see p.34). With the promise of land rights and material goods as a reward, the Crusaders murderously sacked the city. Those Moors that survived were forced out of Alfama to live in the quarter still known as Mouraria, and Alfama was given over to Christian fishermen and artisans.

The one positive outcome of the siege was the establishment of **Afonso Henriques** as the first monarch of modern Portugal. In 1150, Lisbon's cathedral, the Sé, was founded to commemorate the reconquest of the city. It was not until 1260, however – with the Moors finally expelled from the south and the frontiers of today's Portugal almost in place – that the more centrally located city of Lisbon took over from Coimbra as capital.

The discoveries

In 1290, Lisbon University was founded by the far-sighted king Dom Dinis (1279–1325), who also set about strengthening both the city walls and the new country's frontiers – in 1297 these were acknowledged by Spain in the Treaty of Alcañices. Castile, however, still had its eyes on the Portuguese throne, which it looked to acquire by a series of royal marriages between the two countries. War followed when the future Portuguese King João I, backed by Portuguese commoners and English archers, led a famous victory over the Spaniards at Aljubarrota in 1385. To give thanks for a victory that sealed Portugal's independence, the victors set about building Batalha Abbey and the Carmelite Convento do Carmo in Lisbon, which was completed in 1389.

It was only after peace was fully restored in 1411 that King João I could turn his resources towards Morocco in expeditions that were part crusade and part strategic strikes against the Moors. The third son of João I, **Prince Henry the Navigator**, founded a School of Navigation in the Algarve which initiated Portugal's great seafaring traditions and led to the exploration of the islands of Madeira, the Azores and the west coast of Africa between 1419 and 1460.

Over the following centuries, Lisbon was twice at the forefront of European development. The first phase came with the great Portuguese **discoveries** of the late fifteenth and sixteenth centuries. In 1498, Vasco da Gama opened the sea route to India and the Portuguese monarchy, already doing well out of African gold, now became the richest in Europe as a result of taxes levied on the Indian trade. In 1494, the Treaty of Tordesillas saw Portugal and Spain divide up the world between them. As they were discovered, more areas fell under Portuguese control, including Brazil (1500), Goa (1510) and Macau (1557).

THE DISCOVERIES

The reign of Manuel I (1495–1521) marked the apogee of Portuguese wealth and strength. In 1511, he moved into the Terreiro do Paço, a grand palace on Praça do Comércio later destroyed in the Great Earthquake. But his reign found its expression in the extraordinary **Manueline** style of architecture, an elaborately decorative genre inspired by marine motifs, as can be seen on the Tower of Belém and the royal palace at Sintra.

Spanish domination

Despite this enormous wealth there was no entrepreneurial class in Lisbon; the development of a middle class having been stifled by the aristocracy's dominance of commerce. Banking and commerce was also left in the hands of **Jews**, who were banned from taking up most other professions. Though the citizens of Lisbon marvelled at the exotic wares brought back from abroad (such as the elephant which was paraded around the waterfront), few of them could afford to buy any of these goods, most of which were exported to northern Europe.

Popular resentment of Jewish prosperity and pressure from Spain persuaded Manuel I to expel the entire Jewish population from the city in 1496. His successor, João III (1521-57) established the Inquisition in 1536, setting up an Inquisitional Palace in Rossio and victimizing those converted Jews known as New Christians, many of whom were killed in *autos-da-fé* (public executions by burning) – Inquisitions were to continue until the social reforms instigated by the Marquês de Pombal in the eighteenth century. Without Jewish professionals, Portugal found itself with an empire based on commerce but deprived of its commercial expertise. By the 1570s, with the economy close to collapse, the country became vulnerable to Spain once more. After the death of Dom Sebastião in 1578 the next king, Cardinal Henrique, ruled without an heir. When he died in

1580, Sebastião's uncle, the Habsburg Philip II of Spain – Felipe I of Portugal – defeated rival claims to the throne, and in 1581 began a period of **Spanish rule** which was to last for sixty years.

In fact, Felipe I allowed Portugal to continue with a large degree of autonomy, whilst attempting to help develop the city, even bringing over his favourite architect, Juan de Herrera, to begin the construction of São Vicente de Fora. Resentment of Spain came about because of its foreign policy. Part of the Armada was prepared in Lisbon, provoking the enmity of the Dutch and British, old allies of Portugal who were never to be as supportive again, and by the time Felipe III tried to conscript Portuguese troops to quell a rising in Catalonia, Portuguese resentment had reached boiling point. In 1640, a group of conspirators stormed the palace in Lisbon and the **Duke of Bragança** took the throne as João IV. Spain, preoccupied with events elsewhere, accepted the situation formally under the Treaty of Lisbon in 1668.

The second golden age and the Great Earthquake

The opening decades of the eighteenth century witnessed Portugal's second period of splendour, when a colonized Brazil began to yield both gold and diamonds. This new golden age, though more extravagant than the first, had a less brilliant effect. Dom João V (1706–50) virtually bankrupted the state with the construction of the extravagant **Palácio-Convento de Mafra**, created to rival El Escorial in Spain, and also commissioned the phenomenally expensive Capela de São João Baptista in the Igreja de São Roque (see p.44) and the hugely ambitious – albeit more useful – Aqueduto das Águas Livres, which brought supplies of fresh water to the whole of Lisbon for the first time. The infamous **Methuen Treaty** of 1703 established a military and trading alliance between Britain and Portugal. For the Portuguese, it meant the reassuring protection of the British against the threatening powers of Spain and France, as well as a guaranteed export market for its wines. The downside was that it helped destroy the native textile industry by letting in British cloth at preferential rates. João V's apathetic successor José I (1750-77) left almost complete power in the hands of his minister, the **Marquês de Pombal**. The **Great Earthquake** (see p.18) struck Lisbon on November 1, 1755, killing around 40,000 of the city's 270,000 inhabitants. For Portugal, and for the capital, it was a disaster that in retrospect seems to seal an age, marking the end of Lisbon's role as perhaps the most active port in Europe.

Pombal immediately started rebuilding the city to his own designs; the grid-pattern of the Baixa was quickly laid out and a new palace was built around Praça do Comércio. Pombal also set about modernizing post-earthquake Lisbon's institutions, establishing an efficient and secular bureaucracy, renewing the system of taxation, setting up export companies, outlawing slavery and abolishing the Jesuit order, which had long dominated education and religious life in Portugal.

The nineteenth century

Already diminished following the devastating earthquake, Lisbon's trade routes were further threatened by **Napoleon**, and it was only with the protection of the British fleet that Portugal could trade at all. When the country refused Napoleon's demand to call off this protection in 1807, Napoleon's General Junot marched into Lisbon, setting himself up at the palace in Queluz. On British advice, the royal family fled to Brazil, leaving the war in the hands of British generals, Beresford and Wellington. The French were finally driven back in 1811, leaving Portugal little choice but to allow Britain to trade freely with its colony Brazil, which soon declared its independence. The result was that Portugal became almost a colony of Brazil – where its royal family now resided – and a protectorate of Britain under Beresford. The Portuguese army, however, remained intact, and it was they who forced a new assembly and the return of King João VI from Brazil in 1821.

João VI's son, the reactionary Miguel, acceded to the throne in 1826 and at once returned Portugal to its old absolutist ways. The rest of the nineteenth century saw a constant struggle between supporters of an absolutist monarch and those who favoured a new liberal charter, but despite the political turmoil, Lisbon flourished economically and culturally. The Botanical Gardens were considered the best in Europe, the Teatro Nacional de Dona Maria II (built in 1840) became the place to be seen, and the cafés of Rossio – newly laid with its distinctive black and white cobbles – and Chiado were frequented by the likes of novelist Eça de Queiroz. A public works programme was started in 1851 to help curtail unemployment, a national post office established, and the triumphant arch on Praça do Comércio opened in 1873. The development of Avenida da Liberdade during the 1880s began to change the shape of Lisbon, creating a central axis which allowed the city to spread north up the slopes around the new Parque Eduardo VII. At around the same time the Elevador da Glória (1885) and Elevador Santa Justa (1902) were constructed as part of a new network of trams and funiculars.

Meanwhile, **republicanism** took root in the army and among the urban poor, especially after Portuguese claims to Zambesi – the area between the colonies of Angola and Mozambique – failed in 1890, causing Portugal to fall out with Britain. The dictatorial Dom Carlos (1898–1908) was assassinated in Praça do Comércio in a failed coup in 1908 and finally, in 1910, the monarchy was overthrown by a joint revolt of the army and navy and Portugal's last king, Dom Manuel I, sent into exile in Britain. The new republic was declared in Praça do Município, and the palace at Praça do Comércio turned into government offices.

The republic and Salazar

Lisbon and Portugal remained in turmoil because of divisions among Republicans, briefly culminating in victory for the army, which – led by Sidónio Pais – bombed the government offices in Praça do Comércio from Parque Eduardo VII. Pais's rule ended with his assassination in 1918. Economic turmoil followed World War I, with no fewer than 45 changes of government, before General Carmona became president in 1926 and suspended the Republican constitution. In 1928, **Dr António de Oliveira Salazar** became the cabinet's finance minister and managed, with his strict monetarist line, to balance the budget for the first time in years; from then on, he effectively controlled the country, becoming prime minister in 1932 and staying in power until 1968.

Salazar's policies bore many similarities to those of a fascist state: only one political party was permitted, workers' organizations were controlled by their employers, education was managed by the state and censorship was strictly enforced. Opposition to the regime was monitored by the PIDE – a secret police force set up with Gestapo assistance which used torture and long-term detention in camps in the colonies to defuse resistance. During World War II, a neutral Portugal became a hotbed of spies and an outlet for refugees, remaining on good terms with its old ally, Britain, even though Salazar's policies were closer to those of the Nazis.

Salazar's rule produced a modern economy, and much of Lisbon prospered. Despite World War II, in 1940 Salazar staged an exhibition of the Portuguese world which saw

Belém remodelled, with the creation of the Praça do Império and the new Museu de Arte Popular. High-rise blocks appeared around Avenida Roma, the vast Cristo Rei statue was erected in Almada and, in 1959, the city's metro opened. A 1960s boom saw the construction of the brash concrete Discoveries Monument in Belém in 1960, the Ponte 25 Abril suspension bridge in 1966 (originally called Salazar Bridge) and – shortly after Salazar's demise – the Museu Calouste Gulbenkian in 1969.

But although Lisbon prospered, the majority of Portugal's population suffered under the regime, and agriculture was allowed to stagnate. There was internal dissent, but the New State's downfall was largely due to Salazar's imperialism and his obsession with colonial wars. From 1968 Salazar's successor, Marcelo Caetano, attempted to continue with the colonial policies despite growing discontent within the army. Young conscripts had come to sympathize with the freedom movements in the colonies that they were intended to suppress, and from their ranks grew the revolutionary Movimento das Forças Armadas (MFA).

From revolution to EU

On April 25, 1974, the MFA, led by Major Otelo Saraiva de Carvalho, gave the signal for a **revolution**, leading to a virtually bloodless coup, with no serious attempt made to defend the government. Almost immediately the colonies were granted independence, and Portuguese military forces withdrawn, leading to the arrival in Lisbon of some half a million **colonial refugees**, further complicating an already unstable post-revolutionary period. Despite an acute housing shortage, rigid pre-revolution rent laws left landlords with insufficient funds to maintain or improve their properties. Lisbon became a grandly decaying city covered in political graffiti and surrounded by shantytowns, some of which still exist today.

In 1985, Dr Aníbal Cavaco Silva's PSD party came to power, and a year later presided over Portugal's entry into the **European Community**. A massive injection of funds helped Portugal experience unprecedented economic growth, and much of Lisbon was reconstructed with a combination of EU funds and overseas business developments. A massive fire in 1988 was only a temporary setback; though much of the historic Chiado district burnt down, within a decade the area had been impressively rebuilt to its original design.

From the 1990s to the present

In the 1990s, Lisbon echoed to the sound of a building programme on a scale not witnessed for two hundred years. Many of the grand mansions of Avenida da República and Avenida da Liberdade were replaced by gleaming office blocks, cobbled streets served by trams were ploughed under tarmac for fast dual carriageways and underpasses, and decaying houses were either renovated or swept away. In 1992, Portugal's **presidency of the European Community** was commemorated by the hurried and controversial construction of presidential headquarters in Belém – now the Centro Cultural de Belém. Then in 1994 came the recognition of Lisbon as **European City of Culture**, lifting the city's European profile still higher.

Despite the optimism engendered by Cavaco Silva's policies of free enterprise and privatization in the 1980s and early 1990s, there were still noticeable **inequalities** in the distribution of wealth, while large areas of the real estate and the financial sectors were bought up by Spanish companies. The Portuguese reaction to all this was to vote in a fresh government. In 1995, António Guterres was elected prime minister; the following year, Jorge Sampaio, former mayor of Lisbon, became president, giving Portugal a socialist head of state and prime minister for the first time since the revolution.

The new team presided over a further period of growth as more funds poured into Lisbon for the ambitious World Exposition, or **Expo 98**, which saw the redevelopment of the Olivais docklands, the opening of the Vasco da Gama bridge, and a revamped transport network, including a spanking new metro system. Though Expo 98 was a huge success, the social problems and unemployment that plagued Lisbon during the late twentieth century continue into the early twenty-first. Lisbon today remains capital of one of the EU's poorest countries. The authorities' schemes aimed at relieving the city's chronic housing shortage have been poorly planned, producing grim suburbs of Soviet-style estates which now house a sizeable chunk of the city's population. Over the river, the working-class city of Almada has a population nearing that of the capital itself, though most of its residents work in Lisbon, relying on the Ponte 25 Abril bridge, the worst bottleneck in Lisbon's increasingly congested traffic system.

Even so, Lisbon's economic future looks bright. Portugal was one of the first wave of states to join the EMU, a factor that has contributed to Lisbon being Europe's seventh fastest-growing city. The city's cultural life continues to flourish, and social problems largely remain on the periphery of a historic Lisbon which has benefited from substantial renovation, making it look better than it has done for decades.

Books

In the reviews below, publishers are listed in the format UK/US unless the title is available in one country only, or from a Portuguese publisher, in which case we've specified the country.

Fiction

José Rodrigues Miguéis, *Happy Easter* (Carcanet, UK). A powerful and disturbing account of the distorted reality experienced by a schizophrenic, whose deprived childhood leads him to a self-destructive and tragic life in Lisbon. An evocatively written and gripping read.

Cees Nooteboom, *The Following Story* (Harcourt Brace, UK). Dutch author Nooteboom successfully evokes the famous Portuguese feeling of melancholy – or *saudade* – in a tale of a classics teacher who falls asleep in Amsterdam and wakes up in a hotel room in Lisbon – the scene of a romantic past that he realizes he can never fully recapture.

Fernando Pessoa, *The Book of Disquiet* (Carcanet/Pantheon, o/p); *A Centenary Pessoa* (Carcanet, UK); *Lisbon: What The Tourist Should See* (Livros Horizonte, Portugal). The country's best-known poet wrote *The Book of Disquiet* in prose: a kind of autobiography, set in Lisbon and posthumously compiled from a truckload of material. Regarded as a modernist classic, this is the first complete English version. *A Centenary Pessoa* includes a selection of his varied prose and poetry, including his works under the pseudonym of Ricardo Reis. *Lisbon: What The Tourist Should See* is a somewhat dull insight into the city as Pessoa saw it. Written in English and Portuguese (but only available in Portugal), Pessoa's 1925 guidebook describes a Lisbon that is largely recognizable today. *Fernando Pessoa*, another book available only in Portugal (Hazan, Portugal), is a revealing collection of documents and photographs of the author at work, with an introduction by Antonio Tabucchi.

Eça de Queiroz, *The Sin of Father Amaro* (Carcanet, UK); *The Maias* (Carcanet, UK); *Cousin Bazilio* (Quartet, UK); *The Illustrious House of Ramires* (Quartet/New Directions). Queiroz introduced realism into Portuguese fiction with *The Sin of Father Amaro*, first published in 1876. *The Illustrious House of Ramires* and *The*

José Saramago

Portugal's most famous living writer, **José Saramago** achieved global recognition when he won the Nobel Prize for Literature in 1998. Despite comparisons with Gabriel García Márquez, Saramago's blend of magical realism and an almost Joycean stream of consciousness give his novels a uniquely dense but surprisingly readable style. Saramago went to school in Lisbon during the time of Salazar, a background that engendered an antipathy to politics and the Church. As a result, his novels often deal with themes of resistance and the emergence of personal identity. After periods as a metalworker and draughtsman, he moved into publishing and translation before becoming a political commentator for a Lisbon newspaper. In 1969, Saramago joined the then-prohibited Communist Party; in 1989, he was elected as a Communist councillor for Lisbon City Council before he decided to concentrate on being a full-time author. His novels have since come thick and fast. Now in his 70s, Saramago lives in Lanzarote with his Spanish wife.

Maias are both entertaining narratives which give a comprehensive account of nineteenth-century Portuguese society; *Cousin Bazilio* is a gripping story of a woman's daring affair in the confines of Lisbon's middle-class.

Erich Maria Remarque, *The Night in Lisbon* (Fawcett Books, US). Better known as author *of All Quiet On The Western Front*, German author Remarque writes with a similar detachment in this tale of a war-time refugee seeking an escape route from Europe. One night in Lisbon, he meets a stranger who has two tickets, and within hours their lives are inextricably linked in a harrowing and moving tale.

Mário de Sá-Carneiro, *The Great Shadow* (Dedalus, UK). A
collection of short stories set against the backdrop of Lisbon,
as the author describes his obsession with great art and
laments Lisbon's inferiority to Paris. Sá-Carneiro, who
committed suicide at 26, writes with stunning intensity and
originality about art, science, death, sex (including
homosexuality) and insanity.

José Saramago, *Baltasar and Blimunda* (Picador/Harvard University
Press); *The Year of the Death of Ricardo Reis* (Harvill/Harcourt
Brace); *The Stone Raft* (Harvill/Harcourt Brace); *The History of the
Siege of Lisbon* (Harvill/Harcourt Brace). Though many of
Saramago's novels feature Lisbon at some stage, the city is most
wonderfully evoked in *The Year of the Death of Ricardo Reis*, a
book about Pessoa's alter ego, which won *The Independent*'s
foreign fiction award. In *Baltasar and Blimunda*, Saramago mixes
fact with myth in an atmospheric novel set around the building of
the Convent of Mafra and the construction of the world's first
flying machine. In *The History of the Siege of Lisbon,*
contemporary Lisbon is superimposed on an account of the
Crusader siege of the city. A proofreader's own emotions come
under siege when he falls in love with his boss – who had been
appointed to keep an eye on him after he deliberately alters a
historical fact.

Antonio Tabucchi, *Declares Pereira* (Harvill/New Directions);
Requiem: A Hallucination (Harvill/New Directions); *Fernando
Pessoa* (with Maria José de Lancastre; Hazan, Portugal).
Tabucchi is a highly regarded Italian author and biographer of
Pessoa, who lived in Portugal for many years. In *Declares Pereira*
he has re-created the repressive atmosphere of Salazar's Lisbon,
tracing the experiences of a newspaper editor who questions his
own lifestyle under a regime which he can no longer ignore. The
book has recently been made into a film by Roberto Faenza.
Requiem: A Hallucination is an imaginative and dreamlike journey
around Lisbon, with Tabucchi engaging in Saramago-esque

FICTION

conversations with people as diverse as a barman in the Museu de Arte Antiga and a Pessoa-like author. The unifying theme is food and drink, and the book even contains a note on recipes at the end.

Richard Zimler, *The Last Kabbalist of Lisbon* (Arcadia/Overlook Press, Peter Mayer Publishers). Kabbala is the magical art based on an esoteric interpretation of the Old Testament. American author Zimler, now a resident of Porto, writes an intense and compelling story of a Jewish kabbalist attempting to discover the mystery behind his uncle's murder during the massacre of New Christians in Rossio in 1506. Based on historical fact, the story has been a bestseller in Portugal, Italy and Brazil.

General non-fiction

William Beckford, *Recollections of an Excursion to the Monasteries of Alcobaça and Batalha*; *Travels in Spain and Portugal (1778–88)* (Centaur Press/Norwood Editions, o/p). Mad and enormously rich, Beckford lived for some time at Sintra and travelled widely in Estremadura. His accounts, told with a fine eye for the absurd, are a lot of fun.

David Birmingham, *A Concise History of Portugal* (Cambridge University Press). The most recent history of Portugal is also the best for the casual reader; concise, but providing straightforward and informative coverage from the year dot.

Lord Byron, *Selected Letters and Journals* (Pimlico/Belknap). Only a few days of Portuguese travel but memorable ones – beginning with romantic enthusiasm, ending in outright abuse.

Henry Fielding, *Journal of a Voyage to Lisbon* (with *A Journey From This World to the Next*) (Oxford University Press, UK). In 1754 Fielding set sail to Lisbon in the hope that its climate would alleviate his ill health. Written with his usual satirical wit, the journal records the incidents and characters he meets on his voyage to the city where he was to meet his death, though there is little about Lisbon itself.

Damião de Góis, *Lisbon in the Renaissance* (Italica Press, US). De Góis was a friend of Erasmus and lived in Lisbon when it was one of Europe's leading commercial and cultural centres. Written in 1554, the book is a celebration of the pre-earthquake city and its monuments, though the best bits of his work are the reports of mythical creatures such as *tagide* – sea monsters – living in the Tejo.

Lawrence S. Graham and Douglas L. Wheeler, eds, *In Search of Modern Portugal: The Revolution and its Consequences* (University of Wisconsin Press). An academic study published in the early 1980s; heavy-going but rewarding.

Paul Hyland, *Backwards out of the Big World* (Flamingo, UK). Arriving on a cargo boat in the style of Henry Fielding, Hyland goes on to explore modern-day Lisbon before heading up through Portugal, meeting contemporary Portuguese writers, bullfighters, gypsies and the heir to the defunct throne en route; somewhat contrived, but with some interesting insights.

Maite Manjon, *Gastronomy of Spain and Portugal* (Prentice-Hall, US). A comprehensive collection of classic Iberian recipes, including a glossary of Portuguese and Spanish terms and explanations of traditional cooking techniques. Particularly good on regional specialities, including Lisbon dishes and wines.

Paulo Santos, *Lisbon: A Guide to Recent Architecture* (Ellipsis, UK). Neatly designed book detailing the hits, misses and usually adventurous recent architecture in the city, from grand housing projects and the Expo site down to individual shops, bars, and even the public toilets in Parque Eduardo VII.

Edite Vieira, *The Taste of Portugal* (Grub Street, UK). A delight to read, let alone cook from. Vieira combines snippets of history and passages from Portuguese writers (very well translated) to illustrate her dishes; highly recommended.

GENERAL NON-FICTION

INDEX

ROUGH GUIDES: Travel

Rough Guides
on the Web

www.travel.roughguides.com

We keep getting bigger and better! The Rough Guide to Travel Online now covers more than 14,000 searchable locations. You're just a click away from access to the most in-depth travel content, weekly destination features, online reservation services, and an outspoken community of fellow travelers. Whether you're looking for ideas for your next holiday or you know exactly where you're going, join us online.

You can also find us on Yahoo!® Travel (http://travel.yahoo.com) and Microsoft Expedia® UK (http://www.expediauk.com).

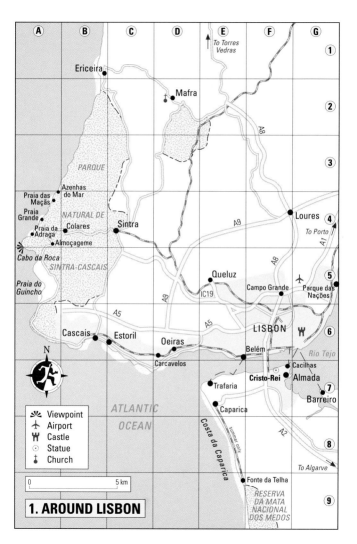

1. AROUND LISBON

Legend:
- ☼ Viewpoint
- ✈ Airport
- ♨ Castle
- ⊙ Statue
- ⌖ Church

0 — 5 km

N

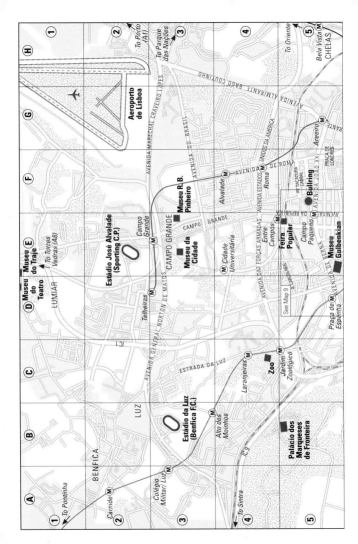

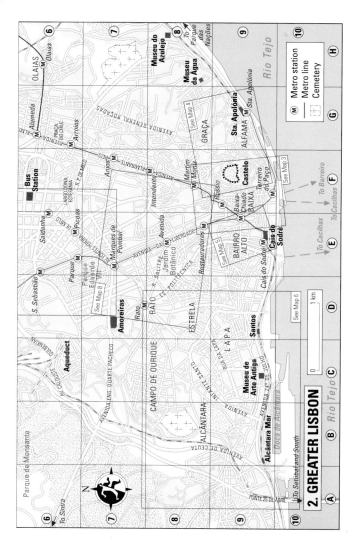

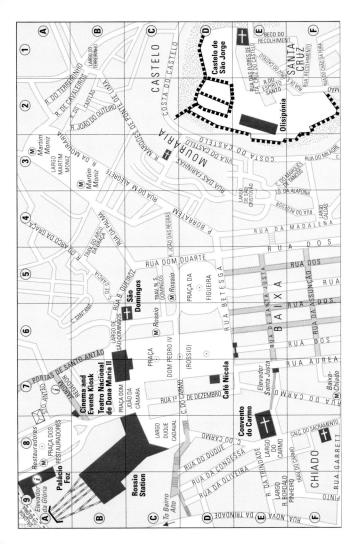

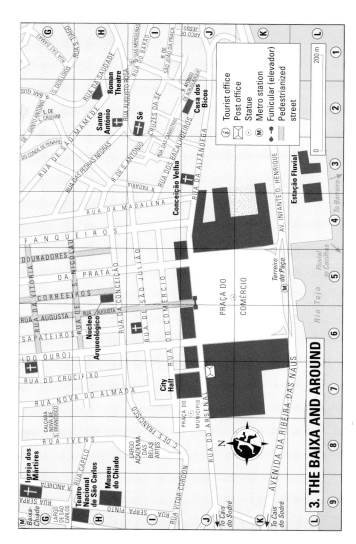

3. THE BAIXA AND AROUND

ⓘ	Tourist office
✉	Post office
⊙	Statue
Ⓜ	Metro station
▮	Funicular (elevador)
	Pedestrianized street

0   200 m

Roman Theatre
Santo António
Sé
Casa dos Bicos
Conceição Velha
Estação Fluvial
Núcleo Arqueológico
City Hall
Igreja dos Mártires
Teatro Nacional de São Carlos
Museu do Chiado

Baixa-Chiado

Rio Tejo

PRAÇA DO COMÉRCIO

Terreiro do Paço

Fluvial to Cacilhas

To Barreiro

RUA DA MADALENA
RUA DOS FANQUEIROS
RUA DOS CORREEIROS
RUA DA PRATA
RUA AUGUSTA
RUA DOS SAPATEIROS
RUA DO OURO (DO OURO)
RUA DO CRUCIFIXO
RUA NOVA DO ALMADA
RUA DOS BACALHOEIROS
RUA DA ALFÂNDEGA
AV. INFANTE D. HENRIQUE
RUA DE SÃO JULIÃO
RUA DA CONCEIÇÃO
RUA DE SÃO NICOLAU
RUA DA VITÓRIA
RUA DE SANTA JUSTA
RUA DOS DOURADORES
RUA DE S. ANTÓNIO
RUA DA PADARIA
RUA DAS PEDRAS NEGRAS
RUA DE SÃO MAMEDE
CRUZES DA SÉ
RUA AUGUSTO ROSA
RUA DA SAUDADE
RUA DAS CANASTRAS
RUA DE SÃO JOÃO DA PRAÇA
R. DE SÃO MERCADEIRAS
ARCO DE JESUS
RUA DE SÃO SAGO
RUA DAS DAMAS
RUA DO CONDE DE PENAFIEL
RUA DE SANTO ANTÓNIO
E. DE CRISPIM
E. DE SÃO CRISPIM
R. DE SANTO ANTÓNIO
ARCO DE JESUS
R. DE S. ANTÓNIO
D. AFONSO DE ALBUQUERQUE

PRAÇA DO MUNICÍPIO
RUA DO ARSENAL
AVENIDA DA RIBEIRA DAS NAUS
CALÇADA NOVA DE S. FRANCISCO
RUA IVENS
RUA SERPA PINTO
RUA VITOR CORDON
RUA ANCHIETA
R. SERPA
LARGO DO CHIADO
LARGO ACADEMIA DAS BELAS ARTES
C. DE S. FRANCISCO

To Cais do Sodré

N

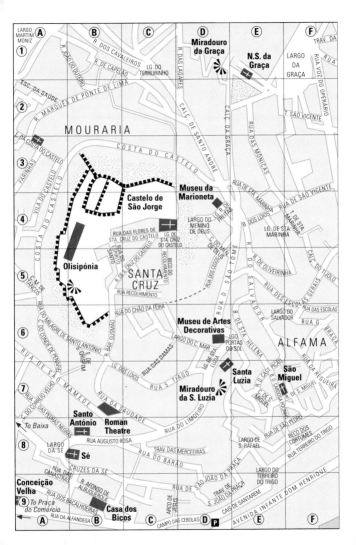

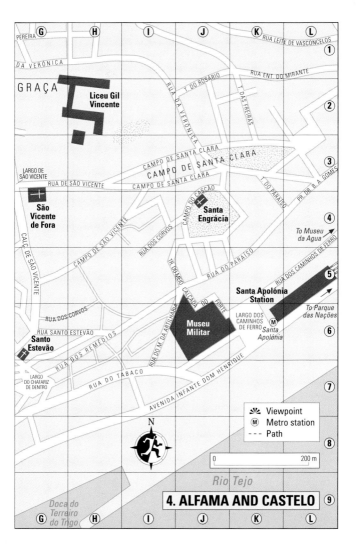

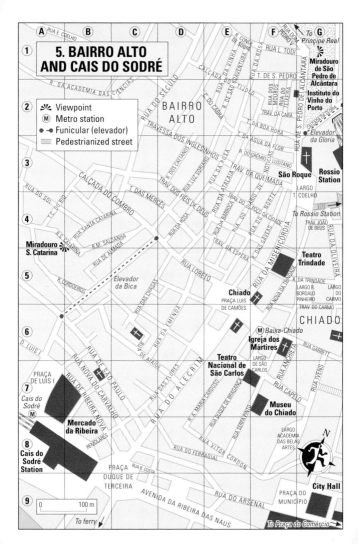

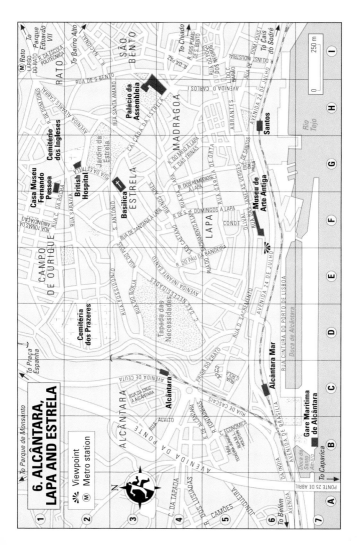

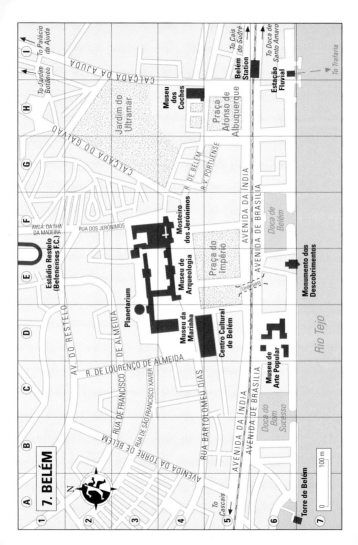

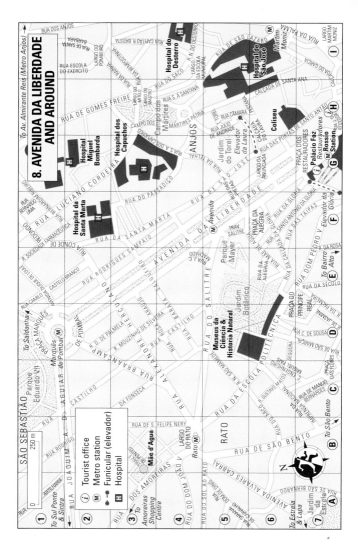

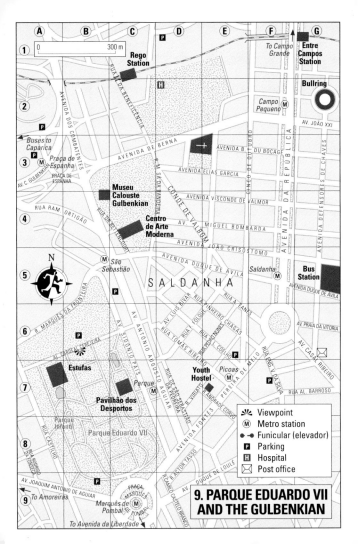

9. PARQUE EDUARDO VII AND THE GULBENKIAN